Sunday Morning Reflections on the Word

Dennis R. Clark

Sheed & Ward
Kansas City

Sheed & Ward™ is a service of The National Catholic Reporter Publishing Company.

Clark, Dennis R.
ISBN: 1-55612-861-4

Published by: Sheed & Ward
                 115 E. Armour Blvd.
                 P.O. Box 419492
                 Kansas City, MO 64141-6492

To order, call: (800) 333-7373

Contents

Cycle A

Sleepers, Awake!

Matthew 24:37-44

A few years ago, *Masterpiece Theatre* broadcast an interesting play titled "Memento Mori." It's about a group of eccentric London aristocrats each of whom receives a series of anonymous phone calls with the same frightening message. "Remember, you must die," says the caller. "Remember, you must die."

The reaction of each of them speaks volumes. The first to receive a call is a very rich, self-centered woman. When her call comes, she's utterly shocked – she'd never even considered that her perfect little self-contained world might come to an end. Her arrogant facade crumbles, fear consumes her, and she dies.

Next in line is an elderly gentleman. After receiving his call, he decides to go for broke and take just one more nubile young wife – his fourth. Unfortunately, it's more than his heart can take. And he too is gone in a trice. Another gent dismisses the caller as a prankster, and thinks no more about it, while the nastiest-tempered of the lot takes the call as a signal to settle old scores and get even with all his enemies before it's too late.

Each in turn reacts thoughtlessly out of a lifetime of habit, till finally the last woman is called. She thanks the caller, "I'm so glad you called," she says. "You know, at my age one forgets so many things. It is good of you to remind me of this most important fact." And with that she sets about rebuilding her life, healing old wounds, and putting aside all that doesn't really matter. She got the message!!

As Advent begins today, the Lord is giving us this same kind of wake-up call: "Remember, you must die." So how are we going to respond? By panicking or despairing or binging or, the old reliable, shopping? None of the above. We're going to respond to the wake-up call by waking up! Waking up to what we may have been missing, namely, the preciousness of the present moment – cherishing each moment, and living it graciously, generously, and single-mindedly – as if this were our only moment. That's all that God asks: if we'll attend to today, he'll handle eternity.

It sounds so easy, just one moment at a time, lived with care. But we have a hard time doing it, because the moments have always been there, as long as we can remember, just rolling in – one after another – like waves. So we take them for granted, treat them as throwaways, and make very little of most of them. We get into little ruts, and fall into habits that numb our brains and let us go through the motions of living without noticing we haven't got a life.

Like the rude guest at the cocktail party, who talks to us distractedly while watching for someone more interesting, we regularly look right over the present, with its special people and unique opportunities, and squander our attentions on trivia or on nothing at all. We settle for the table scraps of life instead of relishing the banquet that's within reach.

Advent's wake-up call is an invitation to stop settling for table scraps or for half a life. It's a call to seize this day and to cherish every single part of it as God's personal gift to us. It's a call to value the things that really matter. And it's a promise that, if we take care of our moments, God will take care of eternity.

May God grant that we learn to cherish the gift of life by giving our whole selves wisely and graciously to each moment. Then, when our life's course is run, and that last moment is upon us, we will walk into the arms of our Lord without fear and without regret.

Amen.

Still Growing Up

Matthew 3:1-12

A wealthy, tough banker died and went to heaven. He was greeted by one of the senior angels who gave him a tour of the place. When they came upon a splendid mansion, the banker asked who lived there. "Oh," said the angel, "you know the man. On earth he was your gardener." The banker got excited. If this was the way gardeners lived, just imagine the kind of mansion he'd get for all eternity.

Next they came to an even finer mansion. "Whose is this?" asked the banker.

"It belongs to a widow woman," replied the angel. Now the man was really getting excited. Finally, they came upon a tiny shack, with no window and only a piece of canvas for a door.

"This is your eternal home," said the angel.

The man was flabbergasted. "I don't understand. The other homes were so beautiful. Why is mine so miserable?"

The angel smiled sadly. "I'm sorry, sir," he said. "We did all we could with what you sent us to work with."

Heaven is not where the real building takes place and angels are not the builders. We are the real builders and what we're building – with God's help – is ourselves and one another. We are trying to grow up into and fill in the outlines of the image God dreamed for us the day we were born. That's a huge task and a confusing one as well because none of us has ever done it before!

It's also a frustrating task because the very moment we think we've mastered one skill or got one good habit nailed down, two new issues, that we haven't even thought of before, jump on stage and demand our immediate attention. We never get done!

It's just like being in grammar school. You work hard to do your best for what seems like an eternity and finally you finish the first grade!

Hurrah! All done! And then, lo and behold, there's the second grade staring you in the face. And behind that is the third grade, and the fourth grade, and on and on! We keep on working, and doing our best, but never finish!

So what are we to make of all this – this being stuck in the in-between state of unfinishedness, having left the station but not yet arrived? What are we to make of this, especially as we hear John the Baptist shouting at us in the Gospel, "Repent, reform"? What does God expect?!

God doesn't expect that we'll get everything right the first time. God knows that all we've got is our "learners' permits," and that learners learn slowly, by trial and error. And God expects that we may get tired or distracted or even thoroughly fed up. We'll do all that, because all of that is just a part of growing up – which we're all still doing, even the oldest among us – still growing up!

God does expect three things:

- First, that we hold onto the big vision and the big hopes God has for us and never let those get worn down or eroded by life;
- Second, that we listen to the rhythms of life, since it's through them that God shows us where to go next; and
- Third, we never quit, never stop trying, even in the face of repeated failure. Jesus has told us over and over, there is no unforgivable sin – none, that is, except despair, because despair locks God out.

As God calls out to us this day through John the Baptist, we are asked just these three things: that we keep our vision, keep listening, and keep trying. With God's help, the growth will come – not in a moment or a day, but it will come. God promises that. And ever so slowly we will be built. We will fill out that image that God dreamed for us the day we were born. Thanks be to God!

Dashed Expectations

Matthew 11:2-11

A young man was walking along a beach after a storm when he came upon a half-buried old lantern. He pulled it out of the sand and rubbed it vigorously. And, of course, a genie appeared and offered him a wish – anything in the world he wanted! Being a clever fellow, the young man decided to ask for a gift that would keep on giving long after the genie was gone. So he asked for the Midas touch. And that's exactly what he got. For the rest of his life, everything he touched turned into a muffler!

False expectations can get us in big trouble! They can break our hearts and kill our hopes. In today's gospel, we can almost hear John the Baptist's heart breaking as his messengers pose his plaintive question to Jesus, "Are you the promised one, or do we look for another?"

As his death draws very near, poor John is hurt and disappointed beyond words. He has given his all with the expectation that, before he died, good would triumph. He imagined a savior who would "beat the stuffings" out of the Romans and would take the throne of Israel as a second King David. Well, it didn't happen, and John was devastated!

We know the feeling, don't we. Dashed hopes and shattered expectations. They are no strangers to us. Whatever the arena, be it marriage or parenting, business or pleasure, leading or following, we have all had the experience of having reality fall short of our expectations – sometimes so far short that we've felt abandoned and betrayed, and cried out, "Where are you, God?"

Like John, at least sometimes we have given our all, invested every drop of our life's blood in the noblest of causes and then seen our best efforts come to nothing, or worse. And we have felt not just disappointed but abandoned and betrayed. "Where are you, God? Don't you care at all?"

Jesus hears John's question and ours, and he responds to it. In effect he says, "You've got your expectations all wrong. You seem to expect that, if you trust in me, I'll bring you happiness by ironing out all the wrinkles in the world around you – fast and on schedule. "Sorry," says Jesus, "ironing is not my job. It's yours. My job is to give you the inner powers, the tools of the heart, that will enable you to carry on your share of the building of God's kingdom. My job is to show you how you can be happy each day of your life, even in the face of troubles and failure.

"Remember what you've seen me do," says Jesus. "'. . . the blind see, cripples walk, lepers are cured, the deaf hear, and dead men are raised to life.' If you'll let me, I'll do the same for you," he says. "I'll heal what is sick in your spirit, if you'll let me.

"I'll open your eyes and your ears so that you'll know what really matters, so you'll know that happiness and peace are available to you every day, even on the worst of days. I'll show you that and let you experience that, if you'll let me.

"I will not insulate you from adversity, challenge, or pain. But I will always see you through them, and never let you come to ultimate harm. I'll take you by the hand, and raise you up; I'll help you to walk and I'll walk with you till your journey is complete, if you'll let me.

"All that is my promise to you, my solemn pledge. And I will not take it back," says the Lord.

The Lord has spoken to us and given us his word. Let us take his word into our hearts with confident, patient expectation!

Habits of the Heart

Matthew 1:18-24

A workman injured his thumb on the job and was told by the foreman to go to the clinic. He stepped inside and found an empty room with only two chairs. At the back of the room were two doors, one marked "illness" and the other marked "injury." The man thought to himself, "I'm not sick, I've just hurt my thumb." So he walked through the door marked "injury."

He found himself in a second room with two more doors, one marked "internal" and the other "external." "It's my thumb," he thought to himself, "not something inside." So he walked through "external" where yet another room faced him, this time with doors marked "therapy" and "treatment."

"Well, I don't need counseling or therapy," he said. "It's only my thumb." So he walked through the "treatment" door into still another empty room with two more doors marked "major" and "minor." "This isn't a major problem," he had to admit, "it's just that my thumb is hurt." So he walked through the door marked "minor" and found himself outside the clinic on the street!

Shaking his head he walked back to work, where the foreman asked, "Were they able to help you?"

"I'm not sure," said the man, "but I'll tell you one thing, that's the best organized outfit I've ever seen!"

We human beings crave orderliness, stability and predictability. That's why we spend so much time trying to organize things. It's why we study history and economics – we're looking for patterns of predictability. It's why we pass laws – to build some order into our lives. It's also why some of us withdraw from life, while others become manipulative and controlling. Disorder frightens us, surprises and scares us.

There was a time, not so long ago, when we thought our scholars and scientists would soon be able to predict and therefore control just about everything. And we'd be able to make neat little rules and procedures for making the world perform exactly as we'd like. But we've learned that life is more complicated than we thought. We're coming to realize that weather forecasters will never be able to predict the weather, economists will never be able to tell us what we really want to know, and, no rules or procedures, however carefully drafted, will ever suffice for all occasions.

It is our destiny to dwell in a land of surprises, in which new challenges and new opportunities await us around every bend in the road. In the absence of an all-purpose rule book or a comprehensive owner's manual, how shall we ever know how to respond? Today's gospel tells us.

Joseph is betrothed to a beautiful young girl, who is living with her parents till he can raise the dowry. She drops by his carpenter shop. His face brightens when he sees his lovely bride, and then she drops the bomb, she's pregnant . . . by the Holy Spirit!? He's devastated. He goes numb, and cannot speak. She leaves crying. As the hours pass, he slowly turns it over and over in his heart. He knows what the rules say: denounce her to the authorities and assist in stoning her to death in front of her parents' house. (What a tragedy that would have been for us.)

But even in his hurt, his heart won't let him blindly follow that harsh rule . . . Perhaps he should just divorce her quietly . . . Still he doesn't act. He prays some more. And in the middle of the night, the Spirit who dwells in all our hearts shows him the way, "Don't be afraid to take Mary as your wife." So with a peaceful heart Joseph puts aside his fears and takes Mary into his house.

On that day of terrible surprise, shock, and pain, a day that Joseph could never have imagined in his wildest nightmares, something very powerful enabled him to reach beyond the narrow, programmed response dictated by his upbringing. What was it? It was the habits of his heart – a lifetime habit of graciousness and compassion, and – a lifetime habit of walking with the Lord and listening to the Lord who always helps us see life afresh.

Out of those habits of the heart came Joseph's ability and willingness in a moment of surprise to look past the rules to the person of Mary, and to act with compassion, forgetting his fears and his doubts, forgetting all else but the person. In doing that, he acted like God himself.

There will never be an end to life's surprises, and no rules or easy axioms will ever fully prepare us for them. Only those hearts whose habits are gracious and compassionate and whose traveling companion is the Lord will be ready for life's surprises. And their deeds will mirror God's face.

So we pray: Lord, grant us great hearts and let us walk with you always!

What God Thinks You're Worth

Luke 2:1-14

There's an ancient legend among the Polynesians about a young man who fell in love and asked for a maiden's hand in marriage. Before a marriage could take place, the groom had to negotiate with the bride's father for the price to be paid for the bride. The price was to be paid in cows. Depending upon the beauty and grace of a bride, her father could demand as many as ten cows, though no one could remember a bride ever being traded for more than eight. For the rest of her life, each woman was known, for better or worse, as a three-cow, or a five- or six-cow bride.

Now as it happens, the bride in our story was not a beauty. Indeed, the unanimous opinion of the villagers was that a single cow, an old cow, would be an extravagant price for any groom to pay for her. And so, with the whole village watching, the negotiation began. As expected, the bride's father asked for a single cow. The groom refused! Instead, he insisted on giving a full ten cows! The villagers were shocked and amazed. "Why," they asked, "did you trade away ten cows – all the cows you owned for this maiden?"

"Because," he replied, "I wanted her to know how much I think she's worth – everything."

It is said, among the natives of Polynesia, that, as the years passed, that "ten-cow bride" became the loveliest woman in the land.

As we gather in the quiet of this night and hear again the story of Jesus' birth in a stable, and as we remember with sadness where this wonderful child's life came to its conclusion – on the cross – we have to ask God, "Why did you do it, God? Why did you give us all you have and hold nothing back? Why did you give us your son?"

From out of the stillness, God is whispering a response, "I gave you all I have because I want you to know, and never forget, how much I think you are worth!"

What Is a Family?

Matthew 2:13-15, 19-23

A very difficult and rowdy little boy was about to turn seven. So his parents were trying to decide what to give him for his birthday. His dad suggested a bike.

"Do you think maybe that will improve his behavior?" asked his mother.

"I doubt it," said Dad realistically. "But at least it'll be spread it over a wider area."

Dad was a realist, and that's what we need to be as we think about our families on this feast of the Holy Family. What is a family? It's a lot more than shared bloodlines or a common residence. It's a lot more than hugs and kisses and Christmas dinner. It's something both messy and wonderful. A family is a gathering together of unfinished, wounded wayfarers who are committed to drawing out the best from each other.

The essence of being family is mutual commitment; intense, bonded commitment that goes beyond sentimentality and self-interest; a commitment that is not casually set aside. That kind of commitment – to the very heart of another – mirrors God's commitment to us. And like God's commitment to us, it brings light into dark places and makes "deserts bloom."

Doing just that, bringing light into dark places and making deserts bloom, is the ultimate vocation of us all. And in the end, it's the way we'll know if we really are families or not, and know if we really are God's people or not. If that is what we're about, then ever so slowly, we'll see one another emerging from darkness and getting better. And every step of the other into the sunlight will feel our own progress.

We'll see tiny patches of those deserts in one another beginning to bloom. And every new flower there will feel like our own. Those will be the signs. We'll still be wounded, unfinished wayfarers. Life together will still have its stresses and its conflicts. But we'll know we're on the way. We've started to be family and to be God's people.

God grant that we may bring light into dark places and make deserts bloom!

A Star is Beckoning You

Matthew 2:1-12

Two friends, Harry and Tom, went hunting in the woods where they got very lost, and very nervous too, as darkness began to fall. Trying to reassure his friend, Harry said, "Don't worry, ole buddy. All we have to do is shoot into the air three times, stay where we are, and somebody'll find us." So that's what they did, shot in the air three times and waited. But no one came. After a while, they tried it again. But still no one came.

When they decided to try one last time, Tom said nervously, "It'd better work this time. We're down to our last three arrows!"

They had the words, but they didn't have the idea! That can be a problem for us all: having the words but missing the idea, living on the outside while missing the inside of life, and worse yet, not even noticing!

If you want to know what that looks like in the concrete, just take a look at the characters in today's gospel: King Herod and his sophisticated entourage of philosophers, scribes, and bureaucrats. The whole lot of them missed the star to start with. When it was finally brought to their attention, they delegated the task of following it to outsiders! And that was that. Back to business as usual. Herod and company liked to think of themselves as "insiders," but in fact they were the ultimate outsiders, living solely on the surface of life, and ignoring the invitation to search for more.

Now take a look at the three wise men. They eventually spotted the star because every day for a very long time they raised their eyes above their desks, books, and charts and looked beyond themselves and up into the skies which is where stars are found! And when at last they saw the star, they did more than admire it and note it on their charts. They followed it and kept on following it, through the cold and quiet of many nights, even though it led them where they had no thought or desire of going: right past Jerusalem to an obscure country village to a peasant's infant lying in a manger.

They had watched and watched, and followed, and kept on following because they knew in their hearts that there was something more to life, something that God wanted them to have, something that God would help them find, if only they were faithful to the search and didn't settle for living only on the surface. Their hopes were not misplaced, for in the end God showed them the way.

For each of us there will always be a star, whether we attend to it or not, a star beckoning us to lift up our eyes and our hopes, and to look beyond the surface of life, beckoning us to lay hold of the very heart of life, and to walk with God.

God grant that we will lift up our eyes to watch patiently for the star which each night brings. Grant us the wisdom follow it, for it leads to the very heart of life. It leads to God.

Watch for the star and follow it. Amen.

Jesus' Formula for Happiness

Matthew 3:13-17

A husband and wife were desperately trying to make it on social security and a small pension, but with no success. One day, as they sat at the kitchen table, sifting through a pile of unpaid bills and trying to figure out how to cut back on their modest living expenses, a sinister visitor suddenly appeared. "Who are you?" the wife asked.

"I am the devil," said the visitor. "And I'm here to offer you a deal. I'll guarantee you that for the rest of your lives you'll never have to worry about money. You'll have enough to get out of debt, finance the grandson's education, buy a new car, and take a Caribbean cruise before you retire to a golf-course community in Florida. Many years from now you will both die in your sleep and your souls will become mine for all eternity."

The couple looked at each other in astonishment and disbelief. Then the husband leaned over the table and in a low, conspiratorial voice, asked his wife: "Do you suppose there's a catch?"

The poor fellow missed the point, just as we do so much of the time. How often do we set out to make a wonderful day or to build another piece of a wonderful life, and before we know it we have gotten lost, distracted, or confused and end up bungling the job – creating instead our own little annex to hell.

God knows this about us. Without God's help, we are never going to get the point of life, never going to "get it together." So, in Jesus, we have the best help possible: God's very own son. And just to make sure we don't miss the point, we hear in today's gospel, "this Jesus is my son; listen to him!"

So what has Jesus got to say to us? His whole teaching, the whole of the gospel, boils down to just two points. First, if you want to be happy, love your neighbor as you love yourself. It's the only way of living that works, the only way of living that guarantees happiness, not just later, but here and now – even in the face of trial and tragedy.

It's a paradox: we get a life only by giving life. Every other way sooner or later leaves us with nothing but a handful of dust. That is the first half of Jesus' message.

The second half is this: if you do want to be happy, and if you are willing to do all the tough things that real love requires, then you have to stay connected to God, the source of power. When our hearts are tied very closely to heaven, when we walk with God day by day, we get the energy we need for loving, and we get it without fail. And when, on the other hand, that connection is broken, we are like burned-out light bulbs: no light, no heat, just dead!

So there we have it. Two points: stick close to the Lord and you will have the energy to love without counting the cost. That is not just the Great Commandment. It is Jesus' formula for happiness. And it works! We have our Father's word on that!

Look Beneath the Surface

John 1:24-39

A local drunk was staggering along Main Street trying to read the morning newspaper when he came upon the parish priest and greeted him politely, "Ga-morning, Father." Now Father was thinking very hard about next Sunday's sermon and was annoyed at the intrusion, so he just ignored the greeting and kept on walking. However, the drunk was not to be brushed off so easily. "Excuse me, Father," he said. "Could you tell me what causes arthritis?"

The priest ignored that too. But when the drunk repeated his question, the priest turned on him impatiently and snapped, "Drinking causes arthritis. Gambling causes arthritis. Carousing with loose women causes arthritis!" And only then, too late, he said, "Why do you ask?"

"Because it says right here in the papers that that's what the pope has!"

He should have seen that coming! So why didn't he? Because he was too caught up in his own thoughts and his own agenda.

John the Baptist knew all about that sort of thing, as he confesses to us in today's gospel. He had known cousin Jesus all his life. They played together as children, and John was sure he knew what there was to know about Jesus. But he didn't. He had missed the very essence of Jesus, and he admits it with embarrassment, "I confess I didn't recognize him."

How could that happen, especially to someone as good and as focused as John? The answer is: very easily. John was so fully absorbed in his work – holy work – and was so blinded by his very narrow expectations of God and of life that he didn't see past the very human surface of Jesus till the very end. He didn't see past the surface because he didn't look past the surface – his busyness and his narrow expectations limited his vision and stopped him short.

If that happened to John, it could happen to us, and indeed, it does happen very often. There are three things in particular that we tend to miss and just not see:

- The first is God's presence, always right here in all power and warmth, but we rarely see or experience either the power or the warmth because we have not looked for it with confident, expectant hearts.
- The second thing we tend to miss is the best of what is inside us, all the goodness already there, and all the possibilities just waiting to be brought to life.
- And finally, we tend to overlook these very same things in one another – both the goodness and the possibilities. And so we give little encouragement to one another.

How do we break this habit of not seeing the good that is there, indeed, of not seeing very much at all?

- First, we have to change our expectations. If we expect the best, that is what we are likely to see and get most of the time. And shouldn't we expect the best if we believe in a loving God?
- And second, if we want to see all the good that's there, we have to take the time to look, regularly and deeply and with fresh eyes, at ourselves, at one another, and at the world.

Such simple changes – just taking the time to look at life with hopeful hearts – but those simple changes can change our lives.

So let us pray for one another:
Lord, you have laid out a banquet before us. Help us to see it in all its richness and splendor, and to rejoice in it always with thankful hearts. Amen.

It's Time to Break Free

Matthew 4:12-23

A patient in a psychiatric hospital was absolutely convinced that he was dead. That was his fixation. He was sure that he was a corpse! The doctors tried to reason with him, but failed utterly. Finally, in desperation they got him to agree to the proposition that corpses do not bleed. He also agreed to allow the doctors to conduct a little test on that proposition. So before he could change his mind, the doctors proceeded immediately with the test by pricking his finger, causing a big drop of blood to come forth. The patient looked at his finger for quite a while, and then at last he spoke. "I'll be darned," he said. "Corpses do bleed!"

Real change of mind and heart comes hard. We cling to ideas that make no sense, and we do so with closed-eyed determination. We hold onto habits and ways of doing things that we see are not working. Year after year, we trudge along in familiar ruts, though we know from past experience we don't want to go where these old trails are leading. Why this reluctance to change? Why this dread of letting go of habits and attitudes, ideas and relationships that are not serving us or anybody else? Why the self-imposed blindness? What is the fear? It's pretty basic, really. To change means to let go of something we have in the hope of getting something better.

The problem in letting go is that we don't have that something better in hand yet – indeed we may not even be able to see its shape yet. We are making a leap, like the man on the flying trapeze. And that means that, at least for a little while, we are likely to be empty-handed.

The big fear, of course, is that we'll end up empty-handed, having let go of what we had with nothing of value to take its place. Now that is a good-sized fear! It's the fear that keeps battered women in ugly marriages, and keeps legions of talented people in the wrong jobs. It's the fear that can keep us stuck in habits of thinking or praying, relating or living that just don't work, that haven't worked for a long time, and maybe never did.

In Sunday's gospel, the Lord is calling us out of the darkness that our fear has made. We are urged to break free of whatever we are clinging to that is trapping or enslaving us or shrinking our lives to midget size. "I offer you a wonderful life now, as well as later, but if you want that wonderful life, you are going to have to re-form and re-shape your life. You are going to have to change . . . a lot."

The Lord knows the fears we are bound to feel when we hear that kind of challenge to change, and therefore assures us we won't be traveling alone. Instead of saying, "I'll see you when you've got this taken care of." It's "Come with me. As you let go of those chains that you've been clinging to, I'll be at your side. And as you set out on a new path, groping for your next step, I'll be there. And I'll give you the light you need to find your way, and the strength you need to keep going and to keep searching. You have my word."

Let us take the Lord literally and let go of the chains our fears have made, and begin to walk the new paths before us. And let us begin that good work today.

Blessed Are They Who Know They Are Poor

Matthew 5:1-12

There's an ancient Hassidic tale about a rabbi who asked to be shown both heaven and hell while he was still alive. He was a particularly fine rabbi, so his wish was granted, and in the twinkling of an eye his tour began. First stop was hell, which, to his amazement, was a fabulous dining room with a vast table laden with the finest foods and the juiciest morsels of every description. Despite that splendid display, however, every single person at the table was just sitting there with arms folded and eyes downcast in sullen, angry silence, because at every place the only utensil was a pair of chopsticks, five feet long. No one could get a bite of food to his or her mouth. The whole lot of them were starving in the midst of a banquet!

After pondering that awhile, the rabbi was glad to be taken next door to heaven, which, to his great surprise, was the exact duplicate of hell. The same long table, the same splendid feast, and a five-foot pair of chopsticks at each place. But every last person at that table was talking and laughing and singing as they picked up the food with their chopsticks and fed the person across from them. No one was starving, and everyone was eating to contentment.

Two identical rooms, side by side, but light years apart. What do you suppose made the difference? Jesus is suggesting the answer to that in the first of the beatitudes which we just read: "Blest are the poor in spirit," he says. Or, a better translation, "Blest are those who know they are poor." Now what's so great about that, knowing we are poor? Actually, quite a lot. Really admitting that whatever we have is just on short-term loan, and not really ours, is immensely liberating.

Knowing and acknowledging before the world that we are poor, frees us from any need to posture or pretend or live behind a mask. It frees us from the blind competitiveness that squanders life on frantically collecting things that can be ours for only a moment.

Knowing that we are poor breaks down the walls that separate us from our brothers and sisters who also are poor; and it lets us see how alike we are. It allows us to ask for help, without fear or embarrassment, when we need it. And it helps us to know from the inside when others are in need of us. It helps us see God's gifts as gifts; and it fills our hearts with thankfulness and the desire to give in return. Knowing that we are poor frees us from all manner of fears and moves us to "pick up our chopsticks" to feed others, and to allow ourselves to be fed.

So let us pray for one another for the liberation that comes from knowing we are poor.

Lord, all we have comes from you, and without you we are nothing and have nothing. Flood our hearts with humble thankfulness. Wash away all the fears that isolate or separate us, and sweep us forward to share your gifts with open hands and joyful hearts. Amen.

We Are Salt and Light for One Another

Matthew 5:13-16

There was a wise nun who was teaching a very difficult class of ninth graders. They were good kids, and bright too, but they had a bad habit of cutting down everyone and everything that crossed their paths – including the persons they saw in the mirror every morning.

Sister, because she was both wise and good, knew she couldn't let this go on. So one Friday morning, she distributed to each member of the class a complete student roster. She instructed them to write down next to each name the best thing they could honestly say about each classmate. "Just tell the truth," she said, "nothing more." And so they did.

Over the weekend, Sister compiled the data, and Monday, she handed to each student a summary of what their classmates really thought of them.

Without exception, the students were astonished. "I never knew anybody noticed that about me," said some. "I didn't realize people liked me so much," said others. And all of them said, "I guess I'm a lot better than I thought."

But the story doesn't end there, because years later one of those students was killed in Vietnam. And that wise nun and many of her former students gathered for the funeral.

After the mass, the dead soldier's father came over to Sister. "I want to show you something," he said. "They found this in my son's pocket." He put in her hand a worn and yellowed piece of paper that had been folded and unfolded and taped back together many times. It was his son's treasured list of all the good things his classmates had seen in him so long ago.

After some moments of teary silence, each one of those former classmates spoke up in turn and admitted that they still had their lists too, tucked in diaries or scrapbooks, in wallets or purses, folded and unfolded many times across the years, reminding them of all the good their classmates had seen in them, and calling them again and again to be true to that good. What a splendid gift they'd given to one another, so long ago!

In Sunday's gospel, Jesus names the good that he sees in us. "You are the light of the world," he says, "and the salt of the earth." Light doesn't draw attention to itself. It lets people see what is around them – what is really there, not what they imagine or fear is there when it is dark and they cannot see. That is what we are for one another, light! That's what Jesus says.

Light lets people see all the beautiful things that are invisible when it is dark. Light lets them see faces and flowers, oceans and paintings, and people's hearts. That is what we are for one another, light. Light lets us see what's worth having and being – and what's not. That is what we are for one another.

But we are salt too. Salt draws out the flavor and the zest and the special character of whatever it touches. In just the right quantities, it brings out the best. That is what we are for one another. Salt is a preservative too. It protects from spoiling and decay and keeps things whole and intact and ready to serve life and not death. We are all of that for one another, salt and light, Jesus says.

So let us pray for one another.
Lord, let us never forget that we are light and salt for one another. Keep our light burning brightly so that all around us may see and have no fear. Keep our special flavor strong so that all whose lives we touch will grow and flourish.

Walk Gently on the Earth

Matthew 5:17-37

It was the first day on the job for the new, young optometrist. The boss, the head optician, was explaining how the office worked. "When customers come in for a pair of glasses, first you examine them. Then you show them some frames."

"But there are no prices on the frames," said the new optometrist.

"Exactly," said the boss. "When customers find some frames they like, they'll ask you how much the frames cost. You say $200.' Then you wait a minute. If there's no objection, you add, 'And the lenses, of course, are $150.' Pause a moment and if there's still no objection, you say, 'Each!'"

How much can I get away with? How far can I go without getting caught? For some folks that's the bottom line for all decision making, the only question that really matters. And for almost all of us, it's a question we still do ask – at least sometimes. It's a way of looking at the world that shows its ugly face in comments like, "She's 2000 miles away, and she'll never find out." Or "What he doesn't know won't hurt him." Or "I'll be long gone, before they find the body." Or "It's okay, nobody's lookin'."

How much can I get away with? What's the least I can do without getting in trouble? Sounds like the formula for an easy, laid-back life, doesn't it. But it's not. In fact, it's a guaranteed, sure-fire formula for sadness, because it goes contrary to our deepest desires namely, our unquenchable thirst for communion, our longing for friendships in which there are no hidden closets and no unshared gifts.

In Sunday's Gospel, Jesus looks at the ten commandments and says quite simply, they're fine, but they're not enough. If you really want a happy life, he says, you've got to go beyond those rules, because they only look at things from the outside. The inside of things is what you need to see and respond to. Look and listen carefully to each person, each creature, each thing that crosses your path, he says, because each of them has a message for you. And the message is always the same: "I am God's good creature," says each one. "Take good care of me."

That is the silent message that Jesus is asking us to hear from every person we meet, from every creature that crosses our path, and from every piece of the earth we touch. "I am God's good creature. Take good care of me," say they all.

If we listen with our hearts to the inside of each of God's creatures, we'll always know how to respond to them, and we'll have the heart to respond – with reverence and care and graciousness. And our heart's deepest desire, our longing for communion, will begin to come true, because to each of God's creatures we will have given not our least but our best – from the heart!

Don't Respond in Kind

Matthew 5:38-48

A distressed farmer was about to lose his farm, so he went to the bank to get a loan, and his old hound dog came along too. Now the banker was a hard, unsmiling man who had never heard the word compassion. So it came as no surprise that, despite the farmer's pleading, and despite his perfect financial record, the banker said 'No, absolutely no!' to the loan.

No sooner had those words been spoken than the farmer's old hound jumped up and bit that banker hard, on the leg. And then he bit one of the customers as well. The banker was astonished. "I can understand," he said, "why your dog might bite me after I turned down your loan. But why did he bite that innocent bystander over there?"

"Aw that's easy," said the farmer. "He just needed to get the nasty taste out of his mouth."

A real part of everyday life is deciding how to respond to people who do us wrong. For some of us instinct says, "Run the other way as fast as you can!" For others, it says, "Get mad," or worse, "don't get mad, get even." In either case we put a big label on the person who hurt or offended us, and that label says "enemy." And sometimes, just for a little while, we may even put that "enemy" label on our dearest friends.

In Sunday's Gospel Jesus offers us an alternative way of responding to people who hurt us. It begins with changing the way we look at them. Instead of seeing "enemy" written across their faces, we need to read what's actually written there, the words "frightened brother" and "frightened sister." That's what those people are even if they've temporarily forgotten or denied it.

So we've got our labels right; now how do we proceed? Sunday's gospel says, "Offer no resistance to injury." That sounds like a recipe for victimhood but it's not. It's just a bad translation. Jesus' real advice is, "Don't respond on the same level. Don't respond to injury with injury. Don't play evil's game. Seize the moment and redefine it into some-thing better."

Jesus gives an example. "If someone wants to go to law over your cloak, give him your tunic as well." Sounds like victimhood again, but actually, it was a very shrewd strategy whose purpose was to shame a sinner into a change of heart by giving him a good look at his sin.

This is how it worked. Jesus' contemporaries wore only two garments, a tunic, rather like the white alb a priest wears, and a cloak or overcoat for going outdoors on cold days. So in saying to your oppressor, "Here, take my tunic as well," you are leaving yourself standing there stark naked. Embarrassing? Yes. Cold? Indeed. But you have also turned the tables on your oppressor. You have taken charge of the interaction and redefined it. And, if there is an ounce of goodness in him, you have shamed him into seeing the ugliness of his sin (bribing a judge to get a cloak he doesn't need), and you have laid the foundation for a change of heart. You have responded to injury with a gift instead of another injury.

Of course, not everyone will be touched by such an appeal. Some hearts are very hard indeed, as Jesus himself knew full well. But don't we owe one another the chance to say "yes" to that kind of appeal? Don't we owe the chance to see hurtfulness for what it is? The chance to retreat from sin and change course – don't we owe that to one another? Of course we do, because we are brothers and sisters.

So let us give to one another the gift of transform ing graciousness. In the face of hurt, gracious-ness neither runs away nor trades hurt for hurt, but strives to draw the best from blinded, frightened hearts, hearts we slowly recognize as brothers and sisters.

Let us give that gift now, without delay, wherever it is needed! We won't run out. We have enough for everyone! And our reward will be peace.

Are You Telling Yourself the Truth?

Matthew 24:37-44

There's an old Jewish tale about a rabbi who went on a journey with his servant Jacob. When they came to a roadside inn, the rabbi went in to rest, leaving Jacob to care for the rabbi's cart and feed his horse. A horse trader came by and plied poor Jacob with strong drink. Before long he had persuaded the fellow to sell the rabbi's horse for a few coins.

The next morning Jacob awakened to the enormity of his mistake, and he was very frightened. What would he tell the rabbi? An idea occurred to him. Quickly he placed himself between the empty shafts of the cart and started to chew hay. Then the rabbi came out. "What's the meaning of this?" he stammered. "Where's my horse?"

"The horse?" replied Jacob. "That's I!"

"Are you insane?" shouted the rabbi.

"Please don't be angry," pleaded the servant. "Years ago a great misfortune befell me. I was a young man then, wild and foolish, and I sinned gravely with a woman. To punish me, God turned me into a horse, and for twenty long years you have been my master. Now, it seems my punishment is over. I'm a man again. Praise God!"

When the rabbi heard Jacob's story he began to pray aloud, praising God for his mercies. But he had a problem. He couldn't continue his journey without a horse. So he went to the marketplace to buy one. And there, at the horse trader's barn, he came face to face with his old horse who was calmly munching hay! Shocked and deeply distressed, the rabbi drew very close to the horse and whispered in its ear, "For goodness sake, Jacob. Again, so soon?!"

Again! So soon! How many times have we had to say that to ourselves! Who can even count! Each of us is different, but for each of us there is a sad pattern: again and again we stumble at the same spots on the same roads. And as the years go by, and the same knee is bruised over and over again, and the same hand is scraped over and over again, two great temptations knock insistently at the door of our hearts.

The first is presumption, which tells us to shut our eyes and say, "No problem. I'm just fine." The second temptation is just the opposite, despair. It says, "There is no hope for me. I'm beyond saving." Both of those temptations are lies, but it is very easy for one or the other to take over and begin to feel like the truth. That is why we have to work very hard at telling ourselves the real truth about ourselves.

Where does this truth-telling begin? It begins with naming the sinful, destructive patterns in our lives, not making them larger or smaller than they are, just seeing those wounded, wounding patterns as God sees them. And how does God see them? In context, and that means with hope. God looks at you or me in our stumbling about and sees a much beloved child who is having the usual troubles growing up. God says to us, "You will grow up if you'll let me help you. But you'll have to be patient, because growing up takes a long time."

One of the kindest words Jesus ever spoke was his response to the charge that he spent too much time with sinners. He said, "Healthy people don't need doctors. Sick people do." He was saying to each of us, "If you are wounded and wounding, if you are flawed, and weak, and not near done yet, I'm your man – if you'll let me be."

Let him be. Open your heart to him. Name your wounds and your sadnesses, the hard places in your heart and the empty places there. Give them all to him and don't take them back.

In God's good time, the healing and growing you desire will happen.

Don't Take Back Your "Yes"

Matthew 17:1-9

A top-level executive was dashing through the airport to catch a plane, when she discovered she'd forgot her watch. So she stopped a stranger to ask the time. The stranger smiled, set down the two large suitcases he was carrying, and consulted his watch. "It's exactly 5:09. The temperature is 73 degrees, and it will rain tonight. In London the sky is clear, and the temperature is 38 degrees Celsius. The Dow-Jones is up 35 points. The dollar is holding steady. . ."

The executive interrupted him, "Your watch tells you all that?" "Oh, yes, and much more. You see, I invented this watch and it's the only one in the world."

"I must have that watch," said the competent executive. "I'll give you $2000 for it right now."

"Sorry," said the inventor, picking up his suitcases, "It's not for sale."

"$4000, in cash," countered the lady executive.

"No," said the inventor, "I made it for my son's birthday."

"Okay, this is my last offer. I'll give you $10,000."

The inventor paused and then agreed, "It's yours for $10,000."

The businesswoman was elated as she took that very thin, handsome watch and snapped it on her wrist. "Thank you very much," she said, and turned to go.

"Hey, wait a minute," called the inventor, dragging over the two heavy suitcases he'd been carrying. "You forgot the batteries!"

I think I want a refund! That's just about the way the apostles were feeling as Jesus led them to the top of the mountain. He'd just told them that he was going to die. And their hearts were broken. So he took them to the mountaintop and let them see him – just for a moment – with all the filters down. He let them experience who he really is, and let them know that even though he would die, he wouldn't be destroyed. He would rise, and he would triumph.

What a moment that was! They were so happy, they just wanted to stay there forever and never leave. "Let us build a shrine for you," they said, "right here,

Jesus, away from all the pain and suffering and ugliness of the world."

But Jesus' work wasn't finished and theirs had hardly begun. So the vision ended, and he led them back down the mountain, back to finish their life's work, back to face all the challenges they hadn't even imagined when they'd said "yes" to Jesus so short a time ago.

They were sad, afraid, and overwhelmed, and wishing they could stay on the mountaintop, and wishing they'd never said that "yes" to Jesus. Jesus knew that. So he spoke to them softly, "Don't be afraid. I'm going to suffer and die, and so are you. But in the end we're going to win. That's what I showed you on the mountain. So don't ever forget it."

Nothing of value is ever bought cheaply. As life unfolds, we come to understand that the price of the things we hold most dear is far greater than we'd imagined in the beginning. Our marriages and families, our dreams, our life's work all looked so simple when we said "yes" to them. We saw only the "watch" and not the "batteries." Later the price of our loves and dreams began to come clear, and, like the apostles, we've experienced the desire to ask for a refund, to put a "no" in place of our "yes" and to retreat to a spot that's warm, cozy and safe, and far from the storms.

It is to all of us that Jesus speaks from that glorious mountaintop. "I know," he says, "I know what it means to be tired and afraid, to want to run away and not come back, to want to hide in a safe place and never come out. I know! But you mustn't do that, you have no need to. You will labor and struggle, sweat and suffer, and sometimes face crushing defeats, but you will never be crushed. You will triumph in the end. That is my pledge to you, and I give you the sign of my own dying and rising from the dead as the guarantee of my pledge.

"Accept my pledge," says the Lord, "walk with me, and be not afraid!"

An Offer We Should't Refuse

John 4:5-42

There was an enterprising young woman who spent years training her dog to speak and tell jokes. Finally, they got a spot on the Johnny Carson show! They were terribly excited, but when they got on stage, the dog just sat there, not saying a word. They were gone by the next commercial! On the way home, the young woman was very upset. "Rover," she said, "this was our big chance, and you went silent on me. What happened?"

"I'm really sorry," said Rover, "but from where I was sitting, I couldn't see the cue cards."

That dog is not the only one who needs cues! We all do. The woman at the well in Sunday's gospel was desperate for a cue. Her life was a wreck. Her mistakes were huge, and she kept making the same ones over and over again. Five husbands she'd had. Now she was working on a sixth. And that was only the tip of the iceberg. What a mess! And it was a mess she didn't know how to escape.

Then Jesus came into her life, ignoring all the rules that said that men shouldn't talk to strange women, that good Jews shouldn't talk to Samaritans, and that nobody should talk about sensitive topics like the number of one's spouses. Jesus ignored all those rules and talked to her. He didn't lecture; he didn't condemn. He just let her know that he knew her sadness and loneliness, her weariness and confusion, and her longing for something more.

He let her know that her story didn't have to go on like this, didn't have to wind down to a sad and bitter end. There was more to life than that, more than she'd ever imagined. And right there, at the side of that well, Jesus offered her that something more. He offered her "living water" which he said would become a "fountain" inside her, "leaping up to provide eternal life."

What was this living water he was offering? Friendship with the Father. Wholehearted, all-encompassing, confident friendship with the Father – which changes everything. It puts energy where weariness was, hope where despair was, and joy where sadness reigned supreme. He offered her the Father's friendship, and she received it and took it in with joy. And her life was changed forever.

This is the very same living water that Jesus offers us now, friendship with the Father, a fountain inside us, leaping up to provide eternal life.

Let us drink deeply of this water, and share it with one another, and let it change our lives forever!

Are You Clinging to Your Chains?

John 9:1-41

About 400 years before Jesus was born, the Greek philosopher Plato told a story about a group of people who had spent their whole lives imprisoned in a cave. They were chained together, facing the back wall of the cave, and they'd never seen anything but that wall. Just outside the entrance of their cave, a fire was kept burning at all times, and it threw some light onto the cave's back wall. So whenever people walked between the fire and the cave entrance, their shadows appeared on the back wall of the cave. Because the prisoners had never seen anything but these shadows moving across their wall, they presumed that the shadows were real people, and that there was nothing more to be seen.

Then one day one of the prisoners broke free from his chains and staggered out into the sunlight. There, to his amazement, he saw the real world for the first time. He saw, in three dimensions and in living color, the real people whose mere shadows he'd been watching on the wall for years.

Overjoyed, he went back into the cave to share with his friends the good news that the real world is a lot bigger and more beautiful than they'd imagined. But they wouldn't believe him – they insisted they'd already seen all there was to see. They held onto their chains, and refused to go outside, and eventually they died in their prison, looking at shadows, and calling them real.

That's a sad ending for a story that should have ended happily, with everyone throwing off their chains and walking out into the light. And I suspect it feels doubly sad because we know in our hearts that sometimes we're like those cave-prisoners. Sometimes we see only the faintest of shadows and declare that is all there is to see. And sometimes we close our eyes entirely, and see nothing at all.

That's why today's gospel story has been read during Lent every single year since the first century: because we need it.

- First, we need to take a hard look at those Pharisees, who claimed to see the truth better than anybody, but in fact didn't see the truth at all. They should make us very nervous.
- Second, we need to remember Jesus' power to cure blindness, even life-long blindness.

In the story, Jesus picked up a little dirt, spat upon it, rubbed the mud on the blind man's eyes, and had him wash his eyes in the pool. Suddenly the man was cured. The case was clear-cut: a miracle, from life-long blindness to perfect sight. But look at how the Pharisees denied and distorted what was right in front of their eyes:

- They denied that it was the same man;
- They challenged whether he had really been blind;
- They tried to discredit him because he was ignorant and poor;
- And when all that failed, they attacked Jesus by saying that he couldn't possibly be a decent man because he had broken the law of Moses by working on Sunday: spitting on the dirt to make mud for the blind man's eyes!

Why did they do all that? Because they were afraid; afraid that it would cost too much to look at the truth, because then they'd have to act on it.

Why do we hide from the truth and settle for mere shadows of reality instead of reality itself? For the same reason: we fear we can't cope with the truth, so we pretend it doesn't exist.

Fear makes us not see our sins. Fear makes us not see our talents and possibilities. Fear makes us not see our unhappiness. Fear makes us not see how anemic and one-dimensional we sometimes are.

Fear makes us settle for very little, because fear persuades us that very little is possible. And that's a lie! Jesus said it very simply: "For those who love God, nothing is impossible."

If our hearts are truly open and one with the Lord, we will have the spiritual energy and power to do whatever needs to be done; and we'll have no reason to close our eyes and hide from the truth.

So that is where our task begins: opening our hearts to the Lord who will let us know in our hearts that we have no reason to fear. Because "for those who love God, nothing is impossible."

And then we can begin to open our eyes.

He Already Knows

John 11:1-45

A priest was teaching his weekly Bible class, and he asked the members how they'd introduce themselves to the Lord when they got to heaven. The first one said, "Lord, I'm Joan. I was married for 47 years; I raised three wonderful children, and I always baked the cupcakes for school. That's who I am."

Another said, "Lord, I'm George. I was the biggest contractor in the county. Almost all of my buildings were good; and I tried to watch out for the little guys. That's who I am."

And another said, "I'm Harry. I was the school janitor all my life. Kept the place real clean, and was never mean to the kids either. That's who I am, Lord."

And so it went till finally it was the turn of the oldest man in the group. He spoke very softly: "I won't need to introduce myself," he said. "The Lord already knows who I am."

The Lord already knows who we are from the inside out, and he looks at you and me with the same love that he had for his dear friend Lazarus. He knows our successes and our triumphs. He knows how much they cost us. And he's very proud of us.

But God also sees what's dead in us, just as clearly as when he looked at the dead Lazarus. God smells the smell. He sees the parts of us that are locked up behind solid rock, as Lazarus was. He sees the parts of us that are so tied up that we can't move. And God calls out to us by name, just as he called Lazarus. "Come out!" he says. "Don't stay in that place of death any longer. Come out into the fresh air and the light; and be released from your bonds, whatever they are. Come out, and live, and share our friendship. Come out!

That is Jesus' call to each of us this day. "Leave behind what cannot give you life, and come into deeper friendship with those who can give you life: the Lord and his good people." That is Jesus' call.

If we are to answer his call, we must name the parts of ourselves that are wounded or dead, imprisoned or in darkness, and then give those parts of ourselves to him to be healed, resurrected, and set free. That is what he'll do for us, if we let him.

So let us spend a little while with him in the quiet of our heart. Let us name our darkness, our prison, our woundedness-whatever it may be – and give it all to him. We can count on him and trust him, because he loves us even more than we love ourselves. Thanks be to God!

All Will Be Well

We have just heard the story of the last hours of Jesus Christ, the best friend we ever had. As we listened to the reading of the Passion, we followed him, step by step, in our hearts through his last hours. And now, having heard Jesus speak those last, dreadful words, "It is finished," and watching his head drop upon his breast for the last time, we have to make sense of it all.

What does it mean, this good, kind, loving young man, the kindest man we ever met – barely in his thirties – dying in so ghastly a way, for no crime at all. What does it mean and what is it for?

What it means is that God loves us so much that he will withhold from us absolutely nothing – not even his own dear son. What it means is that no matter what, God will always be there for us, with ALL his love and power, comfort and grace.

There ARE no limits to his commitment to us, none at all. That's what God our very dear Father is saying to us through this terrible moment in Jesus' life. He's saying, "You can count on me. I'll never desert you, and there's nothing I won't give you, not even my son."

This Passion Sunday is, in one way, a very sad day: Walking with Jesus on this day can break your heart. But it's also the brightest of days, because it tells how very much we are loved, and because it reminds us who view it from the vantage point of the resurrection that, despite all appearances, ALL WILL BE WELL!

So let us rejoice, because, thanks be to our good God, ALL WILL BE WELL!

There's More Beyond the Wall

John 20:1-9

A soldier of World War II, blind and paralyzed, lay in his bed at the Veterans' Hospital. He'd been there a long time, sad and lonely, and now he had yet another roommate. Unlike the grouches who had gone before, the new man seemed jolly and friendly. So the old soldier asked the new man, whose bed was by the window, to tell him what was going on outside. The man responded with gusto. He described the flowers bursting into bloom and the birds hopping across the lawn, the postman making his rounds, the children riding their bikes, and much more.

It became a daily ritual, the man by the window helping the old soldier connect with the wonderful world outside. But one day the man by the window died, and his bed was taken by a new man. With some anxiety the old soldier asked him, "Would you describe for me what's going on outside our window."

The new man looked out the window, paused awhile and said, "I don't know what good it'll do. There's nothing outside this window but a brick wall."

Nothing there! Nothing but a brick wall! That's the fear that eventually haunts every heart, the fear that we're boxed in by the windowless walls of our mortality: we're born, we live, we die, and there is no escape. Just nothing, forever and ever.

That's our fear, but it's not the truth. And somehow that happy old soldier by the window knew that in his heart. "There's more," whispered his heart, and he saw through the wall of that hospital and through the wall of his own mortality, his own dying.

Our hearts are whispering the same words, "There's more than you can see right now, much, much more on the other side of the wall. You are not made for nothingness." That's what our heart is whispering. And all our life long we've hoped against hope that that whisper is not an illusion.

Now at last God himself speaks to us out loud – not in words but in mighty deeds: He has raised our brother Jesus from the dead. And in doing that he's saying to us, "You can trust that whisper in your heart: Life is what I made you for. Not death, but life with me forever!"

Life forever! We have God's word on it. Let us rejoice and be glad!

Will He Be There for Me?

John 20:19-31

An Eskimo and his fifteen-year-old son were fishing with two other men on the edge of the ice. Suddenly without warning, the piece of ice on which they were standing broke away, and very quickly they were pulled out into the Arctic. With the swift currents, high winds, and sub-zero temperatures, their situation was serious. The Eskimo father looked at the other three people and said, "Don't panic, or we die." Then he got into the one kayak that was still tied to the ice. His son expected to get in too – that was the way they always traveled – but his father said, "Sam, you stay here." The boy was hurt and scared, but he did as his father instructed.

After what seemed an eternity, the father returned with another kayak in tow. The strangers got into that one, young Sam took his usual place with his dad, and they headed for home. On the way, Sam asked the question that had been troubling him, "Father, why didn't you let me go back with you the first time?"

"Son," he replied, "I looked into those men's eyes, and I saw that they'd probably panic and die. But I knew that if I left my only son there, they 'd know for sure that I'd be back."

The apostles in Sunday's Gospel were panicked. They were scared to death that the authorities who had killed Jesus would come back to get them too. And worse yet, their hearts were torn with doubt. They had lost hope, lost faith in Jesus. He was gone and wasn't coming back. Overwhelmed and despairing, they'd locked themselves in the upper room. They felt like children abandoned by their parent. Then Jesus appeared. Suddenly they realized: "He hasn't left us after all. He's still with us, and he always will be."

The father had not abandoned them after all, and he never would. At that moment, they knew something else too. They knew that whatever the father asked of them in the future would be possible – no matter how difficult or frightening – for Jesus would always be there with them and for them. Note carefully what happened: their fears and doubts didn't shrink. Instead, they themselves suddenly got a lot bigger inside, here (head) and here (heart), and the impossible became possible for them.

Fears and doubts are part of the rhythm of every normal life. Anyone who doesn't experience fear or doubt, at least sometimes, has probably got his brain turned off – and his heart too. So what do we do when inevitably they appear?

- If we deny their existence or ignore them, we'll wither.
- If we face them and wrestle with them, we'll become the whole persons we want to be.

But where do we get the power to wrestle at the very moment when our doubts and fears are making us feel small, weak, and powerless? The same place the apostles did: From the risen Jesus, the son whom our father left behind, so we'd know he'd never abandon us.

On Good Friday, Jesus settled an important question for us once and for all. The question was, "How much do you love us"? And Jesus answered from the cross, "This much." (extend arms) On Easter morning, Jesus settled a second question. That question was: "Will you always be there for us"? From the door of the empty tomb, he answered, "Yes, always."

My friends, the Lord is not going to take away our fears and doubts, our pains and sufferings by some divine sleight of hand. But to those who listen with trust to his words, he will give great and powerful hearts, hearts big and strong enough to prevail no matter what.

Let the impossible become possible. Let him in and he will fill you full.

Food and Hope for Our Journey

Luke 24:13-35

After a miserable day at the office, a man came home and was greeted at the door by his wife. "How was your day?" he asked, hoping for a little sunshine.

Her response was nervous, "Would you like the good news or the bad news?"

"The good news is all I can take right now," he groaned.

"You know that lovely new car you just bought?" she said.

"Yes," he nodded.

"Well, dear, all the airbags work!"

Sounds like bad news to me! But it was nothing compared to what the disciples had just faced as we find them in today's gospel. Their best friend, Jesus, had just been dragged away, tortured, and put to death. And with him had died their hopes and their dreams. They had hoped that Jesus would save their country and set it on a new and more noble course. They had also hoped that they would have a key role to play in building this new kingdom. Yes, they had dreamed great dreams. But now, on the road to Emmaus, their dreams were dead. And they could not imagine how anything or anyone could ever breathe new life into their broken spirits.

But that is exactly what Jesus did. As he walked that dusty road with them, he helped them see that their dreams had been too small. And that the price they thought they had pay for those dreams was too small as well. As they walked along, Jesus helped them see the world and themselves through his eyes, and helped them see that their real destiny was much bigger and much more grand than they had ever imagined. And finally, as he broke the bread and fed them, he let them know from the inside that, whatever price they would have to pay for the dream that God had dreamed for them, they would have enough and be enough,

because he who had conquered death would be with them always.

All of us have dreamed dreams and held high hopes. It's in our nature. It's the shadow of our longing for God. All of us too have known disappointment and loss, the shattering of dreams, the dashing of hopes large and small. So today's gospel is for us.

It's for us when our dreams turn out to be too small, as we sometimes discover when reaching our goals leaves us sad and empty.

It's for us when our losses are so great we can't imagine anything ever filling our emptiness.

It's for us when the price of going on – and on and on – seems beyond our ability to pay.

Every day of our lives this gospel is for us, challenging us to dream the big dreams that God dreams for us, and to settle for nothing less, calling out to us never to give in to our weariness or pain, inviting us again and again to the table to share this holy food to draw strength for our journey.

So let us pray for one another. May our listening to the Lord Jesus and our sharing in his holy food awaken in us new hope and great dreams. May it give us strength for our journey no matter how long the road. And, when our work is done, may it see us safely into the arms of the One who made us. Amen.

Jesus Our Pathfinder

John 10:1-10

A very crooked lawyer died and found himself facing St. Peter. "What exactly have you done to merit heaven?" asked Peter. The lawyer thought hard and recalled he'd once given a quarter to a beggar on the street.

Peter nodded sourly and looked over to his assistant, the angel Gabriel. "Is that in the records?" The angel nodded, but Peter said it wasn't enough.

"Wait, wait, there's more," cried the lawyer. "I tripped over a crippled child last week and gave him a quarter too."

Gabriel checked the records and confirmed that as well. Peter thought for awhile and then asked Gabriel, "What do you think we should do?"

"Well," said Gabriel with a disgusted look, "I say we give him back his 50 cents and tell him to go to hell."

That man was so bad, he even drew the worst out of an angel! What we're celebrating today is that we have a friend who does just the opposite. Jesus brings out the best in us. And how does he do that? By being shepherd for us. Many times every day, he calls out to us. With quiet prods and nudges, he helps us find our way and shows us where life is to be found and where it's not.

When we wander off the path and get lost, he comes after us and leads us back, not scolding, just glad that we're found. And when brigands and tricksters come – and they always do come – he shows us the path to safety and gives us the strength to walk that path. Day by day, Jesus walks with us, comforting and challenging, feeding and guiding, and urging us forward. He never stops trying to bring out the best in us, even when we haven't listened to his voice for a very long time. Thank God for giving us that kind of friend and brother, who never gives up on us!

But Jesus is more than our friend. He's also our model. What he is for us, we are to be for one another: good shepherds, who bring the best out of one another by comforting and challenging, by feeding and guiding, by urging forward, and by always walking alongside. Each of us will do our shepherding in a different way, but all of us must do it every day. We all must learn to be shepherds.

That's the bottom line of the gospel, and it's a very big order, so we need to pray for one another:

May God grant us attentive hearts that listen to the Lord who shepherds us. May God grant us gracious hearts that know how to shepherd and always bring out the very best from our brothers and sisters. Amen.

It Starts with Remembering

John 14:1-12

A long time ago, before the dawn of recorded history, a clever inventor discovered the art of making fire. Being a generous person, he took his fire-making tools to the snow-clad northern regions, and taught one of the tribes there the art and the advantages of making fire. The people were so excited and fascinated with their new skill, that they forgot to thank the inventor, and didn't notice when he quietly slipped away. But he didn't mind, because all he wanted was the satisfaction of knowing he had made someone else's life better.

The next tribe he went to was just as eager to learn from him as the first. But the leaders became jealous and fearful of the hold the inventor had on the people. So they conspired to have him murdered. After the murder, to allay any suspicion of their involvement in the crime, they installed a huge picture of the Great Inventor in their temple, and they devised elaborate rituals to honor him.

They enshrined his fire-making tools in a golden chest, which people would kiss when they visited his shrine. And the high priest himself undertook the task of compiling the definitive biography of the Great Inventor. This book was handed down with reverence from generation to generation; tribesmen could recite whole sections of it from memory; the penalty of death was imposed upon anyone who failed to acknowledge his greatness. Busy as they were with all these activities honoring the Great Inventor, the people forgot completely the only thing he had come to teach them: how to make a fire.

H ave you ever asked yourself on a Sunday morning, "Why am I going to mass"? I'll bet your kids have – maybe just once! So, what was your answer? (I hope it was good, because if it wasn't you're hating being here right now!) So let's go down the list of possible answers:

- I'm here because it's the law: keep holy the Lord's day. Sort of like taxes. It's the price you pay for having a nice God, and if you don't pay, you're in major trouble. No, not good enough.
- I'm here because it's what decent, God-fearing people do on Sunday. Yawn! Still not good enough.
- I'm here to please God and make him happy. With all the atheists, drug dealers, and terrorists running around, maybe God could use a little encouragement and reassurance that he still has a few friends. Fortunately, God, being God, is already perfectly happy, and nobody can take that away. Try again.
- Well, maybe I'm here to please him in another way, that is, curry favor with him so he'll come through with some big-ticket blessings, or at least overlook some big sins. I believe that's known as manipulation. God's bigger and better than that: He already wants to give you what you need, and he won't be impressed by that immature tactic.

So why do we come here every week? The answer is simple: to remember who we are at the core: God's special people – each one of us. And, as we remember and celebrate who we are – deeper and deeper inside – to draw life from God's son, Jesus, who is here, waiting to touch, heal, feed, strengthen, and draw us forward. That's why we come here. That's why we need to come here!

The tribesmen in the story were good at the details, but forgot the only thing that mattered: how to make fire. The same thing can happen to us, but it doesn't have to. Not if we know how to spend this precious time together: remembering that God is always near, calling us to life, celebrating that we are his very own whom he never forgets, and drawing life from his touch and from the holy food he gives us.

S o, this morning, with everything that is in us, let us remember, celebrate, eat, and draw life!

Listen to What Your Pain is Telling You

John 14:15-21

A good Christian woman read the Bible every day and treasured a favorite passage from Isaiah: "The lion will lie down with the lamb." One day she went to the zoo and came upon the lion cage where something incredulous was taking place. Inside the cage was a huge, ferocious lion and sitting right next to it was a lamb! In total amazement, she called over the guard. "How long have you had a lion and a lamb in that cage together?" she asked.

"Oh, more than a year," said the guard.

"That's amazing. How do you do it?"

"Easy," said the guard. "Every morning we just put in a new lamb."

L ambs are not the only creatures that get wounded and gobbled up by life. We all bear our own wounds and none of us are strangers to pain. We stub our toes and cut our fingers; we get cancers, strokes, and heart attacks. Our children disappoint us. Our parents disappoint us. Our spouses disappoint us. Our most cherished projects collapse. Our best ideas prove wrong. Sometimes it's our bodies that hurt, sometimes it's our spirits. But none of us are strangers to pain.

What are we to make of this? How can a good God permit so much suffering in people he says he loves? It truly is a mystery, and I must confess I don't have a perfect answer. However, I do have a hunch. I suspect that many of our pains are really gifts from God in disguise. They are part of a complex alarm system that warns us when we are doing something hurtful. My bloody, wounded finger throbs and says, "It's bad to cut me." And my aching head says, "Less brandy next time, please." We may not like the messages those pains bring, but they are gifts from God, that help keep us in one piece.

That's fairly easy to see, but much closer to the core of life are pains of the spirit, sadnesses so deep we can't touch/the bottom of them. When our friendships are out of order, when they are not life-giving, we suffer greatly. And the same is true when we are wasting our lives and investing our hearts in what cannot give life. Pain, great pain, always follows, sooner or later.

Those pains are not punishments. They are gifts from God, who doesn't want us to stay lost in a terrible place. Through those pains God is telling us a truth we need to hear: "What you are doing isn't working," he says. "There is no life in it. So isn't it time to change?"

And our pain gives the answer, "Yes, it is time to change."

And what about getting sick, or losing our vigor or our wealth, or being forced to come to terms with failure or loss? Perhaps even those pains are gifts from God, drawing us deeper into the inside of life, peeling away all the distractions and helping us at last to see what really matters.

In today's gospel, Jesus promises he won't leave us orphans, and indeed he has not. At every hour of every day he walks at our side, giving us the strength to face our pains of body and spirit, and giving us the courage both to hear what our pains are telling us and to act on what we hear.

R eceive his strength; he will be enough. Listen closely to what he is whispering through your pains. He is telling you the truth you need to hear, and it can set you free. He is here now, next to you.

Listen to him. Heed his word to you. Act on it. And be free!

How Are We Doing?

John 17:1-11

One fine spring day a holy monk was sitting under a tree saying his prayers. A crippled woman passed by. She was begging food for the small child she carried on her back. The child was terribly misshapen and obviously undernourished and showed signs of harsh beatings. The holy monk watched the two of them till they disappeared over the horizon, and then he sank deeper into prayer. After a long time, he cried out, "O great God, you have told us that you love every one of us. So how can you see such suffering and do nothing about it?"

Out of the depths of the silence, God answered, "I have done something about it, my son. I made you."

So how are we doing? If we were arrested today and charged with being Christians, would there be sufficient evidence for a conviction? I wonder. We know there is only one yardstick that really counts, the great commandment: love your neighbor as yourself. We know the rule, we want to live by it, but sometimes we get awfully confused about how to do it. So maybe it's time we took another look at what Jesus had to say about loving our neighbors.

First of all, who is our neighbor? Jesus answered that with the good Samaritan story. Everyone is our neighbor, he said. No one is to be left outside the circle of our love. No one. And what is to be the shape of our neighborly love?

- Is it friendliness and courtesy? Good, but not enough, he says.
- Taking care never to hurt anybody? Very good, but still not enough.
- Praying each day for all who are in need? Very good indeed, but still not enough.

Jesus showed us by his whole life – and death – what real love looks like and what it does. It does what is needed to bring out the best in our neighbor. And it does that, a day at a time, as long as needed. The love that Jesus showed us focuses its whole attention on the other's need as if it were one's own. It is faithful, it never walks away, and it doesn't count the cost.

Jesus' kind of love is sometimes soft and gentle, and sometimes very tough. It speaks words of comfort, but also speaks hard truths – though only when it can give those truths as gifts and not as acts of revenge.

The kind of love that Jesus showed us takes ordinary people and transforms them. It always transforms the giver, even when the gift is refused. And it can transform us, if we will give it away without counting.

Jesus' kind of love never settles for "have a nice day." Jesus always listened to people's hearts, always heard their real needs, always did what was needed without counting the cost, and never walked away.

God grant that we learn to do the same:
- to listen to our neighbors' hearts,
- to hear their needs,
- to answer without counting,
- and never to walk away.

So let it be, Lord, So let it be for us all!

God Is Wind and Fire

John 20:19-23

A four-year-old was having lunch with his mother. "Mommy," he asked, "is God really everywhere?"

"Yes, of course," answered his mother.

"Is God in this room?"

"Yes, dear."

"And in my cup?" asked the child, pointing to his little cup which was still half full of milk.

"Uhhh, yes," said his mother, wondering where these questions were leading. The little boy smiled, and quick as lightning clasped both hands over the top of his cup. "Got'cha!"

I suspect there is something of that little child in all of us, trying very hard to get a "handle" on God and shrinking God very small in the process. Some of us imagine and treat God like a rich old grandpa who sleeps most of the time. We tiptoe around and try not to wake him. Just avoiding trouble is the best strategy for dealing with the "grandpa" God. And in return for not bothering him, we expect a smooth life and a fat inheritance at the end of the road.

Some of us have cooked up a tougher God who is a real "hangin' judge." God knows all the rules and regulations by heart, knows every single thing we do, is angry most of the time because of our mistakes, and has to be bought off with lots of prayers, sacrifices, groveling and begging. If you are really good at this sort of thing, God has been known to grant an occasional pardon. But don't count on it.

Some of us have imagined a God in our own image, one who likes presents, and can be manipulated – if the price is right. So we try bribery, "I'll do this, if you'll do that." "I'll light a candle every day for a whole year, Lord, if you'll cure my child." "I'll bury Joseph on my front lawn, if you'll find somebody to buy my house." This God is especially fond of incense and kneeling up straight.

All of us, even the wisest, sometimes make God too small. That's why this Feast of Pentecost is so important for us. For on this day we remember and celebrate that God is vastly more grand than our meager, domesticated imaginings of him. As the bible says, God is "wind" and "fire." Wind, unseen and invisible, but breathing life into us from moment to moment. God is wind, powerful and uncontained, ranging far and wide across the earth, yet whispering within us of things we've never dreamed or dared, whispering to us "now is the hour, this is the moment, I will be enough for you." God is wind, always there, always whispering, always breathing life.

God is fire, hot and intense, setting us ablaze with passion for life, setting us alight with hope and caring. Fire, burning away what is dry and dead within us, clearing the way for new growth, making ready for the new seeds the wind will bring. God is fire, warming us when we have grown cold, giving us light when we are in darkness.

God is wind and fire. That is who our great God is, and nothing less. So why is it that we are so often cold and lifeless, lacking in passion and spirit, narrow in vision and love? Could it be that we have not let God be God for us? It could be. It almost certainly is. Can we let that stand? Surely not!

So let us choose this day to let God be God for us, let God be wind and fire for us this day. Amen.

Rest Your Whole Weight on the Lord

John 3:16-18

A very long time ago, when the first Christian missionaries arrived in New Guinea, they found there a cruel and savage culture where cannibalism was still in practice. No one was safe, and no one trusted anyone. In fact, nowhere in their whole language was there a single word for "trust" or "belief."

When one of the missionaries tried to translate the gospels into the native language, he ran into a solid wall almost immediately. The test he was struggling with was from today's gospel, "Whoever puts his trust in the Lord will not die." How do you translate that for people who trust no one? After thinking long and hard, he got an idea. He leaned back in his chair with the front legs off the ground and said to his native assistant, "Tell me what I'm doing."

"You're resting your whole weight on your chair's back legs," came the reply.

"That's it," said the missionary, and he had his translation. It went like this, "Whoever rests his whole weight on the Lord will not die, but will have eternal life."

That is the stunning message of today's gospel. "God did not send his Son into the world to condemn it, but to save it." Jesus came not to punish but to encourage, to bring life, not death. So why is it, so long after Jesus' coming, that we are still so lifeless? Why is our light still so dim? That missionary knew the answer. The clue is right there in the passage he translated: "Whoever rests his whole weight on the Lord will have life."

When did we rest our whole weight on the Lord? When did we trust him enough to let go of our worrying?

- Did we ever say, "Lord, I know you're enough for me, and there's nothing that we can't do together"?
- Did we ever say, "Lord, I know you love me and

see things as they really are, so I'm going to let you set the course for me"?

- Did we ever say any of that with all our heart, and not take it back piece by piece? Probably not.

Compared to what could be, there is not a whole lot of life in us, because most of us have not really trusted the Lord. We have given our assent to the doctrines of the faith, but we have not entrusted our lives into his hands where he can refashion us, reshape us, and rebuild us. Because of our holding back we stay static, wasting our energy trying to control what is beyond our control, and worrying about what does not really matter.

Is that where our story ends, in a dreary et cetera, with our dim bulbs flickering awhile and then slowly going dark? That's not where God wants our story to end. For even after all this time, God still has no interest in condemning, but only in giving life, reshaping and rebuilding our tired old hearts.

We have only to give him our hearts and trust him enough to let him do his work in us. Then our lights will shine brightly, we will give light to all around us, and we will know our Father's joy.

Waste not one more minute! Rest your whole weight on the Lord!

"I'll Always Be Here for You"

John 6:51-58

A high school student was walking down the street, past a house where a child on the porch was stretching to reach the doorbell. No matter how hard the child tried, there was no reaching that bell. The student called out: "Hold on, I'll give you a hand." Then the student climbed the stairs onto the porch, smiled at the small child, and rang the doorbell.

"Gee, thanks," the small fry grinned. "Now, let's run."

R unning away is a temptation that comes to us all. Sometimes, just for a moment, even the bravest of us would like to run away as hard and fast as we can because life seems just too much: work, family, friends, tests, contracts, television, our own selves. Some days all of them or any one of them can make us want to run far and fast and let someone else clean up the mess. "Forget love and duty. I don't care what happens, just get me out of here!"

We've all thought it or said it, and sometimes we've done it. The temptation to run is real, and because it is real, it gives birth to a powerful kind of fear, the fear of being abandoned and left all alone.

We know only too well our own temptation to run, so it's only a short hop to the other side of the equation. What if everybody gets fed up with me, and runs away and leaves me all alone? What if God finally gets fed up with me, and leaves me all alone forever and ever? What if. . . ?

The eucharist is the Lord's answer to that terrifying "what if." In giving us his own body and blood to be eaten as often as we need it, Jesus is saying, "I'll always be here for you, and I'll never run away. Whenever you come to me, I'll nourish your spirit. I'll make you strong when you're weak. I'll be medicine for your heart, and I'll heal you on the inside when you've been wounded there."

That's the promise Jesus made when he first gave us his body and blood, and it's the promise he renews every time we ~~receive the eucharist.~~ ask.

And what does he ask in return? Only that we not run away, not run away from our commitments or our challenges, not run away from ourselves or our need to change, and most especially, that we not run away from those who need us.

At the moment of communion, as the host is held up before us and the priest speaks aloud, "The Body of Christ," the Lord whispers to our hearts: "I'll always be here and always be enough for you. So promise me you'll never run away."

A nd we answer, "Amen. Yes, Lord. I know you are here; and you will always be enough for me. I promise I'll never run away. Amen, Lord. Amen."

Jump into the Pit with Him

Matthew 9:9-13

There was a Chinese scholar who converted from Confucianism to Christianity. After his conversion, he was asked to explain the basic difference between the great eastern teachings of Confucius and Buddha and the Gospel of Jesus. He answered by telling a story: A man fell into a deep, dark, slimy pit. Frantically, he struggled to climb out, but soon it became obvious that he was trapped.

Confucius came along. He saw the man in the pit and said, "Poor fellow, if only he'd listened to me, he never would have fallen into that pit." And with that, Confucius went on his way.

Next Buddha came along. He saw the man in the pit and said, "Poor fellow, if he'll come up here, I'll help him." Buddha waited a little, and when nothing happened, he went on his way.

Finally, Jesus came along. He saw the man down there and said, "Poor fellow!" and jumped into the pit and lifted him out.

He jumped into the pit and lifted him out. Can you think of any better way of summarizing Jesus' life? In every single page of the gospels, the pattern is always the same: Jesus sees a brother or sister in need, and he steps forward and engages that person wholeheartedly without condition or reservation. He never turns his back or looks away. He never holds a person at arm's length – not the crooked tax collector, or the prostitute, or even the leper. He never sits on his hands, or settles for nice words or warm and fuzzy feelings. Always he acts. He connects, and not just for a moment. He stays connected and fully present as long as he's needed. He gets tired and grows weary, and takes proper time out for rest and prayer and just plain laughing, but he never disengages.

How many days and years Jesus had to walk with the apostles before they even halfway understood what he was about. Right in the gospels you can hear him admit that he sometimes found them very frustrating. Yet he never washed his hands of them.

Think of how many days and years he's walked with you and me, slowly drawing us up, closer to our Father. How often we've resisted and temporized, yet he's never washed his hands of us or walked away.

What a friend and brother! But he's even more than that: He's the model, the proto-type of what we're called to become. And he's calling us by name and saying, "Come, walk with me. Follow in my footsteps." We'd like to say "yes." But to do that, we need to discover how Jesus found the energy to do all he did so wholeheartedly.

How did he do it? He began by naming his own gifts, seeing them very clearly, taking real pleasure in them, and then labelling them for what they were: Gifts, which told him in turn how much the Giver, his Father, loved him. And how did that make him feel? Thankful. Not just a polite, "Thank you very much" kind of thankfulness, but a huge, energetic, ocean-full of thankfulness that was too big to be contained, and that overflowed in every direction. That vast thankfulness for being blest and loved was where Jesus got the energy for all the "jumping into the pit" and all the "lifting up and out" that he did for people all his life.

For all of us who want to follow Jesus, the path is clear. So let us pray for one another that we may:

- learn to name the gifts that make us unique;
- learn to see our gifts for what they are: dazzling signs of God's vast affection for us; and
- learn to respond to our Father's affection with thankful hearts whose grateful energy is so vast that it cannot be hemmed in or contained, but overflows and enriches in every direction.

With Jesus, may we find ourselves "jumping into the pit, and lifting our brothers out."

Is Your Door Open or Closed?

Matthew 9:36 – 10:8

The mothers of four priests were sipping tea and discussing their sons. "My son is a monsignor," said the first proudly. "When he enters a room, people say, 'Good morning, Monsignor.'"

"The second mother sat up very straight and said, "My son is a bishop. And when he enters a room, people say, 'Hello, Your Excellency.'"

"Well," sniffed the third, "my son is a cardinal, and when he enters a room, everybody says, 'Hello, Your Eminence.'"

"The fourth mother was quiet for a moment and then she spoke, "My son is six-foot-ten and weighs 300 pounds. When he enters a room, people say, 'Oh, my God!'"

In Sunday's Gospel, Jesus chooses his apostles, but the reasons for his choices are a mystery: Not a priest or a rabbi on the list, not an intellectual or a scholar, not a lawyer or a doctor, not even a monsignor in the whole lot. Nobody of any clout or standing in either Jewish or Roman society. Nobody who'd ever said or done anything worth remembering. Just ordinary folk: Fishermen, tradesmen, and tax collectors. So what was he looking for? Maybe for persons of extraordinary virtue and religious insight, persons untouched by sin? If that was what Jesus was looking for, he must have been blind in choosing these twelve. For the gospels make it clear that the apostles were very flawed people:

- They played little power games, fighting about who was Jesus' favorite, and who should have the best place at table;
- They threw their weight around, trying to brush aside sick people and little children who wanted and needed to talk to Jesus;
- They whined about how much they were giving up to follow Jesus, and talked balderdash about how they'd follow him anywhere.

But when the crunch finally came, they fell like dominoes: Judas betrayed him for money; Peter denied him out of self-respect and fear; and all the rest ran for the hills. So much for the virtue-heroism theory of choosing apostles.

So what was Jesus looking for, and what did he find in the twelve he chose? Just one thing: Hearts that were open enough to let him inside, where he could touch them and begin his work of healing and transformation. Isn't it remarkable that was all he needed: Just their openness, one moment at a time. With it he could do everything and without it he could do nothing for them. And that's all he needs to begin his work in us: openness, a willingness to listen, to see the truth, to be touched, openness to being forgiven, to being changed bit by bit, to enter into a trusting partnership with the Lord, and to let that partnership lead where it will, one moment at a time.

"Come, follow me," Jesus said to the twelve so very long ago, and he intended the invitation for every one of us as well. It's an invitation to friendship and partnership for life. And our being here in this church today suggests that, at some point, most of us probably said, "Yes, I will follow you. I will join you. I will let you in," and threw open our inner door, at least part way. Two of Jesus' chosen twelve, Peter and Judas, abandoned Jesus in his last hours. They shut their doors to him: Judas acted for money; Peter acted for fear. But the greatest tragedy was yet to come. For, while Peter in agony reopened his heart to the Lord, Judas closed his forever, and placed himself forever beyond the touch of the Lord.

The question for this day, and the question we must bring to prayer each day is simple: Is my door still open, or has it drifted quietly shut without my even noticing?" Everything hangs on the answer, so we'd better ask the question carefully: Is my door still open? God knows. Do I?

Building Family: Good People and Good Bridges

Matthew 10:26-33

An angel appeared at a faculty meeting and announced to the dean that, as a reward for her exemplary life, the Lord was granting her a choice of infinite wealth, wisdom, or beauty. Without hesitation the dean chose infinite wisdom. "Done!" said the angel who then disappeared in a cloud of smoke and a bolt of lightning.

Then all heads turned toward the dean, who was surrounded by a halo of light, and was suddenly looking very wise indeed. "Carol," whispered one of her colleagues nervously, "Say something wise."

The wise dean looked round the table at each one of them very slowly and then spoke, "I should have taken the money."

At times we all have second thoughts about the choices we have made and the direction we have given our lives. Doubts and questions rise up and won't be put aside: "Have I set a wrong course? Am I wasting my time? Have I wasted my life?" Those are not happy questions, but like spinach, they are good for us. They are, in fact, gifts from God, invitations from the God of second chances.

Through these self-doubts, God is asking us to let down our guard, pull off our blinders, and take a closer look at how we are living. The message is, "don't be afraid about what you may see, because there is nothing in you that I have not already seen, nothing that could ever cause me to erase your names from the palm of my hand, and nothing that we cannot handle together."

So, trying to trust in that, we close our eyes and face the question, "Does my life make any sense? How do I know? Is it just one long et cetera?" Sometimes it seems that way. How can I tell for sure?

Jesus gave us the ultimate litmus test, the Golden Rule, "Love your neighbor as yourself," which can be shaped into a very concrete question: "Am I building family – big family as well as small?"

That is Jesus' real question to us.

Now listen to what's inside that question: "Am I helping people to grow into themselves and then am I helping to build bridges to link them together?"

If our answer is "yes," we're not wasting our lives. Period! If it's "no," we're in trouble, and no other achievement of ours, no matter how great, can give our lives true value or meaning.

An honest answer to Jesus' question will inevitably make us sad, because every day we do ignore many opportunities to build people and to build bridges to link them. That is sad. And it is a waste of life, ours and theirs. At the same time, an honest answer to Jesus' question should make us glad as well, because most of us really are getting better. More and more we are learning to build what counts: good people and good bridges.

So we have abundant reasons to pray for one another today:

May God help us listen to our doubts without fear. May he help us see our progress as well as our failures. And may he give us great hearts that invest all we have in building family, building good people and good bridges. Amen.

Hospitality:
The Only Road to Communion and Family

Matthew 10:37-42

A young couple invited their pompous pastor for Sunday dinner. While the two of them were in the kitchen making the final preparations, the monsignor asked their young son what they were having for dinner. "Goat," said the little boy.

"Goat?" gasped the monsignor. "Are you sure about that?"

"Oh, yes, monsignor," said the little fellow. "Just this morning I heard mommy say to daddy, 'Don't forget, we're having the old goat for dinner.'"

So much for hospitality! But that is what the gospel challenges us to think about today. Hospitality. There is a lot more to it than "Let's do lunch," or "Drinks are on me." It is a basic attitude towards life – the very opposite of self-absorption which leaves us locked in ourselves, very small, and very alone. Hospitality is a way of living that looks beyond self, opens the inner doors wide, and says with a glad heart, "Welcome, come on in."

That is a very big way of living – it's really like being God – and it can only come from hearts that have grown large and confident and gracious in the warm sunlight of knowing for sure that they are loved beyond measure. To put it in another way, if we have not paid attention to God's hospitality to us, we will never know how to extend it to one another.

Communion, family, is what we are made for and what we long for. Hospitality, the habit of sharing life with a glad heart, is the only road to communion and family, the only road to our heart's desire. But there are rocks on that road, some very large ones, and on each of them is inscribed the same four-letter word, "fear." Fear that I'm nothing and that I have nothing worth sharing. Fear that, if I do share I'll not have enough for myself. Fear of what I may be asked for tomorrow if I put out the welcome mat today. Fear of rejection. Fear of the unknown. Paralyzing, stultifying, isolating fears of every sort.

Which of those fears has your name on it? Probably more than one. How do we dissolve those fears? How do we get those rocks off our road so we can get where we really want to be, in communion and family? Where do we find the energy to give the cup of water when it's needed, and to make sure it's cold, as the Gospel says, and to do that with glad hearts and without counting? The answer is always the same. We push aside those boulders, we find the courage to share life without fear, and we grow in our hearts by confronting our faith and letting it be enough for us.

That is a great and strenuous work. So we must pray for one another this day.

Good and gracious Lord, we thirst for communion and family, yet our fears stand in the way. Help us to know inside that you are enough for us. Let all who come our way will find in us a ready welcome and a lasting embrace. Amen.

I Will Refresh You

Matthew 11:25-30

Certain Christians still practice a method of prayer known as "lucky dipping." It works like this. You begin by praying for divine guidance, and then let your Bible fall open to whatever page happens to open. With eyes tightly shut, you "dip" your finger to the page. The verse your finger rests on is God's answer to your prayer.

One day a pious gentleman found himself in a heap of trouble. So in desperation he prayed very hard, closed his eyes, and lucky dipped into the scripture. Opening his eyes, he read this verse, "And Judas went out and hanged himself." Well that couldn't be God's message, he said to himself, so he shut his eyes and dipped again. This time the verse said, "Go thou and do likewise."

It takes more than lucky stars and lucky dipping to stay the course some days! We all have troubles. Some of them are overwhelming; many of our own making,

- the bad habits we have built over a lifetime;
- the dumb ideas we cling to for dear life;
- the ugly consequences of our sins;
- the loneliness that comes from being too full of ourselves;
- the sadness that comes from seeing what a mess we have made.

We've got lots of troubles of our own making. But we've got other kinds of troubles too, troubles we couldn't have foreseen and didn't make: bad health, accidents, tragedies, and reverses of fortune of every sort, the kinds of things that force us to admit that bad things do happen to good people. We all have troubles. They wear us down and wear us out, and sometimes they leave us feeling trapped.

That's why Sunday's Gospel is especially for us. "Come," says Jesus, "Come to me all you who are weary and find life burdensome, and I will refresh you." It sounds good, but what exactly does it mean? Is he promising to take our troubles away,

to give us an easy out, and a quick escape? No, not at all. He has something else in mind. Listen to what he says. "Take my yoke upon your shoulders," he says, "and your soul will find rest, for my yoke is easy and my burden light."

Taking a yoke on our shoulders like a beast of burden doesn't sound very refreshing or restful. And it surely doesn't sound liberating. But it is all of that. In saying we should take his yoke on our shoulders, Jesus is urging us to link ourselves to him and let him steer us, let him set our course. He's urging us to stop trying to walk away from our troubles, and instead look them straight in the eye, and walk toward them and through them.

"If you are yoked and linked to me," he says, "I can show you the path through anything, and I can give you the energy to keep going. You may get battered in the process – no guarantees against that – but you'll get where you need to go. And, even in the midst of hurts, struggles, and pains, your heart will find peace, rest, and refreshment."

That is the personal invitation and the promise that Jesus is making to each one of us at this very moment. So let us listen to his words with open hearts.

"Come. Come to me all you who are weary and find life burdensome, and I will refresh you . . . Take my yoke upon your shoulders . . . and your souls will find rest."

FIFTEENTH SUNDAY IN ORDINARY TIME

Deep Roots in Good Soil

Matthew 13:1-23

A young man went to a dance and struck up a conversation with a very attractive woman. After three dances with her, the young fellow strutted over to his buddy with a big smile on his face and a scrap of paper in his hand. "She works for the telephone company," he said, "and I'm sure she likes me, because she just gave me her private phone number."

"No kidding," said his buddy, green with envy. "Let's see." So he unfolded the paper which said, "Dial Operator."

Sometimes there is a lot less there than meets the eye!

At times we could say that about our lives, as we find ourselves turning up empty handed and wondering why. "What have I got to show for myself? Why isn't there more?" Those are bitter questions that lots of us have had to ask. Jesus has the answer for us in today's gospel. "If you want the rich, full life that God wants for you, you've got to put down roots, deep roots, in the right place, in good soil." The payoff will be fantastic, "thirty, sixty, a hundredfold." (For you investors, that's a 3000, 6000 or 10,000 percent return!)

Sounds great, but there's a problem, because putting down deep roots goes contrary to deeply ingrained habits. We have short attention spans, and low thresholds of boredom. Our enthusiasms have a half-life that can be measured in hours not years. If you doubt that, check your garage and your closet. We love the new, and, like birds of prey, we scan the horizon for new looks and better offers. Mentally, we keep our bags packed. And, the sociologist Max Weber tells us we even kid ourselves into believing that lateral moves are progress. So we move and move and move some more, getting no better and growing no happier. It's a fact, we have real trouble with putting down deep roots, real trouble making commitments that endure.

But even if we are finally ready to commit, there is still another question. Where do we put down our roots? To what do we to commit our lives? The *de facto* answer for many of us is that we commit to ourselves, to our stuff, and our busy comings and goings. That's awfully thin and shallow soil to plant a life in: self, stuff, and perpetual motion. And the life that springs from such meager soil is bound to be thin, shallow, and meager – a terrible disappointment.

So where do we plant our roots? In the Lord, who is the only entity big enough to hold us, the only entity big enough to satisfy our restless cravings. But how do we root ourselves in a Lord we cannot even see? By setting down our roots amidst his children, our brothers and sisters, whom we can see. If we commit our whole hearts to building communion, building good people and good bridges to link them, we will have the rich, full lives that God wants for us. There is no other place to look for happiness.

So, isn't it time to stop our restless searching, and end our perpetual motion, and put down our roots right here in the midst of God's people? If we do that, we will be astonished at the yield! Thirty, sixty, a hundredfold.

The Growth Will Come, But Not Quickly

Matthew 13:24-43

A preacher was walking down the street when he came upon former classmate who was shabbily dressed, unshaven, and clearly down on his luck. "Frank," said the preacher, "you used to be rich." Frank shook his head and told his sad tale of bad investments and too many afternoons at the races.

"Go home," said the preacher. "Open your bible at random, stick your finger on the page, and there will be God's answer."

Some weeks later, the preacher bumped into Frank who now was wearing an Italian suit and a fancy watch and driving a new Mercedes. "I'm glad to see things really turned around for you," he said.

"Yes, and I owe it all to you. I opened my Bible and put my finger on the page and right there on the top of the page was the answer – Chapter 11."

A nice, quick fix! No waiting. Just closure, now. That's the way we like to deal. When we hear in today's Gospel about the weeds growing up in the midst of the wheat, our first instinct is to act just like the servants: pull the weeds and get rid of them! But the gospel warns us: not so fast! Be sure to look at the whole picture.

In Jesus' day, one of the problems that farmers had to face every year was a weed called "false wheat." It had all the appearances of real wheat, and farmers couldn't tell which was which until it all came to maturity. So they gave every single plant in their field their very best care and then waited. Every plant got a chance to mature and show what it really was. That's what Jesus asks us to do for one another and for ourselves. Wait. Give the time and the help for each to come to maturity and grow into its best self.

Evil is a fact of life. And our first instinct upon seeing it is to pronounce a quick judgment: Weed! Pull it out! Sometimes we're right, but very often, what we call a weed is no weed at all, just an undernourished, stunted, but perfectly good plant that can be made to bear good fruit – if someone will give it some time and some help. If we turn our backs or walk away too quickly, the stunted, undernourished part of you or me with all its possibilities will be lost forever. And, that would be a shame.

The alternative, of course, isn't very neat or tidy. It involves engaging the parts of us that are least attractive, seeing in them the possibility of something very good, and then waiting and working patiently, giving time for the slow process of growth to run its course, even though sometimes we can't be sure any growth is happening at all.

God, who sees us as we are, loves every part of us and has high hopes for every part of us, even the damaged, stunted, sinful parts. All he asks is that we do the same, that we look at every part of ourselves and of one another with compassionate, hopeful, patient hearts. If we do that, the growth will come – not quickly, but it will come. And the harvest will be rich.

An Understanding Heart

1 Kings 3:5-12

A woman married forty years was complaining that her husband never showed her any affection. Her friend suggested that she call in the parish priest, and that's what she did. Father came for visit when she knew her husband would be home and the priest listened to her complaints: "My husband never hugs me, never kisses me, never tells me he loves me." But, through it all, the husband just sat there watching the football game.

Finally, the priest went over to the crying woman, and put his arms around her. He gave her a warm hug and a kiss. Then he turned to the husband and said, "See what I did? Your wife needs something like that at least twice a week."

Without batting an eye, the husband said, "Fine, then, I'll bring her in to see you on Tuesdays and Thursdays."

Not listening and not hearing is as old as the human race, and it has achieved a status equivalent to an Olympic sport between wives and husbands, parents and children, teachers and students, and between all of us and God. That's why Solomon's prayer in Sunday's first reading is so important. When God offered Solomon anything in the world he wanted, he asked for just one thing, "an understanding heart," a heart that could hear the inside of things, a heart that could find peace and then could make peace and so build God's kingdom.

We know that at the very core and depth of everything is God. The understanding heart hears God-at-the-core of every thing and every moment. It sees and knows the world as God sees and knows it. Such a heart knows how to take and to receive the good out of each moment, no matter how dark that moment may be.

Such a heart is not insulated from pain or grief, from wounds or tears, but it will never be destroyed. Such a heart will survive, growing ever stronger and yet ever more subtly attuned to all of life – because it is attuned and listening to God-at-the-core. And God's life fills it full. The alternative, of course, is not pretty. It is a heart deaf to the inside of people, to the inside of each moment, and to the ultimate core of all that is, God himself.

So let us pray with Solomon for the one thing that will open up to us everything that matters. Let us pray for an understanding, listening heart – a heart like God's.

Why Not Give it a Try?

Matthew 14:13-21

A doctor, a teacher, an architect, and an IRS auditor were arguing about whose profession was the oldest. The doctor pointed out, "Well, Eve was made from Adam's rib, so there must have been a doctor available to perform the operation."

"Agreed," said the teacher, "but how would the doctor have known what to do if he hadn't been taught? There must have been a teacher there first, to teach the doctor."

"Maybe so," said the architect, "but before that the world was in chaos. Someone must have brought order out of chaos and that sounds like the work of an architect."

The IRS auditor just smiled and said simply, "But who do you think created the chaos?"

We are all competitive. Each of us likes to be first, best, the champ. That is the best reason I can think of for paying close attention to Jesus. Why? Because Jesus became one of us to show us what being our best selves really looks like. He is what we are called to become. When we look at him, we see clearly where we are supposed to be headed.

Today's gospel captures the essence of Jesus. He had just heard about the brutal execution of his cousin, John the Baptist. So he went off to a quiet spot to be alone with his memories and to pray. But as always someone found out where he was and a crowd gathered. Now here is the point where Jesus showed what made him so special. Despite his own inner pain, the gospel says Jesus looked at the crowd and "his heart was moved with compassion."

That word "compassion" says a lot more than we usually notice. It's from the Latin, *cum passio,* and it means "to be with the feelings of another." In a word, Jesus looked beyond his own grief and took into his heart the feelings and hurts of the crowd, and he felt those as if they were his own. Inside himself, he knew their pains and hurts, their longings and hungers. And being one with them on the inside, he reached out and responded to those needs as naturally as if they were his own. He had to act. To ignore them would have felt like ignoring himself.

Why is it so easy for us to ignore one another's needs, so easy to be cruel or harsh even to those we love? Perhaps because we so rarely listen to the inside of one another and so rarely take what we hear into our hearts. We stay on the outside, where it's easy to judge or reject or simply forget that we are family, all of us. We stay on the outside where it's too easy to fall for the lie that we can live as happy islands insulated from the rest of the world.

Jesus has shown us what a real life looks like, a life that transcends our instinctive competitiveness, a life that leaves no one an island. Jesus has not only shown us what that looks like, he's shown us that it's possible for human beings like us. And he's made it clear that it's the only way to happiness.

So why not give it a try? Why not, indeed!

Keep Your Eyes on Him

Matthew 14:22-33

A very successful banker from New York bought a huge ranch out West where he intended to raise cattle. Some friends came for a visit and asked if the ranch had a name. "Well," said the would-be cattleman, "I wanted to name it the BAR-J. My wife favored SUZY-Q. One son liked the FLYING-W, and the other wanted the LAZY-Y. So we're calling it the BAR-J SUZY-Q FLYING-W LAZY-Y."

"But where are all your cattle?" the friends asked. "Well, actually," said the cattleman, "none of them survived the branding."

L ife is a wonderful gift but it's no picnic – even for the best and the brightest – and many people don't survive. Every day many just sink beneath the waves and drown in their troubles. How many times have we seen a young couple exchange their wedding vows all bright eyed and hope filled. And then, as the years pass, we have watched their light grow dim, their hopes fade, and their dreams sour.

How many times have we held a new child in our arms or bounced it on our knee and imagined all the grand and wonderful possibilities within the reach of its tiny hands. And then, as the years pass, how many times have we watched the possibilities recede, watched them elude the grasp of those now grown-up hands, and watched those hands grow tired and cease to reach out at all? How many times have we seen people sink beneath the waves of their troubles and drown? Too many times!

Why is it that so many sink and are drowned in their troubles? I think Sunday's gospel suggests an answer. Jesus invited Peter to do something quite extraordinary, quite beyond his own powers. "Come," he said, "walk on the water!" And that's exactly what Peter did. He stepped out of the boat – can you imagine that first step! – and began to walk across those rolling waters with his eyes fixed on Jesus.

He was already halfway when he took his eyes off Jesus and looked instead at the crashing waves and heard the roaring wind, and then said to himself, "This is crazy. I can't walk on water." And he sank like a rock. But he had indeed walked on water. He had been able to do the impossible, because his eyes were fixed on Jesus, and because his heart, his whole heart was fixed on Jesus too. Walking on water only became impossible for Peter when he looked away from the Lord.

Jesus is inviting us to walk on water, to do the impossible: to build wonderful lives and wonderful friendships, not off in some safe, other-worldly haven, but here and now in the midst of all the troubles and tragedies that life can serve up. And he is promising more than mere survival as the waters rage and the winds howl around us. He is promising us joy, even while life is battering us.

A nd how do we find this joy? How do we find the power to walk on water and do the impossible? Exactly as Peter did, by keeping our eyes fixed on Jesus, and keeping our hearts fixed on him. He will show us where to walk, and will give us the energy and courage to walk there. And we will not falter or sink into the sea as long as our eyes and hearts are fixed on him.

Prejudice: Stopping the Outside

Matthew 15:21-28

Two pilots were in an airplane, and the plane developed engine trouble. It was clear that they were going to crash. One said to the other, "Well, this is it. We're going to die. Are you religious?"

The other said, "No, are you?"

The first said, "Well, I'm not either, but I think we'd better do something religious, because we're going to be dead in about sixty seconds. Can't you remember anything religious we could do?"

The other man said, "Well, I used to live next door to a Catholic church, and I used to hear those people in there. Maybe I could quote some of it."

"We've only got twenty seconds left," said the other man, "so you better hurry."

The man looked up at the ceiling, and then began to speak, "Under the B, 3; under the I, 9; under the N, 22. . ."

If we live on the surface, on the outside of things, that's where our last words will come from. And they won't say much. Today's gospel story is both embarrassing and confusing. It paints Jesus in very harsh colors. A pagan woman comes to him for help. At first he ignores her. Next he tells her his mission is only for Jews. Then he insults her by saying it's not right to take away the food of sons and daughters and throw it to the dogs.

Is this really Jesus speaking? Well, in fact, it is not. While Jesus did heal the pagan woman's daughter, the account of the event was not recorded by Matthew until about forty years later. In the meantime, the church was embroiled in a bitter internal struggle between its Jewish converts and its gentile converts.

Many Jews believed they were the only people God really loved. And that all the rest of us were just scenery on their stage – tools to be used and discarded when God needed to punish or reward his friends, the Jews. Many Jewish converts brought this prejudice with them when they joined the church. They insisted that any pagans wanting to become Christians would have to become Jews first. So when Matthew, who was one of these Jewish converts, wrote down his gospel, he was still partly stuck in his prejudice against non-Jews – and he put his prejudices on Jesus' lips.

How could he do that? How could anyone who knew anything about Jesus even imagine that Jesus would ever endorse prejudice, would ever agree to rejecting anyone, or would ever fail to open his arms to anyone who came to him, especially someone who was obviously sincere? How could Matthew be so blind? Unfortunately, it was easy. When Matthew thought about pagans, he just stopped at the outside, at the surface; and, of course, that limited what he could see. It created a huge blind spot.

That's what prejudice always does. It reacts to the outside of things, not the inside. It doesn't reach into the heart but responds to the surface. So it sees very little of the truth. And that's what followers of Jesus do sometimes: stop at the surface, seeing little of the truth.

Stopping on the outside makes it very easy for us to reject one another, to say we have nothing in common, to deny that we are brothers or sisters. Stopping outside makes it possible for us to hate, to sneer, to ignore, to exclude, and to reject – and still think we're doing fine. And who are our victims? Almost anyone whose outsides – whose looks and habits and things – don't match ours.

Prejudice is the absolute antithesis of Jesus' way of looking at people. He always went to the inside, and looked to the heart, and listened to what was really there. And no matter how troubled or unattractive or dysfunctional that person was on the outside, what Jesus saw on the inside was always the same: a brother or a sister, a caterpillar ready to become a butterfly.

Matthew's blind spot, which allowed him to insert his own prejudices into the gospel story, is embarrassing, but it is also a gift in disguise – a jarring but healthy warning that even the best of us are susceptible to doing the same: stopping at the outside of things, and living blindly and foolishly – like those two pilots who were so much on the outside of things that they thought the Bingo numbers solemnly spoken could get them to heaven.

The alternative is much happier: looking to the inside and listening to the heart. For what we'll discover there are brothers and sisters beyond number; we'll know we are surrounded not by enemies but by potential friends.

And, knowing all this from the inside, we'll never again walk alone.

Are You with Me?

Matthew 16:13-20

There was a woman from Czechoslovakia who came to this country to visit relatives. She was having trouble with her eyes, so the relatives took her to an optometrist. The doctor showed her a standard eye chart that displayed the letters C V K P N W X S C Z Y, and then asked if she could read it. "Read it?" the woman replied. "She's my neighbor!"

Sometimes we all misread situations and miss the point. That's why Jesus asks his pointed question in today's gospel. "Who do you say I am?" he asks. He's really asking, "Are you with me? And, if you are, how does it show?" That's the question we have to answer now as Jesus calls us by name and looks us in the eye as he looked at Peter: "Are you with me? And, if you are how does it show?" How are we to respond to that? Only the truth will do. So let us speak the truth to our Lord here and now as best we can.

Let us pray. "Lord, you know all things, so you know I'm with you. You are the best friend I've ever had, and you have picked me up and pulled me back together more times than I can count. But, Lord, my attention span leaves much to be desired. So often you help me to understand something about life, and I get it . . . and then I get distracted and forget it, and blunder along as if you had never taught me anything. So you start over with me at the beginning again and yet again.

"But, Lord, all your efforts have not been in vain. I am really starting to remember and to believe on the inside what you have been trying to show me: that loving with all my heart and with all my gifts is all that really matters. I think I've been doing a little better at that, Lord, and you know what, I'm a lot happier than I used to be. Thank you for the help, Lord, and for your patience too.

"I've been holding out on you, Lord. I guess I don't have to tell you that. There are parts of my heart that just seemed too dark to look at, too hard even for you to fix. The idea frightens me, but I think I'm ready to give you those parts of myself. I know that deep wounds don't get healed in a day, but they'll never even start to get healed if I don't give them to you. So that's my decision. They're yours. Tomorrow I'll probably want to take them back and pretend they don't exist. But we'll worry about that tomorrow. And when tomorrow comes, you'll be there to help me.

"A little while ago, I heard you ask me a question. 'Are you with me?' you asked. Well I am with you, Lord, more and more every day. And I know you are with me. So I think my life is going to get better and better.

"For all that, I thank you, Lord. Amen."

World-Class Friends

Matthew 16:21-27

More than 3000 years ago, when he was just getting started, the great Jewish leader Moses hired a press agent named Sam. When Moses and his people arrived at the edge of the Red Sea, with the Egyptian army in hot pursuit, Moses called for Sam and asked, "Where are the boats?"

"Oh, sorry, Moses," replied Sam. "I was so busy with the press releases, I forgot to order the boats."

"You idiot!" Moses exclaimed, forgetting for just a second that he was a spiritual leader. "What do you expect me to do – raise my staff and part the Red Sea?"

"Hey, boss," said Sam, "if you can do that, I can get you two full pages in the Old Testament!"

Even the smallest and humblest of us has a hankering for greatness. For most of us it's not a hunger to see our name in lights or in the history books. For most of us it's much simpler. We just want to know that our lives are adding up to something. We want to feel that, when we're done, we'll have something worthwhile to carry home to God. Our hearts are very insistent about this and about telling us what is worthwhile and what is not. And Jesus confirms our hearts' message. He says the only thing that really counts is communion – family – and that comes only from a lifetime of building good people and good bridges to connect them.

So how do we go about building good people and good bridges? Jesus' answer to that is: not by running out on people or quitting on them in mid-course. In today's Gospel Jesus makes it clear that the only way we can build the communion we desire is by holding to course, persistently facing and wrestling with all the things we'd like to flee, and sticking around and following through when we'd like to walk away. That's the task of a lifetime, but it can only be done a day at a time. That's all we ever have and all we are ever responsible for, one day, one moment at a time. Even the smallest of us can handle that!

Think of the people who have made the most difference in your life, the people who have drawn the best out of you, and whose fine imprint is still visible in your life. Think of that special teacher or parent, grandfather or friend. How did they make such a difference for you and me? Rarely through anything spectacular, but almost always through hundreds and thousands of tiny moments and tiny choices that slowly added up to something very good in us. They loved us for the duration, and they didn't just fade away when the road got bumpy or boring.

That is what Jesus is calling us to do and to be for one another: faithful friends who love for the duration and don't fade away; steadfast friends whose tiny moments and tiny choices slowly add up to something very good in those we befriend.

We are called to be world-class friends!

A surprise awaits those of us who accept that challenge: as we give away our lives a day at a time in faithful friendship, we will find our inner selves being transformed and enriched beyond all our expectations, and the joy of the Lord will be ours, not just later on but here and now.

Hope Mightily in the Hidden Goodness

Matthew 18:15-20

A boy and his father were taking a train trip. Because it was their first time on a train, the father accidentally broke some minor railroad rule. This drove the ticket collector into a rage. He shouted and scolded and denounced the man at length. But the man did not respond.

The man's son was puzzled. He couldn't understand why his father was putting up with such abuse. So he asked him why he chose to remain silent. The father smiled, "It's this way, son. That poor man has to put up with himself all his life. Surely it's a small thing for me to put up with him for just a few minutes."

Sad to say, getting hurt and inflicting wounds are part of daily life, and every day we have to deal with the consequences. We all know what to do about the hurts we cause: ask forgiveness, repair the damage, and don't do it again. Easier said than done, of course, but at least we know what to do.

The harder question is what we're to do when other people hurt us and do us wrong. How are we to respond? Our ideas on this are a bit fuzzy. We know as Christians that revenge is no option. We've been told to "forgive and forget," "turn the other cheek," and "don't hold a grudge." We've heard all that, and we do fairly well at resisting the temptation to get even. But our response to being wronged and hurt still tends to fall short. Like the man on the train, we may put up with the offense – and we may even smile – but then we distance ourselves from the offender, maybe just a little, or maybe a lot. And inside our heads we say, "Forget you!" – which is not the kind of forgetting Jesus had in mind.

In today's Gospel Jesus tells us what he does have in mind. "If you've been wronged or hurt," he says, "don't just sit there waiting for the offender to make the first move. Take the initiative, go to that person, name the problem, build a bridge across the chasm that separates you, and then walk across it. That's a tall order: opening up a tender subject, talking it through reasonably and respectfully, and then leaving it alone.

Fear makes us want to run the other way, fear of anger or rejection, fear of being hurt again. Those are reasonable fears, but they account for only one side of reality, because hidden in the heart of even the most hardened sinner – right next to all the meanness – is an untapped reservoir of goodness. That goodness can be drawn forth and made to grow. But first it has to be seen, and named, and hoped in.

As good teachers and good coaches know, to fail to see and name the good in another, and to fail to expect the good from another is ultimately to condemn that person to death. But to see and name another's goodness, and to hope in that goodness, is to give the gift of life.

That is the gift that Jesus gives us every day, and the gift he asks us to give one another: the gift of hoping mightily in the goodness that is buried in your heart and mine.

Surely we cannot withhold that gift. Surely we cannot withhold the hope that bridges great chasms and causes dead hearts to come alive! Surely we cannot. Surely we will not!

With What Measure Are You Measuring?

Matthew 4:12-23

Three convicts were sitting on death row in the state penitentiary. For years they had been arguing about who was the smartest. And now their day of execution had come. The first man is strapped into the chair, the switch is pulled, but nothing happens. So the warden commutes his sentence and sets him free. The same thing happens to the second man, and he too is set free. Finally, the third man is strapped in the chair, and again nothing happens. But before the warden can say a word, this "smart" guy interrupts and starts pointing excitedly, "Hey, dummies, can't you see? All you gotta do is cross the black wire with the yellow one . . ." And so they did!

Even the smartest of us are pretty foolish a lot of the time. Every day we shoot ourselves in the foot. We do what we know isn't good for us. We repeat yesterday's mistakes with the accuracy of a Xerox copier, and we make choices we know can't possibly lead to a happy day much less a happy life. And yet, God dearly loves us, and so do a number of his people.

Is it because they don't see our shortcomings or don't recognize our dark side? No, God and our true friends see all that—even when we think we've got it hidden. But they see something more as well. Side by side with our flaws they see the goodness that is trying to grow up inside us. And, like God, our true friends say to themselves, "This person needs my help and my understanding." And that's what true friends give, help and understanding.

Today's Gospel story is a shocking reminder that we all need help and understanding in large doses every day. We need it every bit as much as that official in the story who was drowning in debt and had no way out. And we owe it to one another as the only fair payment for God's always giving us

his help when we need it. Yet, paradoxically, we're tempted every day to withhold from our neighbors the very help we know they need if they are to survive. We hold back our compassion as if it were a non-renewable resource. Our lives are soured because of that.

There is no surer path to happiness and peace of heart than to name honestly the full extent of our own need for help and understanding, and then to use that as the measure for the help and compassion we are willing to extend to one another. In doing this we enlarge our own hearts and make them ready and able to receive all we need. Jesus said it perfectly. "The measure you measure with will be measured back to you." That's just the way that hearts work.

May God grant that our measures and our hearts be very large indeed. Amen.

The Lord is Always Near

Matthew 20:1-16

On a freezing morning in January of 1982, an Air Florida jet crashed into the icy waters of the Potomac River just after taking off from Washington's National Airport. There were only six survivors, all in the water, clinging to a fragment of the plane's tail section. Only minutes were available for a rescue before they would succumb to the freezing waters, so there was no time to send for a boat. There was only a small helicopter, which could handle just one person at a time, hovering over the survivors, lowering a lifeline and a flotation ring, waiting till the person was holding tight, and then dashing to shore for safety.

Each time the helicopter returned and lowered its line, one of the survivors, a middle-aged, balding man with a great mustache, would grab hold of the flotation ring, and pass it to one of the others with him in the water. When at last the other five had been rescued and the chopper returned for him, the man was gone. Overcome by the cold, he had slipped quietly to his death in the dark waters, and was not seen again.

What could possibly prepare a person to respond instinctively with such greatness of heart? What would cause him to act so decisively and so generously when the costs were so great and there was no time for deliberation? Where do such big thoughts and noble deeds come from? Surely they don't just happen.

Today's psalm tells us where to look for the answer. It says, "the Lord is near to all who call upon him." Whatever that man's religious persuasion, whatever name he used for God, however it was that he prayed, he must have allowed the always-near God to enter the innermost places of his heart. Very often, he must have experienced the warmth and vastness of the Lord's unfailing love for him. So when his moment of decision came, he knew what he wanted to do: be as generous as the Lord. And he had the power to do it. His heroism was not a fluke, but the final act of a life lived consciously in the presence of a generous Lord.

All of us like to think of ourselves as winners, people who are beyond the ordinary, persons who think big thoughts and do great deeds. What music to our ears are the compliments of others that label us as gracious, big-hearted, generous, and large-minded. Yet, every day we experience the contrary tug and pull of smallness, of meanness of heart, of miserliness, and narrowness of spirit. Only too easily do we emulate the folks in today's Gospel who were angry and envious at the employer's special generosity to the neediest and poorest of his workers.

How do we resist that tug to smallness? How do we find the power to leap over its narrow walls into that broad and sunny place where only the large of heart dwell? We don't find it in an instant, but only through many days and years of receiving the always-near Lord over and over again into our innermost space, and allowing him to work there.

And what is this work? To help us experience inside that he is our very dear father whose generosity knows no bounds; and thus to empower us to become persons of such great spirit, that no one can mistake us for anything but the sons and daughters of our great and generous God.

The Lord is never absent and is always near. What a tragedy it would be to pass a lifetime unconscious and unaware of his presence, untouched by his transforming power.

Open your inner doors; welcome him. Experience his comfort and bask in his warmth. Be transformed by his presence and become great of heart as he is great.

Let no one doubt that we are sons and daughters of a gracious and mighty father!

Does My "Yes" Really Mean Yes?

Matthew 21:28-32

A well-known cardinal died and went to heaven, where he arrived at the same time as a rather scruffy looking New York cab driver. The two of them were assigned their places. The cardinal got a walk-up flat on the very outskirts of heaven, while the cabby got a mansion full of servants, just a few blocks from the throne of God.

The cardinal was pretty upset, so he complained to St. Peter, "I devoted my entire life to God, and this is what I get, a walk-up flat in the boondocks, while this cab driver who never even went to church gets a palace. Surely I deserve better."

"Our policy," explained Peter, "is to reward results. So let's talk about your results. What happened, Your eminence, when you gave your sermons?" The cardinal had to admit that most people fell asleep. "Exactly," said St Peter. "Now, on the other hand, when people rode in this man's taxi, they not only stayed awake, they prayed."

A t this moment each of us has in our possession a very personal gift from God, our very own slice of God's creation. That gift has many parts: our selves, our relationships, the communities we belong to, the bit of earth we tread on. And God has said to us, "Take what I have given you and make it grow. Help it become whole and complete. Help it bear the fruit it was made to bear."

It takes some of us quite a while to hear those words of God because he speaks so softly. But when we do hear them at last, very few of us say "no" outright like that disobedient son in the Gospel. Most of us say "yes." But what does our "yes" to God really mean? Does it have guts and deep roots? Is it a pledge spoken with conviction? Or is it the "yes" of the cocktail party, as in, "Oh yes, we really must do lunch"?

In some parts of our lives, our "yes" can generally be taken at face value. Those are the parts where our competitiveness or our desire for a tangible goal drives us forward. So, for example, when most of us pick up a tennis racket or a golf club, we play to win, and we say "yes" to whatever is necessary to make that happen. We practice, we take lessons, we focus and concentrate as if nothing else in the world matters or even exists.

The same pattern is equally apparent as we plan our investments, build our homes, and seek to advance in our professions. We spare no effort to achieve our goal. Our "yes" means exactly what it sounds like: Y E S.

In light of all this, our behavior in what we say are the really important parts of our lives may seem a bit bizarre! If we did a quick poll right now and asked what each us values most deeply, it's likely that the answers would not be: winning at tennis or golf or bridge, or having the best house, fastest car, most glamorous wardrobe, or fattest wallet. The answers would almost universally sound like this: what I really want is to be a good person, a faithful friend, a loving spouse, a parent who is bringing up wholesome kids, a person who is at peace with God and the world, and who is making the world better for everyone.

Right on the mark! That sounds like a "yes" to all the right things. But is it really? Or is it a "yes" that really means "no," just like the response of that first son in the Gospel? "Yes, father, I'll work in your vineyard," he says, and then doesn't go. It could be, but how can we be sure? In fact finding out for sure is as simple as taking what we say we value most, and then spelling out exactly what we do, all the time, or almost all the time, to make it happen.

The results of this little review may well be shocking, because what we are doing in many cases has no hope whatever of achieving what we say we want.

For those of us who thus find ourselves seriously under-invested in the very core of life, today's Gospel offers both comfort and challenge. In praising that second son, Matthew is telling us there is still room in the kingdom for us, even at this late hour, if we change our bottom line, if we put some muscle into our commitments and some weight behind our "yes." Ambivalence has had its way with us for too long. The day for clear choices is upon us.

S o let us pray for one another:
May God grant us the insight to choose wisely and the grace to make our deeds match our words. And together may we make his kingdom to come in this place in our time. Amen.

Are You Ready for the Consequences?

Matthew 21:33-43

The employees of a large company were offered a once-in-a-lifetime chance at a terrific pension plan. The only conditions were that all employees had to join, and it all had to be done within thirty days. Within a week every employee had signed up – except Seymour. He was adamant, "It's too complicated," he said. "I don't understand it." His co-workers, supervisors, and union representatives begged, pleaded, cajoled, and threatened. But Seymour wouldn't budge.

On the last day of eligibility, the president of the firm called Seymour into his office on the top floor of corporate headquarters. "Seymour," he said, "I have the approval of your union for what I am about to say. We are now on the seventeenth floor. If you do not sign this paper by the time I count to ten, I will have you thrown out of that window."

Without waiting for the president to start counting, and without any sign of anger or resentment, Seymour signed on the dotted line. The president took the document, inspected the signature, placed it in his pocket, and then asked, "Now, why on earth couldn't you have signed before now?"

Seymour replied, "Because you're the first person who explained it to me clearly."

Bad choices bring bad consequences. That's what the president helped Seymour remember. That's what some of us may have forgotten.

A nationwide survey of Catholics several years ago brought some good news about the success of our teaching efforts. It revealed that, in the last twenty years, we Catholics have experienced a pronounced shift in our concept of God. Gone almost entirely is the image of a fierce Old Testament God who is ready at any moment to rain down punishment. In its place are images of God as loving Father and Jesus as caring brother.

That is remarkable progress in a short time. It frees most of us from the terrible idea that we need to bribe or placate a harsh and vengeful God. It frees us, instead, to talk to God as a friend and a mentor. What a liberation!

Unfortunately, there's a down side to the good news. Some of us have taken this wonderful image of God as loving and always-forgiving Father and cheapened it. Some have reduced God to a doddering King Lear, a senile grandfather who smiles perpetually and absolves his children from responsibility for anything at all, so long as they smile back. That's a "have-a-nice-day" God; someone to be ignored.

Once we got liberated from our unwholesome fear of God, some of us concluded that there was no reason at all to be afraid. We were wrong. There is something very big to be afraid of, our own foolishness, which takes the form of an illusion that we can make bad choices and not worry about consequences. Even Seymour knew that wouldn't work!

In today's Gospel story about the tenant farmers, Jesus gives us a stern and pointed warning on this very matter. His warning is not that the Father will smash us if we sin or make a mistake. That's not the kind of Father we have. Jesus' warning is that our foolish choices, our sins, have built-in consequences that no one can escape. And that's not God being mean. God always forgives; it's just that nature never forgets. If we ask him, the Lord will forgive us for those ten martinis before lunch, but the hangover will proceed just the same.

We are very fortunate people. But one of the hazards of affluence and good fortune is the illusion that we can insulate ourselves and our loved ones from the ugly consequences of bad choices. We simply cannot.

- Untended relationships will wither.
- Unguided children will become monsters.
- Recklessly-driven cars will get wrecked.
- Unjust societies will generate criminals and revolutionaries.
- People who live beyond their means will run out of means.

None of these ugly consequences is punishment from God. They are simply the inevitable results of our bad choices. And Jesus spent his ministry trying to warn us about them and telling us where we'd find the power to make good choices.

God has given us a great work to do: building up one another and making his kingdom come. Will this great work be done? The question is still open, but the answer lies in our choices and the consequences we cannot escape. Our loving Father has us by the hand. He offers us strength and guidance, and he cheers us onward, but only we can choose.

Let us pray for one another that we may choose wisely, and share in the joy of seeing his kingdom come both within us and around us.

Fear-Habits Keep Us from Life's Banquet

Matthew 22:1-14

There's an interesting fable from Holland about three tulip bulbs named No, Yes, and Maybe. They lived at the bottom of a bulb tin, content to be round and fat, and dressed in silky brown garments. When autumn came, they fell to discussing the destiny of tulip bulbs. No said, "I don't think there is any other life for tulip bulbs. We were made to live in bulb tins and I'm quite content to be right here." And with that he rolled over and went to sleep.

Maybe disagreed. "I'm not satisfied with things as they are. I feel something inside me that I must achieve and I believe I can." So he squeezed and squeezed himself, turning this way and that. But nothing happened, and finally in frustration he gave up.

Then Yes spoke up. "I've been told," he said very softly, "that by ourselves we can do nothing, but that we can achieve our destiny, if we put ourselves in God's hands." The others just sniffed and looked away.

Now one day a hand reached down into the bulb tin, groping for a bulb. No and Maybe scurried out of reach, and hid in a corner. But Yes rolled right into that hand, which took him out and buried him in the cold, damp earth of winter!

"What a fool to fall for that trick," laughed No and Maybe, who were warm, dry, and safe in their little bulb tin. And with that they went back to sleep. When spring came, No and Maybe were nowhere to be seen. No had shrivelled up and died in his sleep; while Maybe had worried and fidgeted himself to death. Nothing remained of them but a few dry husks and a handful of dust. And what about Yes who had let himself be buried all winter in the ground and had seemed to everyone to be dead? Well he was a sight to behold. For you see, he had burst out of the ground and blossomed into a whole new life.

God is inviting us to blossom into a new life, a life so rich and full that Jesus describes it as a banquet hosted by a king. Everything we could ever want, everything our hearts have ever longed for, is on the table, put there by our Father. Yet, we find it hard to say "yes," hard to accept his invitation to the banquet. Our fear-habits hold us back, our fears of letting go, our fears of losing we're-not-quite-sure-what. And so, in response to God's invitation, we hedge our bets and mutter a "maybe," which leaves the door open but leaves most of life's banquet out of reach.

What's the problem? The problem is trust. For if we really trusted that God does love us and would never lie to us or do us harm, then we'd have to believe him when he tells us where happiness is to be found. And we'd have to say "yes" when he calls us to get up and walk with him to the banquet, for he knows where the feast is . . . and where it's not.

The key is trust, and that doesn't come easily. So we need to offer a quiet prayer for one another.

Lord, every day of our life you've shown how vast and how tender is your love for us. And from the moment of our birth, you have given us good reason to trust you. So now at last we commit ourselves into your hands to be shaped and transformed into your likeness. Again and again you have invited us to a new life. Now with your help our answer is "yes," and so may it be for the rest of our days. Amen.

Use Your Life as He Uses His

Matthew 22:15-21

A man walked into a roof-top bar and ordered a drink. The man next to him began a conversation about the unique wind currents in the area. The first man said he didn't understand what was so special about the wind there, so the other said, "Let me show you." With that he went to the window, jumped out, did a spin in mid-air, and then came back in. "See how great the currents are! You can do the same thing."

After a few more drinks and much prodding, the first man decided to test the wind currents. He went to the window, jumped out, and dropped like a rock. The bartender looked at the other man and said, "Superman, you're really mean when you're drunk."

Most of us are neither mean nor a drunk – but is that enough? Is just staying out of trouble and avoiding notable nastiness enough to make a life? It's a start, but it's not nearly enough. So what is enough? Jesus gives us a clue in today's gospel. His enemies were trying to entrap him into an indictable offense. But he just brushed them off, "Give to Caesar what is Caesar's." And then he returned to his core message, "but give to God what is God's."

So, what do we have that is God's? Very simply, our life. But how do we give that back to him? By becoming nuns or priests or martyrs or missionaries in darkest Africa, or perhaps by throwing ourselves on a live grenade to save our friends? For most of us that is not what God wants. What God does want from all of us is for us to learn to use our life the way he uses his life: by helping those who need help and giving life to those who need life. So how do we begin? By being alert and paying attention to one another, and developing the deeply ingrained habit of asking ourselves: How's he doing? What does she need? Is he OK? How can I help?

Most of the time most of what people really need is within our power to give. For example, some of us are getting a little forgetful, and what we need is just a little reassurance – and a little patience. And for all of us there are those days when nothing is wrong but nothing is right. Most times a friend is all that's needed to lift the fog.

And think about the times someone has been very bad, and needs to say so, but doesn't know how. A dose of encouragement from an understanding friend will light the way and draw him out of the dark. At any given moment most of what is needed by the people right around us is within our power to give. And better yet, all we have to handle – all we have to give – is one moment at a time: if we take care of the minutes, God will take care of the days – and the years.

God has given us the gift of life, and the power to give life to one another – in many shapes and sizes – every day. We can be real supermen and wonder women if we learn how to give our gift, if we learn to pay attention to one another, see what is needed, and give what is needed – one moment at a time – and never withhold our gift. From such humble stuff the kingdom of God is made.

With God's help, let us make it here and now together.

You'll Be Surprised at What's Inside

Matthew 22:34-40

A college student was telling his friends how taking a first-aid course had prepared him for all emergencies. "The other day, I saw a woman get hit by a car," he said. She had a broken arm, a twisted knee, a fractured skull, and was bleeding all over the place."

"How horrible!" gasped his friends. "What did you do?"

"Thanks to my first-aid training, I knew just what to do. I sat down on the curb and put my head between my legs to keep from fainting."

Guess who is the center of his life! Today's Gospel gives us a very different view of life. Jesus says, "If you want to be happy, love God with your whole heart, and love your neighbor as you love yourself."

We have heard those words thousands of times. Most of us know them by heart and have taken them to heart: love is the key to life. But that still leaves a question: how do we do it? How do we get disentangled enough from our own agenda and from our own wants and needs, feelings and prejudices, to have both the clarity and the will to love wisely and well?

It's not easy, but the word "compassion" points the way. It means "to feel with." And that's exactly what we have to do. With some regularity, we have to take off our own shoes and walk in another person's moccasins. We have to lay aside our own thoughts and feelings and get inside the thoughts and feelings of our friend – or our enemy.

It's amazing how different things look and feel from inside there. Some things look bigger, some look smaller, and some things you can't see at all. There are dark and scary places there, and some horrendous wounds hidden behind closed doors, and some marvelous, secret gardens as well. We have only to look inside.

Who'd have thought all that was there? Most of us would never have imagined it. But when at last we begin to see within our brother's heart, and see how the world looks when viewed through our sister's eyes, we begin to understand their need of us and of our help. We begin to understand what loving them calls for here and now. And we begin to have the heart to give and forgive as needed – without counting. This is our calling as Christians. It's what makes us like God.

So let us pray for one another. May God grant us compassionate hearts – great, wide and welcoming. May we learn to feel with one another that we may give and forgive wisely, and well, and always without counting. Amen.

Love Never Forgets and Always Acts

Matthew 23:1-12

A wealthy man lost his wife when their only child was very young. He hired a woman to serve as nanny for his little son, and that she did with much affection for many years. Just as the boy was preparing to go off to college, he was stricken with a deadly disease and died. His father's heart was broken, and before long he died as well.

No will could be found and there were no known relatives. So the state held an auction at the mansion. The Nanny was there, clutching her worn black purse. She had only a few dollars, but was determined to buy one special keepsake – a painting that had hung above the fireplace as long as she'd been there, a portrait of the boy she'd loved and nurtured all those years.

When the painting came up for auction, no one else wanted it, so Nanny got it. She took it home and began to clean it and to polish the frame, cherishing all the memories the painting evoked within her. As she made a final adjustment to the frame, a paper fell out from behind the cardboard backing. It was the old man's will, which stated that all his wealth should go to the person who loved his son enough to buy the portrait!

True love never forgets. True love always acts, and it never fails. The old man knew that, and so did Nanny. But do we? Or are we the ones Jesus is rebuking in today's Gospel? "Their words are bold," he says, "but their deeds are few." Sometimes that is who we are. Sometimes we do forget those who love us and those who need our help. Sometimes we do settle for talk, talk, talk, and for cheap token acts.

But we're not willing to let things rest there. Every week we gather here because we know that forgetting one another and settling for talk and tokens won't get us to our heart's real desire – won't get us to communion and peace. We gather here not just to remember the Lord's love for us,

but also to ask ourselves in his presence: who is it that needs our love and our help this day, this week?

The Lord always answers very specifically and never in the abstract – we'll hear the answer if we're listening. And we'll receive the energy and power to act, if we ask.

So let us listen and act, that when our work is done, the Lord may say to us, "Your words were few, but your deeds were bold."

At that moment, we will not need to be invited us to enter into the joy of our Father. For we shall already have lived there for many years.

Be Ready on the Inside

Matthew 25:1-13

A little more than a hundred years ago at the 1893 Chicago World's Fair, a group of distinguished scholars took a long look into the future and predicted what the country would be like in 1993. Here are some direct quotes: "Prisons and poorhouses will almost disappear, and so will divorce. Taxation will be reduced to a minimum. The entire world will be open to free trade, and there will be no need for a standing army. In 1993 the government will have grown simpler and smaller because true greatness always tends towards simplicity."

There you have it, our world! But before we laugh too hard, who among us can predict with confidence even what is close at hand, like the weather on Monday, the price of gold on Tuesday, or who will be here with us next Sunday, and who won't? We can make educated guesses, but none of us can really predict the future because the endless and ever-changing interplay of the billions upon billions of factors that make up the world and even our own bodies are just too complex ever to track with certitude.

So how in heaven's name are we to respond to today's Gospel? How do we avoid getting left outside, like the foolish virgins in the Gospel story? How are we to prepare and get ready for a future we can't even see? What is Jesus talking about? He's not talking about getting our things, our stuff in order. He's not talking about updating our fire insurance, or reviewing our wills, or checking the roof and the gutters before it rains. He's talking about preparing our insides, our spirits, for whatever our unseen future may bring.

Life eventually confronts us all with hard times and sometimes even disasters. It also surprises us often with incredibly good fortune. We have all seen people who weren't ready for either the good or the bad. We have seen them "crash and burn," or flail about like beached whales, or wander aimlessly into the sunset, or break apart on the rocks of prosperity. So we all need to hear what Jesus is saying: "Be ready on the inside."

But how do we get ready for the good fortune and the bad that our unseen future surely holds? There is only one sure way, and that is by rooting our hearts very deeply in the Lord now, and getting in the habit of seeing the world through his eyes. If we have done that, when the future at last takes its shape and becomes the present, we'll find ourselves standing on rock. We'll know what to make of it. We'll have the power to respond to it. We will survive, and the Lord's joy will be in our hearts, even when pain is there too.

"Be ready," Jesus says. Be ready on the inside. Put your hopes and your roots in the Lord, and you will stand firm all the days of your life. And God's peace will dwell in your heart.

Are You Fully Invested?

Matthew 25:14-30

In the 1960s when the President of France, Charles de Gaulle, was regularly aggravating most of the world with his monumental arrogance, there was a fictitious story making the rounds which caught the essence of his character rather nicely. It seems that one day de Gaulle decided to go up to the church of Sacré Coeur on Montmarte to pray at the Shrine of the Sacred Heart. He strode down the aisle of the church and then stood for a long while in silence, staring intently at the tabernacle. Finally, he spoke his prayer, "Sacred Heart of Jesus, trust in me!"

It's just a story, but quite by accident it opens the door onto a profound truth: God does trust each one of us very much – so much, indeed, that he has entrusted to each of us a rich and entirely unique combination of gifts. For each of us, the gifts are different, some are spectacular, others quite ordinary. But all of us have received everything we need to complete our life's mission well. That's the point of today's Gospel: we already have what we need. What remains to be seen is how we'll use it. Will we live up to God's trust in us?

The three servants in the Gospel story spell out our options. The last of the three is a decent, honest man. He wants to do the right thing, but he's terrified of making a mistake, so he hides his treasure in a safe place where no one can find it. He doesn't even think of stealing or spending it; but he doesn't do anything with his treasure. He simply has it for awhile, and then is made to give it back – after which he finds his hands are empty and the game is over. Too late he discovers that just staying out of trouble isn't enough. A holding pattern isn't a life!

The other two servants offer us a different model. They take the treasures that are entrusted to them and they invest them. Think for a moment what investing means: pondering, imagining, calculating, using all our ingenuity, and then, finally, making a commitment – writing a check that can't be taken back – spending our limited treasure with the hope – but no guarantee – of a return. That is hard work. It's worrisome. And it's risky. But it's the way God calls us to live: fully investing all our gifts and expending every ounce of our lives to help the kingdom come inside us and around us.

God has already entrusted us with everything we need to complete our life's mission well.

May fear and weariness never cause us to hide our gifts or to doubt them. Rather, let us use them with joy, expend them without fear, and invest them all, that his kingdom may come here and now. Amen.

We're All Kin, So Be Kind

Matthew 25:31-46

Two men, Tom and Bill, had been best friends all their lives. So when Tom died suddenly, Bill was devastated. One evening, watching a beautiful sunset, Bill was sure he felt the presence of his old friend nearby. "Is that you, Tom?" he asked.

"Yes, it's me," came the reply.

"What's it like where you are?"

"Well, it's kinda nice," said Tom. "I get up in the morning, have a big breakfast, maybe go for a swim in the lake, chat with my buddies and flirt with the ladies. Then it's time for lunch and a nap. And so it goes."

"Wow!" said Bill. "I had no idea heaven was like that."

"Who says I'm in heaven?" replied Tom. "I'm a moose in Wyoming!"

Life is full of surprises! And so is today's gospel story which is about life's ultimate winners and losers. In the story, both the folks who got invited into heaven and those who got left outside were surprised and shocked, and couldn't figure it out. The good guys couldn't remember doing anything particularly good – there wasn't a single Nobel prize winner in the lot. And the bad guys couldn't remember doing anything especially bad – not a felon among them. "How did we get here?" they asked.

So in this very last story in the whole gospel, Jesus gives the answer and explains what it is that makes some people real winners and others real losers. It's not something outside us, something wonderful we've made, or achieved, or got possession of. It's something inside us that makes us life's winners. It's a habit of the heart, a carefully cultivated habit of seeing who really needs us, and then answering their call.

That kind of habit doesn't come from a hope of reward – out there. It comes from inside, from a deep sense of kinship: we are kind because we see one another as kin, and we recognize in one another's faces the face of our brother, Jesus. This open-ended habit of kindness, which sets no narrow limits as to person or place, carries within it its own reward, and makes us life's real winners. For every time we reach out and give away a part of ourselves, we come closer and closer to our heart's real desire which is communion, kinship with one another and with God, kinship which never leaves us abandoned or alone.

The deeply-rooted habit of kindness changes us and sows the seeds for a new kind of world. And it readies our spirits to hear with confident assurance the words of our Lord's final promise: "I will wipe every tear from your eyes, and there shall be no more death or mourning, weeping or pain, for the old order has passed away. . . Behold, I make all things new!"

Take That Walk

Luke 11:27-28

Lk 11:27-28: In November 1860, shortly after he was elected president, Abraham Lincoln was urged to appoint a certain individual to his new cabinet. The president-elect pondered the appointment for a long time, and then decided against it. When asked why he'd said no, Lincoln replied, "I'm afraid I just don't like the man's face."

"But the poor fellow isn't responsible for his face," protested the advisor.

Lincoln disagreed, "Every man over forty is responsible for his face."

Every day, as the minutes and hours pass one by one, we make hundreds of tiny choices. We sort out our experiences and choose what to see and what to ignore, what to remember and what to forget, what to take inside and make a permanent part of ourselves, and what to discard forever. As time passes, our choices become patterns, and slowly, usually unconsciously, we remake and reshape ourselves. And it shows in our faces.

The key to what we become, the key to the future shape of our faces and our hearts, is not what happens to us, but what parts of our experience we choose to claim as our own and take inside. Sometimes we make very sad and strange choices. Sometimes, in defiance of reality, we edit out "the sun, and the moon, and the stars," and take inside only darkness and a handful of dust.

That's why today's gospel can be such a help to us. In it, Mary bares her soul and shares with us what life has taught her – and what it should have taught us – namely, that God's love for us is immense, and that the life he gives us is no curse but a gift that we can embrace with confidence and hope, and without fear.

If we haven't learned that from life, we haven't been paying attention. We've been filtering out the gold and throwing it away; and our sad, angry, troubled faces show it.

If we want hearts that are serene, confident, and hope-filled as we face a challenging today and an invisible tomorrow, Mary has shown us where to look: in the trash can of our long-ignored memories where the full scope of God's affection and care is writ large.

Go back to the beginning. Take your infant self by the hand, and walk through the years with attentive eyes. See the Lord's love of you in action, day by day across the years, probing and prodding you, nurturing you through so many good people, showing you the way out of so many dead end streets, picking you up when you fell, and never, ever abandoning you.

Take that walk in the quiet of your soul, and receive the peace and confidence, the strength and hope that our Lord has always wanted you to have.

Receive the Holy Spirit, and let your heart be warmed at last!

Cycle B

Stay Awake or You'll Miss the Best Part!

Mark 13:33-37

In celebration of Thanksgiving, a genteel widow went to a pet shop to buy a parrot. She found a rather splendid one, but the manager warned her it had been raised by a sailor and had a foul mouth. The woman was confident she could reform him, so she took him home, where she soon discovered just how foul a mouth he had.

Not a person to be trifled with, the woman took that bird and locked him in a dark closet for half an hour. Then she put him back in his cage and addressed him solemnly, "Now, have you learned your lesson?" The parrot was unbowed, and responded with the same curses as before.

Back to the closet he went, this time for an hour. Again he was asked, "Have you learned your lesson?" And again, undaunted, he squawked his curses. With that, the woman opened the refrigerator door and thrust the parrot inside. When at last she pulled him out, he'd turned blue, his feathers were frozen stiff, and an icicle was hanging from his beak. "Well now," she asked triumphantly, "Are we going to say those words anymore?"

"N-n-no, m-m-ma'am!" said the parrot humbly and with the greatest courtesy, "B-b-but could you please tell me, ma'am, what that turkey in there did?"

Some parrots are slow learners. And so are some people – probably most of us. That's why Jesus calls out so urgently to us in the gospel, "Stay awake! Pay attention!" He knows we regularly miss a good portion of what's really going on around us. We see events but don't get their meaning; we hear words but don't grasp their significance. And so very often we stay stuck where we are, and don't grow, and don't flower as we could.

Think of the wonderful things that happen to us every day: the sunrise, the freshness after a rain, the smell of a rose, small kindnesses, laughter, a hug, a winter fire, a new idea, an old friend. So many

lights to light our day and to teach us that life is a blessing, and that our good God is with us for sure. So many lights that go unnoticed and unnamed every day.

And think of the sad and hard things that come to our days as well. They, too, have much to teach us. Our failures and our sins, our bodily pains and pains of the spirit, our disappointments and our losses, our grieving and our weeping: these are part of all our lives and God does not shield us from their pain.

But hidden in each – no matter how terrible – is an invitation to life, an invitation from God to become more: more whole, more true, and more happy. And hidden there along with the invitation is always God's promise to give all the power and strength that are needed. But alas, too often we sleep through those messages too. And their light does not lighten our darkness.

Jesus is calling to us now, "Stay awake!" He is pleading with us to see and receive the light that God is sending us in so many different forms at every moment.

Let us not turn our back on that light. Let us watch for it at each moment, and take it in, and let it give light to our whole house.

The Script is Ours to Write

Mark 1:1-18

Somewhere deep in the New England countryside, a vacationing family stopped at a gas station and the driver told the old gent at the pump to "fill 'er up." While waiting, the traveler asked, "What are the people like in the next village down the road?"

The old fellow wasn't much for taking chances so he answered with a question, "What were they like in the last village you passed through?"

"Actually very friendly and hospitable," the traveler responded.

"Well, you'll find these will be just the same," said the old boy. And as it turned out, he was right.

Now as it happened, the very next person to drive into the gas station asked exactly the same question: "What are the people like in the next village down the road?"

And again the station attendant responded with his question, "What were they like in the last village you passed through?"

"Oh, very sour and unfriendly," came the reply.

"Ah well, you'll find the people in the next village will be just the same," said the man with a smile. And once again the wise old fellow was right. For each man received exactly what he had prepared himself to receive.

In today's readings we hear the advice of both Isaiah and John the Baptist: "Prepare the way of the Lord." "Get yourselves ready because he's coming soon." Now even the little children in our congregation know that Jesus already arrived nearly 2000 years ago. That's old news. So why are we rerunning these old tapes? Because, while Jesus has already arrived out there, in the world, to some extent or other he has not yet been received in here, in our hearts. So how do we make it possible for that to happen? How do we prepare ourselves to receive the Lord into our very center?

Today's story gives us a clue. Those villagers who lived down the road from the gas station were just like us, a confusing and contradictory combination of good and bad, of meanness and grace. When the two travelers came along, they both encountered the same villagers, but for some reason each of them took something very different from that encounter. What made the difference? Not something outside, but something inside them.

What made the difference were the eyes and hearts with which each of those travelers viewed the world. Those eyes and hearts had been prepared for that visit to the village by a whole lifetime of choosing what to see and what to ignore. The understanding heart of the one was prepared to see through all the contradictory surface data and into the hearts of the villagers, and so as to recognize them as brothers and friends. Whereas the hardened heart of the other traveler was prepared to receive only the negative, the ugly, the worst, and that is exactly what he took home from his village encounter.

The Lord is dwelling here in our midst, where he has always been, showing himself to each of us in diverse and subtle ways every day. Some of us will recognize his face and invite him inside because we have prepared our hearts and made them receptive. We have done that through many years of recognizing and trusting the good, wherever it appears.

Some of us, on the other hand, will see little if anything of his face and will have to live with the hollow sadness of disappointed hearts. For our blindness to the goodness visible all around us each day has left us with eyes and hearts unprepared and unable to recognize or welcome the Lord.

Where will your story end? Where will mine? With a heart that recognizes and delights in the good when it sees it, a heart that is prepared for the Lord? Or with a blind heart that can receive nothing but sadness?

The script is ours to write and we are writing it at this very moment.

Have You Seen Your Prison?

John 1:6-8, 19-28

There was a bright but very hyperactive little second grader who found himself headed home one day with a report card that was a major disaster. After stalling through dinner, he finally got up his courage and showed the report card to his dad. "Son," said the father, "we're going to have to do something about these grades." "We can't, Dad," replied the boy. "They're in ink!"

They're written in ink . . . so he's stuck! That little boy was the prisoner of an idea that was too small. So today's Old Testament words from Isaiah are just right for him as well as for us. Isaiah says with absolute assurance: the Savior is coming to release prisoners and set captives free. Now most of us have never even seen the inside of a jail, much less been guests there. But we've all been prisoners, all been captives. That's because most prisons are inside the head and the heart, and not outside.

Think about the prisons we've been locked in, often without knowing it till long after the fact. Think of the narrow, fixed ideas that keep us blind to our life's real possibilities. Think of the close-mindedness – or even stubbornness – that cuts us off from so many people and so many opportunities. Think of the compulsions and addictions that leave us no freedom at all to build a real life. Think of the pessimism and fearfulness that trap us inside a tiny cell. Think of the long-cherished grievances that lock out so many people and so much love. And think of the self-absorption and self-centeredness that condemn us to what is, in fact, solitary confinement. Think of all that, and so much more.

Those are mighty strong prisons we're locked in, with thick walls and no light and no fresh air. It's hard to see inside a prison. And sometimes, when we've been there a long time, we don't even know we're in prison – or at least don't want to admit it, because we fear we'll never get out. So it is to us that the Lord is saying, "I want to set you free from everything that enslaves you." We have only to ask, from the heart, and God will do it. But if we are to ask for freedom, we must first name our prison, which may not be so easy, for that's where our resistance lies. That's where our work and our prayer must begin.

So let us begin by praying for one another: Lord, give us light to see our prison walls. Give us hope to look beyond them. And give us courage to walk through the doors that you open. Amen.

It's Time to Re-Imagine Ourselves

Matthew 4:12-23

Some years ago on a sunny fall day in New Hampshire, I took a long walk through the fall colors, and eventually wandered into an old churchyard. The gravestones there dated as far back as the 1700s, and some of their inscriptions were so worn with time as to be altogether unreadable. But one of them caught my eye, and I've never forgotten it. It said, very simply, "He did what he could."

Who could ask for anything more? Which one among us would not be honored to have that on our gravestones as the final verdict of our family and friends? "He did what he could." "She did what she could." That thought has warmed and comforted me many times over the years. But I must confess that reading Sunday's gospel side by side with that ancient epitaph has given me second thoughts. Did the man whose bones have lain so long beneath that gravestone really do what he could or only what he and his friends thought he could? I wonder.

For a clue let's take a closer look at Mary. The angel delivers his extraordinary announcement and Mary's first response is, "That's impossible. You must have come to the wrong address. I'm just a peasant girl, and besides that I haven't even got a husband!" She wasn't saying "No." She wasn't trying to be difficult. She just couldn't imagine how something so wonderful could be true. And, had the dialogue stopped there, that would have been that. And it wouldn't have come true.

But the Lord's messenger prodded her further, and she finally spoke her "yes," not because everything had suddenly become clear, but because she trusted the one who'd sent the message. She trusted the Lord, and, with his grace, she became what she thought was beyond her; she did what she thought was impossible. In doing that, she has confronted us with a very large question: In the things that really matter, have we perhaps unconsciously defined ourselves down into flyspecks? At the core of our lives have we imagined ourselves into "munchkins"? Have we shrunk our vision and our hopes and spoken the word "impossible" too often and too fast?

For at least some part of ourselves an honest answer for all of us is "yes." We have settled for being less whole, less happy, less at peace, less bonded to one another than we could be, because we've told one another that less is all that's possible. Now in one sense, we're right. Not much is possible if we're working alone. But we're not working alone. God has given us one another as helpers. And as Mary discovered, he's given us himself. For all time he is our help and our strength, and nothing is impossible with God.

So now is the time to re-imagine ourselves as Mary did, to imagine ourselves as God imagines us: large and noble, enlivened and yet at peace, truly whole and wonderfully bonded to one another in friendships that will last into eternity.

That is God's vision and hope for us!

God Has Spoken

Luke 2:1-14

There's an ancient legend that when God created the heavens and the earth and everything in them, they were created through the use of words. "Let there be light," and there was light. "Let the waters teem with living creatures," and it was done.

Everything that God made with words was good. But God was especially proud and fond of the man and woman because they contained God; a part of God's life-giving spirit. This made the devil jealous and angry. And so, one day, when God was enjoying the company of the man and the woman, the devil "happened" by. He walked up to God, and with a sneer asked him what he liked so much about these creatures.

When God was ready to speak, the devil craftily put a bond upon his tongue. God could not talk! God's creative power was in words and the devil had bound that power! The devil laughed at God and struck the man and woman many times very hard. As time passed, the devil came back to mock God. He scoffed at God's silence and helplessness. God responded by holding up one finger. "One?" asked the devil. "You want to say one word, is that it?"

"Yes," nodded God, pleading with sad eyes and urgent hands.

The arrogant devil thought to himself, "What harm can God do with just one word?" So he removed the bond from God's tongue.

Then God spoke one word in a whisper in the middle of the night. God spoke it for the man and woman, and it brought them great joy. It was a word that gathered up all the love and forgiveness and creativity stored up the whole time of the long silence. The one word spoken was "Jesus!"

God has spoken this "word" to us once and for all and won't take it back: Jesus is with us and for us for all time. And he will always be enough. Thanks be to God!

What Are We Really Handing On?

Luke 2:22-40

If you ever want to provoke a severe attack of melancholy, just read the newspaper or watch the TV news. They are full of unendurable sadness: Gang warfare, drive-by shootings, bombings of innocent bystanders in London, in Oklahoma City, in Bosnia, serial killings, ubiquitous muggings, the battering of helpless infants, biological warfare against one's own people, and on and on.

Where does that kind of ugliness and hardness of heart come from? Not out of the air or from flouridation in the water! And don't try to blame it on the devil either. Our values, good and bad, have their roots in our families and our friendships. Now mind you, each of us is free to sort out and pick and choose. But most of the time what most of us choose are the values of the people we value: Mainly our families and friends. That's a lot of subtle power – for good or ill – that we have over one another, as we sit at the supper table, and watch TV together, and chat on the golf course, and stand and sit and sing together here in church, and do all the things we DO with one another each day.

As we do what we do, even without speaking a word, we're quietly revealing our true selves, and making very clear what we value and what we don't. But we're doing even more than that. We are silently teaching – usually without intending to – subtly inviting those who value us to be like us. What exactly are we teaching to the people we say we love? To answer that, we have only to look at the pattern of our actions, and not at our words. What we ordinarily choose to do is what we really value. And that's what we teach to others even without speaking a word – just by doing it.

If, for example, I tell you that Sunday mass is the most important event of my week, but you see me getting here late and distracted, and with homily unprepared, week after week, you'll know that the mass isn't all that important to me, and you'll wonder whether it should be all that important to you. I'll have taught the wrong value, quite like you're saying that family is the center of your life, but spending no time with your family or talking with them. Your deeds will swallow up your words. The truth will speak itself and all will see it. And like me, you'll have taught the wrong value brilliantly.

Mary and Joseph understood all this very well. And that's why we find them in Sunday's Gospel taking their tiny new baby on the difficult journey up to Jerusalem. They knew that everything they'd ever say or do could touch the spirit of their child – for good or ill. So they went to the temple, not just to do the customary rituals, but to commit their lives to handing on to Jesus the very best of what was in them – with God's help. We have no written record of their subsequent life as a family. We have only the man Jesus, whose life speaks for itself, and speaks eloquently for his family.

We call one another "friends," and that is what we long to be. So let us do for one another what true friends do: Listen to what the patterns of our deeds tell us about our real values. And then, with God's help, make our deeds match our best words and our highest hopes. Our good deeds, even in the smallest of things, will not be lost upon those who value us. Those good deeds will teach and encourage silently and powerfully. They will find an echo in the hearts of those who know and trust us. Our goodness will draw forth from deep inside them all that is good.

By God's grace, may we be true friends for one another.

Keep Your Eyes on the Star

Matthew 2:1-12

At the very top of a high mountain, there was a monastery. The monks were rarely seen in the village below, but the people there held them in high esteem. One day, one of the monks trekked down the mountain to the village. An excited villager, honored to meet such a holy man, struck up a conversation: "Father, surely yours is the best of all lives, living so close to God up in the clouds on the top of the mountain. Tell me, what do you do up there?"

After a thoughtful pause, the monk replied, "Well, I'll tell you, we fall down and we get up. We fall down, and we get up. We fall down, but, with God's help, we keep getting up."

The three wise men in the gospel for Epiphany would have understood that monk. They knew about mistakes. You will note that, although it's more than a week since Christmas, we're only now celebrating their arrival at the stable. That is because the wise men arrived late! They had made a wrong turn! After spotting that star – which nobody else paid any attention to – and after following it through many lands, the wise men just couldn't imagine that a newborn king would be anywhere but in the capital city. And thus, when they'd got so very close to Bethlehem where Jesus was, they turned away, turned their back on the star, and went instead to Jerusalem. They got dazzled and distracted by the lights of the big city and lost their way.

The reason we call them "wise" is not that they made it straight to Bethlehem on the first try. No, we call them "wise" because they didn't give up their search for Jesus when they got lost. They recognized they were lost. They asked for help, turned their eyes back to the star, corrected their course, and found their way to the stable!

What a perfect model for us as we begin a new year and continue our search for the Lord. Even the youngest of us have already made our fair share of wrong turns and spent more than enough time on dead-end streets. And at times we have all ignored our "star," ignored the very clear guidance God has been giving us through the circumstances of our lives and through the unique pattern of our own special gifts.

None of those mistakes of ours is any surprise to God. After all, as our maker, God knows we are slow learners. All God asks is that we not look backward but that we attend to the present – which is all we have – and then get up and try again. All God asks is that we open our eyes, pay attention to our "star," change our course if need be – just as the wise men did – and follow that star wherever it leads, for in the end, it leads to the Lord.

So as we begin this new year, we really do need to pray for one another:

Lord, help us to see the special star you have sent to each of us. Help us to see your gifts to us and to recognize how you are calling out to us through those gifts. Help us to keep our eyes on your star and follow it. For, in the end, we know it leads to you. And you are where we want to be. Amen.

Baptism into God's Likeness Is a Lifetime Task

Matthew 1:7-11

A poor traveler was making his way across eighteenth-century England. Exhausted and famished, he came to a roadside inn, which had a sign over the door identifying it as "St. George and the Dragon." The traveler knocked on the door, whereupon the innkeeper's wife stuck her head out an upper window. "Could you spare some victuals for a poor vagabond?" the traveler asked.

The harried innkeeper looked at his shabby, dirty clothes, shouted "No!" and slammed the window. The vagabond knocked again. "What now?" screeched the woman.

"Ma'am," he asked most respectfully, "do you suppose I might have a word with George?"

There's a combination of the dragon and St. George in us all. And helping the saint to flourish and prevail is hard work. Indeed, it is the task of a lifetime. Nobody could make that clearer than St. Peter does in Sunday's reading from the Acts of the Apostles. At the time of this writing, Peter has already been pope for ten years. He's been a close personal friend of Jesus for three years. He's seen every miracle, and heard every story Jesus ever told. He's witnessed the resurrection, and he's received the Holy Spirit at Pentecost.

Yet, through it all, he's been the prisoner of a really small, truly bad idea: he has been absolutely certain that God doesn't really like anyone but Jews! Indeed, Peter has insisted that a Gentile who wants to become a follower of Jesus has to become a Jew first! He has insisted, but, for quite a while, he's been feeling uneasy about it. And now, haltingly, he admits it. (It's so hard to give up a cherished idea.) Listen to his words: "I am *beginning* to see how true it is that God shows no partiality!" Fifteen years it took him to figure that out! Fifteen years!!!

Figuring out life, getting the important things straight, helping the saint to prevail over the dragon is hard and slow work, and not work that can be done alone. But it is work that must be done, if we are to become our best selves, the selves God imagined the day we were made. Our work, our task, has two parts: first, holding onto what is true in us and helping it to grow; and second, letting go and changing what is not true. That means first seeing and then acting.

It is to do this holy work of holding on and letting go, seeing and then acting – that we gather here every week. We come here, not to change God, but with God's help, to change ourselves. We come, not to reshape God into our way of thinking, but to let ourselves be reshaped into God's likeness. If that kind of change is to happen our hearts must be open, trusting, and attentive. For the spirit whispers softly and only those who are listening closely will hear. Only those whose inner doors are open will receive the light and the energy the Holy Spirit is sending even as we speak.

So let us listen now with open, trusting, attentive hearts, that like Peter, we may begin to see what is true, begin to live what is true, begin to say "farewell" to the dragon in us, and begin to let the saint in us prevail.

You Come with Me

John 1:35-42

A woman and her elderly grandmother were sitting on the porch discussing a member of the family. "He's just no good," said the young woman. "He's untrustworthy, not to mention lazy!"

"Yes, he has his problems," said the grandmother as she rocked back and forth in her rocker, "but Jesus loves him."

"I'm not so sure of that," replied the younger woman.

"Oh, yes," said the old lady. "Jesus loves him." She rocked some more and thought some more, and then added, "Of course, Jesus doesn't know him like we do . . ."

Well, of course, the Lord does know us all clear through. And today's gospel gives us a hint of what that really means. Jesus is meeting Simon for the first time. He looks intently at him, and sees there the seeds of greatness just waiting to grow. Then Jesus names what he sees, "You are Peter, the rock," he says. "You, come with me." So Peter follows him, and, very slowly, he becomes the strong one, the rock on whom all the others depend.

In a very true sense Jesus is calling each one of us just as he called Peter. His call is not just generic – "Y'all come." His call is supremely personal. For he is able to see and name what is best in us – something we often fail to do. He sees past the parts of us that cause us to be discouraged and downhearted, and like a laser, he comes to focus on what makes us special and like no other. Then he calls us by name. He says, "You, come with me and I will teach you how to grow into your best self. I will show you how to give your gift to the world."

That is the Lord's invitation and promise to us this very day. It would be a terrible shame, a real tragedy, to ignore it. So let us pray for one another:

Lord, we thank you for the gifts we carry within us, and we bless you for calling out to us every day. Walk with us always as our teacher and guide. Let us know the joy of growing up with you at our side. And let us know the joy of giving to one another what you have made to grow in us. Amen.

Loving Is Giving Your Gift

Matthew 1:14-20

A young man was walking along the beach when he stumbled on a magic lantern. He rubbed the lantern and a genie popped out with a hearty greeting, "Have I got good news for you! This very afternoon you will receive three gifts: a miracle cure for all ailments, a huge diamond, and a dinner date with a famous movie star."

Of course, the young man was elated, so he rushed right home where he was greeted at the door by his mother. "Some odd things have being happening this afternoon," she said. "At noon someone delivered a barrel of chicken soup. A half hour later, a telegram came saying a long-lost relative has left you a minor-league baseball stadium, and just a few minutes ago, MGM called inviting you to dinner tonight with Lassie!"

So much for good news! As with so much of life, that fellow was raised up for a moment and then let down fast. We know the experience well: a hungry longing for something more, a momentary hope that it's within our grasp, then disappointment and back to hungryh longing.

It is to all of us who know that hungry longing that Jesus is speaking his invitation, "Come with me! Follow in my path." Many of us are ready to say "yes" to him, but we still have a question: how do we follow him? What is his way? We know the generic answer: Jesus' way is the golden rule: "Love God with your whole heart and your neighbor as yourself." But how does that translate into the concrete? How do we actually put together a life out of that?

We begin by remembering that love is never in the abstract – general good feelings are nice but they aren't love. Love is always in the concrete. We give our love and care to this specific person or that one at this specific moment or that. Furthermore, we love and care with what we have and with what we are and not with what somebody else has or is.

The specific shape of the loving and caring to which we are called individually is defined by the specific gifts that God has entrusted to our personal care. That means, on the one hand, that you are very probably not called to be Mother Teresa and I am definitely not called to be our parish organist. But it also means we have to work very hard at seeing, naming, and developing what are our own special gifts so that we can share those gifts with those who need what we have to give.

The deep and hungry longing for joy, which we all know so well, will never be fully satisfied in this life. But if we see, and name, and develop our own special gifts and then share them open-heartedly with all who need them, we'll begin to experience the joy we've always longed for. We'll begin to know the peace for which we were made.

That's the good news for which we've been waiting! Joy and peace can be ours here and now! Thanks be to God!

God Will Set You Free

Mark 1:21-28

There's a fat, wily little cat named Garfield who's the star of a popular comic strip. In a recent installment, Garfield is shown curled up in his cozy chair with a can of beer in his paw and watching television, while outside a fierce storm is raging. Through the window Garfield sees one of his buddies, just standing there shivering, freezing to death with icicles hanging from his nose. Garfield is overcome with emotion, and exclaims, "I can't just sit here and watch him freeze. I've got to do something!" And with that he jumps up, runs to the window, and closes the blinds!

Garfield is not alone. Drawing the drapes and closing the blinds on ugly reality is not reserved just for the comics. In every one of us there's a little voice that speaks up when we're faced with evil. And that voice says, "What you're looking at is too much for you, so you'd better run." It's the voice of fear. And very often we listen to it, and run. Fear makes us run from what's ugly or sinister or wrong outside us and around us. It also makes us run from the dark and broken parts of ourselves.

Mentally we close our eyes and draw our inner blinds, hum a happy tune, shop till we drop and have another Valium, keep the chatter going and the music blaring, and pretend that I'm OK and you're OK. In doing that we're agreeing to remain prisoners of our dark side, prisoners of what is broken in us, permanent prisoners of fear. It's a despairing choice which says there's no alternative. It says, "I don't dare look at the problem because it can't be fixed – now or ever." It settles for trying to put a pretty face on what will never be pretty at all.

Today's gospel makes it clear that God has an alternative for us. On a Sabbath evening, right in the synagogue, Jesus sees an evil spirit that has some poor man in its total control. (We should note that the Jews use that term "evil spirit" to refer to anything evil that could take over a person's life and possess him or own him.) So Jesus sees the "evil spirit" and he doesn't look away. He confronts it: "Be quiet, and get out!" he says. "Have no more power over this man." and that's exactly what happens: The man is set free.

God has no intention of letting evil triumph in the world or in us. God has no intention of abandoning us to the prisons that our fears and failures keep locking us into. God is calling out to us, urging us to pull back the blinds and open our eyes, to see what's there, what needs healing, what needs heavenly light. God is telling us not to be afraid to name the parts of us that are broken and ugly, and need help. God already knows which they are, but we have to speak their name. When our work is done and we see the Lord face to face, we'll have joy in full measure.

That is God's desire for us. And God has the power to make it happen if we will trust enough to open our eyes, name what needs to be named, and put it all in God's hands.

May God grant us the grace to answer the call, and be set free at last. Amen.

We Owe as Much Help as We Need

Luke 2:22-40

This is the weekend of leftovers, so I have a few leftover Christmas stories for you this morning. The third grade at one school was putting on their annual Christmas pageant, which centered on the story of Jesus' birth. As scheduled in the script, Mary and Joseph arrived at the door of the inn and asked for a room. The little boy playing the part of the innkeeper just couldn't bring himself to say "No room in the inn!" So instead he said, "Come on in!"

That left Mary and Joseph (and the audience) with their mouths open, wondering what would come next. But Joseph was a resourceful fellow. He walked into the inn, looked around and then said to Mary, "This place is a dump. Let's go stay in the stable!"

In a similar play at the neighboring school, there was an equally kindly "innkeeper" who also couldn't say "no." Instead, his response was, "I'm terribly sorry we've haven't got a room for you, but won't you come in for a drink."

And finally, the four little angels in the same play were instructed at just the right moment to hold up lettered cards spelling out the word star, s-t-a-r. Well, of course, they got it backward, and the message they beamed out to their mommies and daddies, uncles, aunts, and teachers, was r-a-t-s, rats!

All of us human beings – not just our kids – have a dickens of a time getting things right. So, as we celebrate this Holy Family Sunday and think about our own families, the one thing we need to get clear and remember more than anything else is this: we all need all the help we can get; and that means we all owe all the help we can give.

So let's give our help, and never hold back! Our reward will be watching one another grow whole in the sight of God! And that will be some reward indeed!

Walk Through It With Him

Mark 1:29-39

There was a man who was feeling very poorly, so he went to the clinic for a complete checkup. When it was all over, his wife asked what the doctors had decided was the problem. "I really don't know," replied the man, "They wouldn't tell me a thing. But I did eavesdrop a little, and I heard one of them say something I can't quite figure out. He said they'd find out for sure at the autopsy!"

Not all news is good news. Bad things do happen to good people. Sooner or later, every heart gets broken. And even the youngest and tiniest among us know what big hurts feel like. Just in case we've forgotten, Job reminds us in Sunday's first reading. He's lost everything, his wealth, his health, and every last one of his ten children. So he cries out, "My days come to an end without hope . . . My life is like the wind; I shall not see happiness again."

What's a person to do with losses like that? What are we to do with hurts that break our hearts, especially the hurts we know we didn't earn? The childish side of us wants to get angry and shout at God, "I did my part. I went to church, played by the rules, and kept my "insurance policy" with you paid up in full, O God! How could you let me down like this?"

The childish side of us thinks we can manipulate God and curry favor with little bribes: pious prayers, happy hymns, and well-scrubbed faces. And when, inevitably, the bad times come, the childish side of us gets angry, and walks away; and the anger poisons our life and kills our love.

In every church and every synagogue there are always empty seats left there by angry souls who walked away when they found they couldn't buy good luck from God.

So how are we to respond to the hurts and losses that stab our hearts? We respond by receiving them without fear, naming them with eyes wide open, taking them in, not running away, but walking through them. As we do that, we find that tucked in right next to the hurts is the Lord. God always comes – with healing – and never stays away. The Lord is always enough, and is never found wanting.

God's promise to those who trust is not that they will be insulated from pain, but that they will find the power to walk through the pain when it comes, the power to become more on the inside. God's promise to each of us who trust in the midst of hurt and loss is a heart grown larger and a spirit grown more peaceful.

Our future is as yet invisible, and what it holds for us is not yet known. But already we know all we need to know: the path we walk we do not walk alone. The hurts we face we do not face alone. In the midst of darkness we shall be transformed, and by God's grace we shall live forever!

We Have the Gift of Healing

Mark 1:40-45

Some years ago Bishop Fulton Sheen had a prime time TV show opposite Milton Berle every Wednesday night. One night he told about his visit to an African leper colony. He had brought along a supply of little silver crucifixes so he'd have something special to give to each of the 500 lepers in the camp. The first leper he met had only the stump of his left arm. And his right arm and hand were covered with ugly, open sores. Sheen took one of the little crucifixes, held it a few inches above the leper's hand, and then let it drop into his palm.

In a flash, he was struck by what he'd done. "All at once," he said, "I realized there were 501 lepers in the camp, and the most leprous of them all was myself. I'd given a crucifix – the symbol of God's absolute love for us all – but then I'd pulled back and closed my eyes to what that symbol implied for me. "So I looked again very hard at that little crucifix, and I knew what I had to do. I pressed my hand to the leper's hand with the symbol of love between us, and then I proceeded to do that for all of the remaining 499 lepers!"

None of us, thank God, are lepers. But there's not one of us whose heart hasn't been wounded or even broken many times, not one of us who doesn't need healing. So it is to all of us that Jesus is speaking by his actions in Sunday's gospel. In stretching out his hand, touching that leper and healing him, Jesus is telling us – once again – that God does love us all no matter how damaged or broken we are. He's telling us that no matter how bad we've been, our Father will always be there for us, always be waiting for us to open our hearts so he can heal us.

That's the first half of Jesus' message, but there's more. In addition to what God wants to do for us, there's the matter of what God wants us to do for one another. And it turns out to be exactly the same thing: we are to become healers too, healers of one another. That sounds wonderful, but how do ordinary, wounded people like us become healers? Very simply by remembering how our own wounds feel and remembering what we need when we're broken. What we'd like, of course, is a quick fix for our wounds, but what we need is a friend who'll reach out just as Jesus did, take us by the hand – when our hand isn't looking so good – and walk through the darkness with us and not let go of us halfway!

If that's what we need as we try to walk through our hurts and losses, it's also exactly what our brothers and sisters need. And it's something each of us can give.

So let us give our healing gift, a hand extended in friendship, a hand that will not pull away till the walk through the darkness has reached the light. Let us give our gift, and not hold back!

He Wants Us to Make a Difference

Mark 1:12-15

An old man was walking along a beach at daybreak, when he noticed a girl ahead of him picking up starfish that had been cast ashore by a storm the night before. The old man hurried to catch up to her, and asked what she was doing. "Rescuing starfish," the young lady replied. "They'll die if I leave them here when the sun comes out."

"But this beach goes on for miles," argued the man, "and there are millions of starfish stranded here. How can your effort make any difference?"

The girl looked intently at the starfish in her hand, then threw it back to the safety of the sea and said, "It makes a difference for this one!"

We'd all like to make a difference, however small. So, as we hear Jesus calling out to us, "Repent, re-think your lives," we say to ourselves: "Maybe we need to make some changes; better take a look." So we give ourselves a fast once-over. "I don't lie, or cheat, or steal. I don't abuse my kids or cheat on my spouse. I'm scrupulously honest on the golf course, and I always use the designated receptacles for cigarette butts and candy wrappers. I'm not perfect but I'm not doing too badly. Of course, there are some things I need to attend to, like losing about ten pounds, quitting smoking, and cleaning up my language a bit. And I really need some exercise. Okay, I can make some changes."

All true. We're pretty nice folks and we could do some fine tuning of our private lives that would make us even nicer. But Jesus is calling us to think bigger than that – bigger than just "nice," bigger than just staying out of trouble.

He's urging us to ask ourselves two questions: First, what am I doing to justify the space I'm taking up, and the air I'm breathing? And second, are the people around me enriched each day because I'm here? Would their lives be noticeably poorer if I were gone? As we consider those questions, Jesus is reminding us pointedly that staying out of trouble is good but not enough. We've got to make a difference!

So how do we go about making a difference? We begin by identifying and naming the tools God gave us to work with. We begin by naming our gifts. And then we ask quite simply, who needs what I have to give? If we ask that question honestly and thoughtfully, we'll be amazed at what we discover: there are lots of people who need even the youngest and oldest of us. There are lots of people for whom we can make a real difference every day.

God has entrusted special treasures to each one of us. We are gift bearers charged with the life-long task of bringing God's gifts to those who need them.

So let us give thanks for the gifts we are privileged to bear and give thanks that we are partners in building the kingdom. With glad hearts let us bring the gifts we bear to those for whom they were intended. We will make a difference, a very real difference! What more could we ask?

Are You Watching and Listening?

Mark 9:2-10

There once was a king whose greatest desire was to gain absolute power over every square inch of his kingdom. He had succeeded in removing all the obstacles to his complete control except one: the people still put their ancient god above the king. The king summoned his three wisest advisors to find a way to put an end to such worship. "Where," asked the king, "where might the people's god be hidden and so be made to vanish from their lives and cease to challenge my rule?"

The first advisor suggested hiding the god at the summit of the highest mountain. "No," said the king, "The people would abandon their homes and climb the highest mountain to search for their god."

The second advisor proposed hiding the people's god at the bottom of the sea. But the king rejected that idea as well: "The people would probe the ocean's depths to find their god," he said. Finally the third and wisest advisor, a wrinkled and bent old man, spoke his advice in a hoarse whisper. "O mighty king," he said, "hide the people's god somewhere in their everyday lives. There they will never find it!"

The trusty advisar understood how we are! God is hidden, but not in some remote, faraway spot. God is right here in our everyday lives. Yet we rarely see him and rarely recognize his presence. All too often we fear that we are walking alone and we dread that our journey may have no destination, may be just a long walk to nowhere. All too often we are deaf and blind to God. So it is for us – doubting and weary wayfarers – that Jesus was transfigured and, just for a moment, shone like the sun on the top of that mountain. And it is to us, the blind and the deaf, that God is speaking through that stunning event.

And what is God saying? "I am with you always, walking at your side. And your name is written on the palm of my hand. If you listen carefully, you'll hear me whispering to you. If you watch closely, you'll see that I am here. So watch and listen!"

It takes time to learn how to listen attentively and respectfully to everyday life. It takes time to learn how to hear what's really going on around us and to see what's always been right under our nose. It does take time, but if we persist in paying respectful attention to everyday life, very slowly we'll begin to catch a glimpse of God when we look at a rose; we'll begin to feel the nearness of God in the cool of an evening breeze; we'll begin to hear God's voice echoing inside the voice of a friend. And we'll begin to know the warmth of God's presence as we hold a newborn child.

The road we walk is a long one, often rough, and sometimes dangerous. But God desires that none of us walk that road alone. God desires that at every moment of every day we have the comfort, the strength, and the delight of divine company. A friendship that is ours for the taking.

What a tragedy to settle for anything less! What a tragedy to walk forever alone! Let that tragedy not be ours!

Compassion Is Our Chance to Say Thank You

John 2:13-25

One foggy, stormy night at sea, a ship's captain caught sight of what looked like the lights of another ship heading straight toward him. He ordered his signalman to relay a message to the oncoming ship: "Change your course ten degrees to the south."

Immediately came the reply, "Change your course ten degrees to the north."

The lights were getting closer, so the captain responded firmly, "I'm a captain. Change your course south."

But the reply was equally firm, "I'm a seaman first class. Change your course north."

Outraged at such insolence as the lights loomed nearer and nearer, the captain fired back the message, "You idiot! I'm giving you one last chance to change your course south. I'm on a battleship!"

To which he received the cool reply, "I'm giving you one last chance to change your course north. I'm in a lighthouse."

How easy it is to misunderstand or ignore what is right in front of us. How easy it is to ignore the "lighthouses" in our lives.

Today's Gospel ends with some chilling words on this very matter: "Jesus needed no one to give him testimony about human nature. For he was well aware of what was in the human heart." Do those words make us a little nervous? They should. And if they don't, we really ought to be worried, because that's a pretty sure sign that we haven't yet seen a good photo of our innards. So let's think about the dark side of our inner selves for a moment. What would Jesus see – what does he see – there at the core of our insides? An awful lot and a lot that's awful.

We started sinning young – was it fighting over toys or hating a new sibling or trying to manipulate the family with tantrums? Who can even remember where we started. But with the passage of time, we all developed our own particular specialties, truly rotten habits, stupid, mean, faithless, hateful things

we could do regularly without even thinking about them. And every time we made a mean or faithless choice, a little dose of spiritual poison was released into our system and headed straight for our hearts. That has occurred many times over, day in day out, year after year, up to this moment. The result is the damaged and wounded heart that Jesus sees this morning with perfect clarity.

So why didn't Jesus just wash his hands of the whole lot of us long ago? Why was he willing to die on our behalf when he knew what was in us? Because, in seeing our hearts with perfect clarity, Jesus saw more than the damage and rubble left by our sins. He also saw our striving, our hungering for what is true and good, our longing for wholeness, our willingness to start over again and again, even though we know in advance that our greatest successes will be mixed with failures. And seeing all that, he took pity on us. He took us into his heart and encircled us with his compassion. We didn't earn any part of that; it's all a free gift!

What does he ask in return for such a gift? Only that we tell ourselves the truth about all this. And the truth is that without his gift of compassion we would die. If we have understood that inside, our hearts will have to soften and we will have to give the same compassion as freely as we have received it.

Compassion is not optional. We owe it without any charge because we have been given it freely and without charge. Compassion is not a burden but a unique opportunity. It's the one chance we have to say, "Thanks, Lord, for the gift of life and for that very long line of second chances that stretches back to childhood and that reaches forward all the way to the end."

So let us begin now to speak with our deeds as well as our words. May every day of ours – every act and every choice – speak loud and clear: Thank you, Lord. Thank you very much!

He'll Always Be There for Us

John 3:14-21

In 1989 a deadly earthquake struck Armenia and in less than four minutes over 30,000 people were dead. The moment the quake stopped, a terrified young father rushed to the local elementary school to search for his little son. But where the school had been, he found only a huge pile of rubble.

Standing there in numb disbelief, the father remembered the promise he'd made long ago to his son, "No matter what, I'll always be there for you." So, with tears in his eyes and terror in his heart, he ran to the spot where the boy's classroom had stood and began digging through the rubble. Around him on every side grieving parents were weeping and crying out, "My son! My daughter!"

After a while some friends came and tried to pull him away, saying, "It's too late! They're all dead! Go home to your wife." Even a police officer tried to persuade him to leave. But he labored on alone for 8 hours, then 12, 24, and 36 hours. Finally, in the 38th hour, as he pulled back one more boulder, he heard his son's voice. He screamed the boy's name, "Armand!"

The voice answered, "Daddy? It's me, daddy!" Then the boy added these priceless words, "I told the other kids not to worry, Daddy. I told 'em that if you were alive, you'd save me, and them too. You promised, 'No matter what, I'll always be there for you!' And you did it, Daddy. You did it!"

The father worked more feverishly now, clearing the way for his son and his classmates. "Come out, my son," yelled the father. But Armand replied, "No, Daddy, you can let the other kids come out first, because I know you'll get me. No matter what, You'll be there for me!"

It's a true story about a recent event but the message matches exactly both today's gospel and the whole of Jesus' life. Both say that God is and always will be there for us.

Just think what that means. If we let God in we'll never have to walk alone. Someone will always help us get up when we fall; someone will help our wounds to heal – and not just the ones that others have inflicted, but the ones we've inflicted on ourselves. Someone will remind us where we're going when we've forgotten or lost our way. And someone will help us know how to bring our gifts to those who need them.

Someone will gently hold up the mirror in front of us when we've let our hearts grow ugly or hard. And he'll help us not despair when we see how much unfinished work we still have to do. God will always be there for us and always be enough for us, and never let us come to ultimate harm. God will do and be all this for us if we trust enough to walk with him and not turn away when we are challenged to keep moving, and growing, and changing. For God is always there for us.

And what does God ask in return? Just that we do the same for one another, that we accept our vocation to be family, to help one another grow whole in the sight of God, and to leave no one outside the circle of our love. It is a messy vocation, never neat or tidy, and never without its price. But it is a holy work, God's work.

Isn't it time we embrace our true vocation with all our hearts? Isn't it time, indeed!

Invest or Die!

John 12:20-33

Actor George Burns' wife, Gracie Allen, has been gone for more than twenty years, but a lot of her scatterbrained lines still hit home. In one of her shows she called a repairman to fix her electric clock. The man fiddled with it for a while and then told her, "There's nothing wrong with the clock; you just don't have it plugged in."

Gracie replied, "I don't want to waste electricity, so I only plug it in when I want to know what time it is."

Sorry, but that's not the way it works. It's not the way life works either. Plugging in occasionally isn't enough to make a life. Sticking one's toe in the pool isn't swimming, and it won't do a thing for the heart and the lungs. Half-hearted cameo appearances don't make a relationship and they don't do much for the heart either.

We're all bargain hunters. We like to get something for nothing. But some things, the important things, can't be had on the cheap. The best things in life are not free. They are bought at great price over a long time. And they are bought only by those who consistently invest everything they have. Those who hold back and stand off on the sidelines of life with arms folded will, in the end, find themselves with exactly what they paid for: leftovers, mere fragments of a life!

That's the real point of today's gospel. Jesus says, "Unless the grain of wheat falls to the earth and dies, it remains just a tiny grain of wheat. But if it dies, it produces much fruit." There is no middle ground for that grain of wheat. Either it risks everything and goes down into the ground in the hope of a harvest, or it sits on the shelf and dries up and dies anyway. The only way to save its life in the long run is to spend its life, all of it, now – and hold nothing back.

The same is true for us. If we cling blindly to what we have and are now, we'll never become what we're really called to be. Indeed, we'll lose what we have. We'll dry up and die. We were made for more than that. We were made for more than the dry crusts and cold leftovers.

God made us for a rich, full life together as a family. And in Jesus, he has shown us the only way to make that kind of life, and that is by investing all we have and all we are in building God's kingdom (which means, building up one another), holding nothing back just as Jesus never held anything back, but instead bearing all our gifts to one another as Jesus brought all his gifts to us.

That is the only sure formula for a happy life, the only way of living that will bring us our hearts' desire. The clock is ticking, so let us save our life by investing all of it . . . wisely . . . now!

All Will Be Well

We have just heard the story of the last hours of Jesus Christ, the best friend we ever had. As we listened to the reading of the Passion, we followed him, step by step, in our hearts through his last hours. And now, having heard Jesus speak those last, dreadful words, "It is finished," and watching his head drop upon his breast for the last time, we have to make sense of it all.

What does it mean, this good, kind, loving young man, the kindest man we ever met – barely in his thirties – dying in so ghastly a way, for no crime at all. What does it mean and what is it for?

What it means is that God loves us so much that he will withhold from us absolutely nothing – not even his own dear son. What it means is that no matter what, God will always be there for us, with ALL his love and power, comfort and grace.

There ARE no limits to his commitment to us, none at all. That's what God our very dear Father is saying to us through this terrible moment in Jesus' life. He's saying, "You can count on me. I'll never desert you, and there's nothing I won't give you, not even my son."

This Passion Sunday is, in one way, a very sad day: Walking with Jesus on this day can break your heart. But it's also the brightest of days, because it tells how very much we are loved, and because it reminds us who view it from the vantage point of the resurrection that, despite all appearances, ALL WILL BE WELL!

So let us rejoice, because, thanks be to our good God, ALL WILL BE WELL!

Pay Attention to That Tug

John 20:1-9

A little boy and his grandfather were high on a hill flying a kite. They watched the kite soar higher and higher till finally a low cloud hid it from sight. "Bobby," said Grandpa, "maybe some robber up in that cloud stole your kite."

But the boy shook his head, "No, Grandpa!"

A little while later, Grandpa spoke up again, "Bobby, I'll bet some robber up in that cloud did steal your kite."

But the boy's answer was still the same, "No, Grandpa!"

Finally Grandpa asked, "Bobby, what makes you so sure you've still got a kite up there?"

The boy replied, "Because I can feel something you can't feel. I can feel the kite tugging at my string."

All our lives, at least when we've been paying attention, every one of us has felt little tugs at our hearts, soft whispers inside that somehow let us know we're not alone, and hinted that we're destined for something very special. Now, most of the time those inner tugs have been so quiet, and so hard to name or put a finger on, that we've hardly noticed them, or just brushed them aside, or didn't dare trust them. But always they've been there for each one of us.

Jesus, when he came, talked to us about those quiet tugs and inner whispers. And he told us we can trust them because it's God who's whispering to us – telling us we're God's own dear children, and no mere throwaways. We want to believe that, but it's hard, because the routineness of life and the pains and sadnesses of life so often seem to tell us just the opposite. And we're afraid of being fooled by our own wishful thinking or by pretty words. Talk is so cheap!

But, fortunately for us, Jesus never settled for just talking. He always acted. And in the end, he gave us a sign we can count on: He gave us the sign of his own dying, and being buried, and rising from the dead as guarantee that his words to us and the tugs we've always felt in our hearts, can be trusted.

That's the message of Easter. That's the meaning of Jesus' resurrection: God didn't make us for pain and suffering, for sadness and dying. We were made for life, for exciting, eternal life in God's very own embrace!

On this Easter morning, let us trust at last in this good news that's always been there, tugging at our hearts. Let us rejoice in it, and be very, very glad!

Entrusted with Part of God's Power

John 20:19-31

Two strangers struck up a conversation at a Washington, DC, cocktail party. After a few minutes of small talk, one said, "Have you heard the latest White House joke?"

The second fellow held up his hand. "Wait, before you begin, I should tell you I work at the White House."

"Oh, don't worry," replied the first man, "I'll tell it very slowly."

Some folks are slow learners. That surely seems to be the case with the apostles in Sunday's gospel. As they come face to face with Jesus for the first time since he died, they're not only surprised, they're scared stiff! Because they remember what they were doing the last time they saw Jesus, or rather, the last time he saw them: they were running in the opposite direction; and Peter was whimpering to the high priest's maid that he didn't even know Jesus.

So Jesus starts over with them. "Peace be with you," he says. In effect he's saying, "I understand: you're not bad guys, just slow learners. So don't be afraid. I'm not interested in dredging up the past. All I want is for you to get better now. So we're going to start over. And slowly, together, we're going to get it right."

"Peace be with you." It's an ancient Jewish blessing which means, "May you become whole in the sight of God." In speaking that blessing, Jesus is summing up his mission and his life's work which is to help us grow whole in the sight of God. But at the same time he's showing us our mission and vocation as well. "As the Father has sent me," he says, "so I send you. Receive the Holy Spirit. If you forgive men's sins, they are forgiven. If you hold them bound, they are held bound." What a truly astonishing vocation!

Jesus is saying that each of us has been entrusted with a part of God's power to help people take heart and take hold of their lives. We have been entrusted with a part of God's power to help people break free from whatever is wounding or killing their spirits, free from whatever is isolating them or shrinking them down, free from whatever is freezing them or preventing them from investing their gifts where those gifts can grow and flourish.

That is an astonishing and exhilarating assignment! But it's frightening as well, because we can fail to use the gifts entrusted to our care. Fear, blindness, or plain old self-absorption can leave our gifts sitting on the shelf or thrown uselessly away. And absent the gifts we were entrusted to bring to them, many people will languish; many will stay bound up in blindness and fear, despair and hurt; many will never taste the joy of growing whole in the sight of God – if we fail to give our gifts.

So we have ample reason to pray very hard for ourselves and for one another:

May God grant that we see the gifts entrusted to our care. May we carry our gifts to those who need them. And together, in the giving and receiving of our gifts, may we all grow whole in the sight of God. Amen.

Closer Than Your Heartbeat

Matthew 4:12-23

There was a little girl named Allison who always had a hard time going to bed. And this night was no exception. After a story and prayers and a drink of water and a visit to the bathroom, Allison was tucked in and the lights were turned off – but not for long. "Mommy," she called out in a pitiful voice. "I can't go to sleep; I'm afraid of the dark."

"Now, Allison," her mother replied patiently. "There's no reason for you to be afraid. You know that God is always right there with you."

"I know, Mommy," said the little girl. "I know God's here. But I want somebody with skin on!"

Little children aren't the only ones who get scared in the dark. We all get scared in the dark times, and we all need someone to hang onto – someone with skin on. Jesus understands that, as he makes so clear in today's gospel. "I'm not a ghost," he says to his friends. "I'm very real; I'm here; and you can count on me. So don't be afraid. I'll always be here for you, closer than your breath, closer than your heartbeat. I'll always be here, even when its very dark."

Jesus' words comfort his friends and calm them, and that's good. But it isn't enough so far as he's concerned. He wants more for them and for us, a lot more than just peace and quiet. He wants to transform us into new people, who see the world in a new way – and respond to it in a new way.

He wants to transform us into people who understand what it means to be made in God's own image and what it means to be entrusted with wonderful gifts. He wants to transform us all into people who understand that our greatest joy – our only lasting joy – is to be found in building family and bringing one another to wholeness in the sight of God.

He wants to help us see that the cost of being transformed – and being transformers – is always high, but the cost of not being transformed, the cost of staying mired in ourselves and stuck in our fears is higher still. For that choice leaves us with little or nothing of the only joys that truly warm the heart and enliven the spirit.

Our being transformed is God's hope and desire for us, God's will for us. And it will happen and continue happening for each of us, if we trust in God's presence which is closer than our breath, if we draw strength from the love which is closer than our heartbeat.

God wills us to be whole and to be filled full. How can we settle for anything less?

More Than Just Watching

John 10:11-18

There was a little boy who was asked what his father did. "He watches," said the boy.

"You mean he's a night watchman?"

"No," said the boy. "He just watches."

"Well, what does he watch?" asked his friend.

"I don't know if I can tell you everything," replied the boy, "but I can name a few things. He watches television, he watches Mom do the housework; he watches the weather; and I think he watches girls, too. He watches the stock market, football games, and all the sports. He watches Mom spank us, and he watches us do our homework. He watches us leave to go to church and PTA and shopping. He watches Mom write letters and me play with my dog, but mainly," said the boy with a touch of sadness, "he just watches."

Cool detachment, being an impartial observer, just watching, is the very opposite of what Jesus is telling us about himself in the today's gospel. In defining himself as the Good Shepherd, Jesus is making it clear that he's definitely not cool and impartial when it comes to us. He's prejudiced in our favor, and there's nothing he won't do for us. That question surely got settled on Good Friday.

So as we engage the ups and downs of life, the very good days and the very bad ones, we can go forward with confidence. Because we know now we'll never have to walk alone, we'll always have the guidance and the inner power we need as we need it because he is there and because he wants nothing more than to see us succeed and get better day by day.

Remembering that is a real "shot in the arm," but it's only half of Jesus' message. Because every time he tells us something about himself, he's also showing us what we are to become. So the second half of today's message is that we are called to become good shepherds too. That begins with our recognizing the partially grown goodness in one another, and then loving and actively hoping in what we see inside our neighbor. That means loving and hoping deeply enough to engage and intertwine our lives with theirs and not to pull away when our friend's growth is not swift or certain or when the cost of his or her growing up is greater than we'd thought – or would've liked.

Good shepherding is often silent, but never passive. It is always engaged, but never controlling. The good shepherd is sometimes disappointed, but never gives up hope. The Good Shepherd's greatest joy comes from seeing his friend thrive and flourish, and grow a little closer to the masterpiece God has in mind.

The Lord has given us each a share in the work of shepherding. May we be faithful to this holy work, and never despair, never walk away, and never settle for just watching. Together may we know the joy of seeing one another grow whole in the sight of God. Amen.

Are You Connected to Him?

John 15:1-8

There was a man who was facing a birthday, one of the "Big 0" birthdays, and he was feeling mighty nervous about the state of his soul. So he went to a holy monk to talk it over.

"What have you done all your life?" asked the monk. "What are you especially proud of?"

"Well," said the man, "I've gone through the Bible seven times."

"Very good," replied the monk, "But how much of the Bible has gone through you?"

Good question for us all! And it's really the question Jesus is asking us to think about in today's gospel. "I am the vine," he says, "and you are the branches." Just think how close that connection is: a vine shares everything it has with the branch, and gives the branch everything it needs. All the branch has to do is stay connected and take in and use what the vine is sending. The fruit comes all on its own, and there's lots of it.

That's the way our relationship with Jesus is supposed to work. That's how connected to him we are supposed to be. The alternative is not pretty: being cut off, withering, and dying, no fruit, just the fire where dead branches are disposed of. Not an option we'd choose!

So there is the question: are we connected to Jesus? Or are we just living in the same general neighborhood? The answer is probably very clear to our friends. And here's how they know, and how we can find out.

If we are connected to the Lord, we'll see things the way the Lord sees them. We'll value the things that God values, the things that really matter. And, at least most of the time, our deeds will match our words.

If we're connected to the Lord, we'll see ourselves as he sees us, with love and compassion, but with no illusions. And that's exactly the way we'll see one another, with love, and compassionate understanding, but with no illusions.

If we are connected to the Lord, we'll regularly surprise ourselves with the brave and noble deeds that rise out of our hearts almost without thinking. We'll wonder, for a moment, where did all that goodness and courage come from, and then we'll know: it came from God!

If we're connected to God, our hearts will sing the words of a new song; and no sadness, no power on earth, can take from us our hope and our joy.

So let us pray for one another. God grant that nothing within us or around us will ever stand in the way of our being connected to you, or ever cut us off from you. May your spirit touch our innermost being, and day by day may our hearts be reshaped and transformed more fully into your likeness. Amen.

Love That Lasts

John 15:9-17

When God made the world and all that is in it, he left his fingerprint on every creature that came from his hand. And so, even today, if we look very carefully, we can see his mark on every creature.

Have you ever watched geese fly in a V formation? It is a thing of beauty to see, and if you listen you can hear the beat of their wings whistling through the air all in unison. It's a quiet sound, but it hints at the secret of their strength: the lead goose with his flapping wings cuts a swath through the air's resistance, and creates a lift for the birds behind it. They, in turn, as they flap their wings, create a lift for those coming behind them.

And so it goes through the whole formation: those who go before give a lift to those who follow. The tired ones fan out to the far edges of the V to take a breather, and the rested ones surge toward the point of the V to pull the flock along. Each one takes its turn. If a goose grows too weary or too sick and has to drop out of the formation, it is never abandoned. A stronger member follows it to a resting place, and waits till it is ready to fly again.

Sticking together, taking turns at giving one another a lift, watching over and taking care, and leaving no one behind. It doesn't sound "lean and mean" – quite the contrary. But it works! It doubles their range, it cuts their work in half and it sees every one of them safely home.

God surely has left his fingerprint on them. And through them he is speaking to us and to the longing he put in our hearts. We long for communion, for peace, but most of all, for love that lasts. If you doubt that, just look at the powerful feelings that show themselves on days like Mother's and Father's Day, Thanksgiving, and Christmas. We long for love that lasts.

Jesus tells us in the gospel what the geese have been telling us for millions of years: if you want love that lasts, you have to give love that lasts, love that watches over and takes care, love that takes turns at giving one another a lift, love that sticks together and leaves no one behind.

That is our hearts' desire, our deepest longing. So let us pray for one another:

May God help us all to give and to receive love that lasts. Amen.

The Truth Can Set You Free

John 17:1-19

A holy person died and went straight to heaven, where one of the senior angels was assigned to give the grand tour. The tour began in a long, white, gleaming hallway, with many doors on either side. As the two of them floated up to the first door, the sound of gospel music was so loud that the door shook. "That's the room for the Baptists," explained the angel. Continuing along the hall, they came to the next door which was very quiet, so quiet in fact, that even when they put their ears right up against it, they could just barely hear a few people inside. "The Quakers are in there," said the angel.

And so they went, door by door, the full length of the hallway, passing the rooms designated for Lutherans, Presbyterians, and Methodists, Jews, Moslems, Buddhists, and every other group you could possibly imagine. Finally, at the very end of the corridor, the angel tiptoed up to the last door, whispering to the new saint to be very, very quiet. "But why?" asked the newcomer. "Who's in there?"

"Oh, we always have to be very quiet at this door," said the angel. This is the room for the Catholics, and they think they're the only ones here."

Those folks weren't seeing reality. And that means we've got a lot in common with them! For, in our own way, most of us are every bit as blind to the truth. And what is it that we're blind to, and missing, and not seeing? Something very important: When we look at ourselves and at one another, most of us don't see what God sees.

Just thinking about what God sees makes most of us nervous, because we imagine we know what God sees in us and what God thinks about us – and we're sure it isn't pretty. We're sure, but we're wrong! So today let's try to get it right.

Imagine for a moment that you're sitting face to face with the Lord all by yourself, and that the Lord looks you straight in the eye and tells you exactly what he sees. What do you think he'll say? Will he rant and rave? Will he be sarcastic and biting? Will he nag, or shout, or just shake his head and walk away? No, he won't do any of that. Instead, I think the Lord will start by saying what we adults say so often and with such pleasure when we re-encounter young friends: "Look at how you've grown." And then he'll remind you of many days and many events that you've long forgotten, times when you struggles against great odds and prevailed, times you were frightened or confused but didn't give up, times you were brave and generous, large-minded and large-hearted, times you were discouraged or just plain tired but kept on going, times you made a total mess of things and then brushed yourself off and started over.

God sees all that effort and striving of yours. He knows what it has cost you, and how much more there is to you now than there was not so long ago. And he says with a parent's delight, "Look at how you've grown."

"But what about my failures and my sins?" you say to yourself as you wait for the other shoe to drop. The Lord hears your unspoken question and says very simply, "I know you're not done yet. I don't expect you to be. And what's more, I know that before you're done, you'll stumble many times more and fall many times too – that's no surprise. Remember, I'm the one who made you; and I made you able to learn a little bit at a time from your mistakes! So keep learning, my child. Keep your heart open. And remember always how I rejoice at your every step forward and delight in even the smallest of your victories."

That is how God sees us, with the affection and delight, the understanding and compassion of a very dear parent. And what God sees is the real truth about us, the truth that can set us free, if only we'll take it inside our hearts and believe it. So let's begin again this process of taking it inside our hearts by praying for one another.

Lord, you give sight to the blind and hope to the weary. Open our eyes that we may see in ourselves and in one another all the goodness that you see. Open our hearts that we may love all that you love. Amen.

Alone and Afraid

John 20:19-23

Two brand new work crews were installing some telephone poles. At the end of the day, the foreman asked the first crew how many poles they'd put in. "Twelve," was their answer.

"Not bad," replied the foreman. Then he asked the second crew how many poles they'd put in.

"Two" was the reply.

"Two?!" shouted the foreman. "The others did twelve and you only did two?"

"Yeah," said the leader of the second group. "But you should've seen how much they left sticking out of the ground!"

I think the apostles would have identified with that second group, because they really knew what it meant to make big mistakes and lots of them. After Jesus' death – and even more – after his ascension, the memory of their past mistakes, past failures, past inadequacies, and past hurts overwhelmed them. As they looked out into the future, and tried to imagine how they could "teach all nations," they felt very small, very alone, and very afraid. So they locked themselves in a room and stayed there, helpless and hopeless, frozen in place by their fears, feeling their smallness and knowing their inner poverty.

And then, suddenly, with the power of a mighty wind and the intensity of a burning fire, the Holy Spirit showed himself to them. The Spirit showed them they were not alone, never had been, and never would be. The Spirit showed them that, despite their smallness and despite their flaws, they could do what Jesus had asked them to do, and they could do it well. Because they had a mentor who was with them always, a wise and powerful guide for life, a permanent friend to encourage, comfort, and strengthen them at every turn of the road till their work was finally done and their path had led them all the way home.

This had always been true, but at last they recognized it was true. At last their hearts were set free. And they burst forth from that locked room to carry to the whole world the gifts that God had entrusted to their hands.

As we walk our path burdened by the memories of our mistakes and failures, and frightened by the reality of our smallness and inner poverty, the Holy Spirit who dwells always in our hearts is crying out to us. "Let me walk with you and set you free from your fears," says our mentor spirit. "Let me show you the way. Let me show you your gifts. And let me show you that, with me at your side, you – as small as you are – will always have enough and be enough. You will be able to bear your gifts and you will find your way home."

The Holy Spirit, our mentor spirit, is calling out to each one of us. So what is to be our response? Very simply: Come, Holy Spirit. Walk with us. Show us your path. With you at our side, we will carry our gifts and find our way home!

In God's Image and Likeness

Matthew 28:16-20

There was a married couple who were avid golfers and they were discussing the future. "Honey," said the wife, "If I were to die and you were to remarry, would you two live here in this house?" "I suppose so," replied the husband. "It's paid for."

"What about our car?" continued the wife. "Would the two of you keep that?"

"I suppose so – it's paid for too."

"Well, what about my golf clubs? Would you let her use them too?"

"Heck no," blurted the husband. "She's left-handed!"

At times we all talk too much – and listen too little. We fill our lives with chatter and we end up making foolish mistakes and missing so much of what really matters. So as we celebrate the feast of the Holy Trinity, the church says to us, "It's time to stop talking, be very, very quiet, and stand in silent wonder at the vastness and goodness of God."

Be still and watch God our Father in the continuing act of creating new things before our very eyes: this morning's flowers, this evening's sunset, tiny new infants and ourselves – still here, the universe still growing, all manner of good things continuing to tumble forth from creative, fatherly hands. Be still, and see, and give thanks!

Be still and see God's son, Jesus, who at this very moment is in the process of liberating us and setting us free from whatever has trapped or enslaved us or narrowed down our lives. Where would we be at this moment, if day by day Jesus had not been helping us break free over and over again? Where, indeed? Jesus our liberator is here now, and his quiet work continues in us. Be still, and see, and give thanks!

Be still and listen to the Holy Spirit, our wise and caring mentor, who dwells always within us, and silently guides and challenges, comforts and encourages, shows us the way, and helps us to walk in it. Be still, and listen, and give thanks!

And finally be still and remember what the Lord has told us about ourselves: we are made in God's own image and likeness: father-creator, son-liberator, spirit-mentor. And there indeed we have our own vocation spelled out for us: to be creators, liberators, and mentors; to make what is good, to set one another free, and to comfort, challenge, and guide those who need us.

We are made in God's image and likeness: Father, Son, and Spirit. God grant that we may build our lives in your image and likeness. Amen.

Meals Are for Families

Matthew 14:12-16, 22-26

There'd been a long dry season, and there wasn't enough hay to feed the cows, so two good ole boys decided to go into the hay business. They got a truck and drove to another state, where they bought hay for $3 a bale. Then they brought it home and sold it for $2.50 a bale! After a few weeks in the business one of the old buddies said, "You know, there must be something wrong. We're just not making any money."

"I know," said his friend. "Maybe we ought to get a bigger truck."

Nobody could be that crazy! Right? Wrong! And if you doubt it, just take a look in the mirror. All of us some of the time and some of us all the time have been just as foolish as those good ole boys when it comes to making choices and deciding what counts.

At times, we've all looked for happiness where it can't be found. We've invested our hearts in things that can give our hearts no return. We've longed for purpose and fulfillment, but excluded from our lives the only things that can fill us full. We've lived as little islands and developed a special fondness for two little words: "Mine" and "Lots." And then we've been surprised to find ourselves feeling empty and alone.

At times we have all been as foolish as those fellows with their hay – selling our lives at a discount, and winning no joy. That's why every one of us needs to hear what Jesus is saying to us as he gives each one of us his own body and blood. He's telling us what our lives are really about, and where our true happiness is to be found. So listen quietly and hear him.

"Take this holy food and eat it," he says, "so that I can heal your heart and refresh your spirit.

"Take this holy food and know inside that you'll never be alone or empty. I will always be with you and for you, and so will my family.

"Take this holy food," says the Lord, "and share it with your brothers and sisters. Let me show you that your heart was made for sharing and not for living on an island. And let me help you see that your greatest joy will always come from giving and receiving and not just from getting and having.

"Take this holy food and know inside that you are a part of my very own family and that our friendship and love for one another, our communion, our community will last forever.

"Take this holy food," says the Lord, "and be a special part of my family forever."

What Will It Be?

Mark 3:20-35

There was a tiny chapel in the French Quarter of New Orleans where the evening mass had been attended by the same little group for as long as anyone could remember. One year when Mardi Gras rolled around, a huge downpour occurred right in the middle of mass, driving many costumed party-goers indoors wherever they could find shelter. As it happened, a very large man, dressed as Satan himself, sought shelter in the chapel just as mass was ending. In the dim light, he looked so much like the real thing that the congregation panicked and went scrambling for the exits – all except a little old lady who caught her coat in the kneeler. And she really panicked as "Satan" came her way. "Satan," she cried, "I know I went to mass here every evening for the last fifty years, but all the time I was REALLY on your side."

That was just a story – something made up just for fun. But, the truth is that people do things like that in real life. How does that happen? Why do so many of our commitments come unglued and disappear without a trace? Why is it so easy for us to walk away after so long without looking back? I suspect it's because many of our commitments have no roots.

If we keep our hearts insulated, disengaged, and in neutral, how can we bond to anything? How can there be any power to our love? And if we haven't rolled up our sleeves and wrestled with our own selves, with one another – and with God – how can we expect that there'll be anything inside us but a barren waste? We haven't built anything to fill the place.

So often we walk awhile with this person or that along nicely-insulated, parallel paths, because it's convenient and safe, and then we wander away or they do. And we're surprised! We shouldn't be. There was nothing to hold us there. Lots of mar-riages and families stumble along that way, and come unglued that way. And so do lots of friend-ships, including the most important of all, our friendship with God.

None of this is what God has in mind for us. That's why he sent Jesus: To show us what a real human being looks like, one who digs down and draws upon the deepest and best parts of himself as he engages each moment and each person. That rich, deep, full human being whom we call Jesus is our model. He is what we are called to be. But, of course, we draw back and resist, because we get scared.

Sunday's Gospel lets us watch this happen when Jesus brought the Good News to his own neighborhood. At first the people were fascinated by him, but then many of them, his family included, got frightened and resisted and called him crazy. You see, they liked the illusion they were living in, where salvation could be won by external compli-ance with rules. It didn't really work. But they dreaded having to look inside and wrestle with the big things that make us God-like. So they found an excuse; "Jesus, you must be crazy, or maybe you're possessed by the devils" And with that excuse many of them held him at arms length, and kept him on the outside of their lives.

The Lord will never leave us. He'll never cease knocking at our inner door, urging us to let him in, and to let one another in. But he'll never force entry. That means it's a real possibility that any number of us will go through the whole of life never having really known or loved ourselves, our God, or even one of our neighbors. Will that happen to us? Will we settle for impoverishing our inside by living only on the outside? The decision is ours, and we get to make part of that decision this very day. What will it be?

We Have Seeds to Sow

Matthew 4:26-34

In 1984, a woman in California was driving a Porsche after having had several drinks. While speeding along at 60 in a 25-mile zone, she had an accident in which her passenger was killed. In the lawsuit that followed, the court ordered Porsche to pay $2.5 million for having designed a car that was too high performance for the normal driver!

In 1985, an overweight man with a serious heart condition bought a lawnmower from Sears. Later he had a heart attack while starting the mower. He got $1.8 million from Sears!

While attempting to burglarize a school, a man fell through a skylight. The company that insured the school was ordered to pay the burglar $250,000 in damages and $1500 a month for life.

A few years ago, a man was injured when a drunk driver rammed into the phone booth while he was making a call. California's chief justice ruled that the company that designed the phone booth was liable for the man's injuries.

Sometimes the world surely does seem crazy and out of control. If you doubt that, just repeat to yourself a few words like "drive-by shooting," "Bosnia," "Washington," "Gnatcatcher," or – one of my favorites – "building inspector." At times, so many things seem broken and out of control and too big for anyone to fix. We can become overwhelmed with a sense of utter powerlessness and say to ourselves, "I can't do anything about anything!"

In every era life has always seemed that way at times. And Jesus knew long ago that we'd need some help on this very matter; so he speaks to us about it through Sunday's gospel. "You are not powerless at all," he says. "You have the power to plant seeds, and those tiny seeds – if nurtured patiently – can grow large, and bear fruit, and give shade and comfort to many. God will see to the growth – and that will be a mysterious process. But you must plant the seed and care for it and then wait and wait and wait some more."

Whether in our personal lives or in our lives together there are many things that need fixing, many challenges that are truly enormous. For many of those things there is no quick fix, no ready solution. But as the Lord keeps telling us, we do have the power to plant a seed. God has put in our hands the power to bring the kingdom one step closer to fulfillment within us, among us, and around us – if only we'll plant our seeds when and where they're needed. That is our vocation: planting good seeds and tending them. What a privilege – to help God's kingdom come! What a responsibility!

So we truly do need to pray for one another: Lord, help us to see clearly the special seeds you have entrusted to our hands. Help us to know where and when our seeds need to be planted. And help us to trust and never despair of your promise, that you will give them growth and make them flourish and bear fruit abundantly. Amen.

Is Fear Shaping Your Life?

Mark 4:35-41

A woman with five small children decided that their summer vacation should begin with planting a garden. So she took her little brood to the nursery where, for the next two hours, they squabbled over who got to push the shopping cart, insisted on seeing every plant in the five-acre greenhouse, cried very hard when there were no pink petunias, and broke a large pot. Home at last, she complained to her patient husband, "All I want is peace and quiet and some beautiful flowers."

"My dear," said her husband, "I believe they call that a funeral."

For those of us who aren't quite ready for a funeral, peace and quiet and beautiful flowers are not on the menu most of the time. What is on the menu for all of us – young and old – is a steady diet of new things we haven't tried before.

For some of us the story inside our head goes like this: I haven't been a little kid before. I haven't gone to school before, or stayed home alone before, or gone to sleep without a night light before.

For others among us the inside story sounds like this: I haven't had to look for a job before, or been entirely on my own before, or had to name and share my inmost feelings before, or been really poor before.

And for some the story goes like this: I haven't been old before or been widowed and alone before, or had cancer before.

There are lots of different stories. We each have our own and for each of us the story keeps changing! But the big question for all of us is always the same: as the next door opens and we come face to face with our next challenge, will we freeze in fear and pull back or will we walk through the door and come to grips with whatever we find there?

The question is not whether being alive is dangerous and difficult. We know it's dangerous and difficult! There's always some kind of "storm" rocking the boat. The real question is whether we're going to let our fear of life's dangers and difficulties take over and shape us. Will we let fear master us and shrink our life small?

The answer we give to that very big question will come right from the core of our relationship to the Lord. For if we know deep inside how much God loves us and what marvelous gifts we've already received, there's no room for fear or for the "living death" that fear imposes on its victims. There's only room for the peace, hope, and joy that no sadness can take from us.

So let us embrace what remains of this day and what remains of our lives with a serene confidence that is rooted in the sure and certain knowledge that God is with us and for us now and always.

The Child Is Not Dead, but Only Asleep

Mark 5:21-43

A father, whose five children were all young adults, bought an answering machine and recorded the following, very revealing message: "If you require financial assistance, press one. If you are in emotional turmoil over an impending breakup with a romantic partner and require a few hours of sympathetic discussion, press two. If you are being treated unfairly at work or school and wish to vent your anger on your parents, press three. If your car or household appliances need immediate repair or replacement, press four. If you are telephoning to inquire about our well-being or to pass a few moments of pleasant conversation, please check the number you intended to dial!"

Life eventually beats up on everybody. We all get our turn – it starts when we're very young. And as we get knocked around and tried and tested, we begin to decide what we really think about life; we begin to find out what we're really made of. Sometimes what we find is that we've become like the man in the story who loved his kids but had long since stopped hoping for anything from them except "gimme." Sometimes what we discover is that we've given up on life and ceased to hope.

Sunday's gospel is about a man and a family who gave up and gave in to despair when the crunch came. Their beloved little girl died while Jesus was on the way to their house to visit her, so they told him, "don't bother coming. It's all over. She's dead and nothing's going to change that. So don't waste your time." Those words should sound familiar, because we've all spoken their equivalent about some parts of our lives, maybe some very big parts. "Dead, finished, kaput," we've said. "That's that. I've been hurt enough already. If I hope for something better, if I hope for change, I'll just get hurt again. I really can't face the pain and the disappointment. So let me be. I'll make do with what little I have."

Whether we know it or admit it, we've all spoken those words inside our hearts at times. We've all let our fear of disappointment and our fear of more hurts kill our hopes, shrink our expectations, and blind us to life's possibilities. Yes, we've looked at parts of our lives and said, "Dead! Period! Paragraph!"

So it is to all of us that Jesus is speaking: "Fear is useless," he says. "What is needed is trust. . . The child is not dead, but only asleep." He's telling us that the parts of us that seem dead and beyond help are not that at all. They're asleep. But the Lord can awaken them and give them life and growth, if we let him, if we abandon our fears and let his life flow into us and raise us up.

What a shame it would be to turn our backs on such a generous offer of life. What a tragedy it would be to miss all the wonderful things he still has in mind for us.

Let that tragedy not be ours!

Why Don't You Tell Your Face?

Matthew 16:13-20

On Sunday morning a man showed up at church with both of his ears terribly blistered, so his pastor asked, "WHAT happened to YOU?"

"I was lying on the couch watching a ball game on TV while my wife was ironing nearby. I was totally engrossed in the game when she went out, leaving the iron near the phone. The phone rang, and keeping my eyes on the TV, I grabbed the hot iron and put it to my ear."

"How dreadfully gasped the pastor. "But how did the other ear get burned?"

"Well, you see, I'd no sooner hung up and the guy called back!"

He just didn't get it. Lots of folks never get it, never understand how LIFE really works, even at the simplest levels. That's why Jesus is pressing his followers – and us – so insistently in Sunday's Gospel: "Do you understand who I am?" he asks, "and what my being here means for you?"

It's a crucial question. And there's one sure way of finding the answer, and that is by checking how we're living. Are we living like people who know for sure that a loving God is walking at their side at every minute? Let's see:

• Have we stopped wasting our time worrying?

• Have we put aside posing and posturing and fretting about our image?

• Have we stopped closing our eyes to our dark side? And stopped avoiding things that seem too much for us?

• Do we welcome life with a happy heart? Are we glad to wake up in the morning?

• Do we see how gifted and special we are? At least sometimes, does seeing our own giftedness just make us want to smile?

• Do we have hearts so full of thankfulness that we instinctively work at helping others be as happy as we are?

If that's the way we're living, then we understand who Jesus is, and we know what it means to have him walking with us. It means that we've been set free from all kinds of chains and fears and sadness. It means that no matter what, we're going to be okay. It also means that we have the power to help set other people free from all manner of sadness by showing them HIS face mirrored right here in our own.

A long time ago there was an old Indian chief whose little granddaughter was something of a Sourpuss. "Are you happy?" he asked her one day.

"Yes, Grandpa," she replied.

"Well then, my dear, why don't you tell your face?"

We have every reason to be very happy right here and now because we already have everything we really need: We have God himself. Why don't we tell our face, and our heart?

We've already got it all!

So East to Get Stuck, So Hard to Break Free

Mark 6:1-6

There was an old Baptist preacher who always preached on the same topic, baptism by immersion. Christmas, Easter, the Fourth of July, the sermon was always the same: baptism by immersion. No Baptist would think of disagreeing with that idea, but they surely did get mighty tired of hearing the same old thing year after year. So the deacons got together and hatched a plot. "Reverend," they said, "You're such splendid preacher, we'd like to try an experiment. Just before you go into the pulpit next Sunday, we'd like to give you a scripture reading you haven't seen. We're confident you're so good that you can preach a fine sermon on any topic with no preparation at all."

The preacher got all puffed up with pride and accepted their challenge. So the next Sunday, as he ascended the pulpit, the deacons handed him a text. It was the very first verse of the book of Genesis: "In the beginning, God created the heavens and the earth." Nothing at all about Baptism. The preacher read the verse aloud very slowly, then turned his eyes to the congregation and said, "If I remember my geography, the earth is one-forth land and three-fourths water. And water brings me to my subject for this morning, Baptism by Immersion."

How easy it is to get stuck and how hard it is to break free. Two hundred and eleven years ago, when our War for Independence was finally won, tens of thousands of Americans – people born and bred here – piled into ships and went into permanent exile because they couldn't imagine how a government without a king could be made to work! They were stuck in a dead idea!

Nearly two thousand years ago – as today's gospel tells us – Jesus' own neighbors and friends thought he was some kind of "nut," and refused to listen to him. They were sure they already knew and understood everything there was to know about themselves, about life, and about God. They were so sure, and so wrong! They too were stuck in a dead idea.

There's a lot about every one of us that is very right. There are parts of us that are so good and so true that we just "glow in the dark." And we need to take delight in all that goodness that we and God have built together. But at the same time we need to look at the parts of us that have got stuck and frozen, the parts of us that are like that old preacher: repeating the same old words, making the same old mistakes, stumbling on the same rock on the same road every time we pass.

Whether we are young or old, the Lord is calling each of us to let go of the parts of us that don't work, let go of the parts that are stuck in the mud, and let go of the parts of us that are lifeless and unfree. Let go of it all and let God take over and show the way. It is the way to freedom and life.

Let us walk free with the Lord this day and always!

No Previous Experience

Mark 6:7-13

There was a news photographer who was assigned by his editor to get some quick pictures of a major forest fire burning in the area. His instructions were to rush down to the nearby airport, board a small plane that would be waiting for him, and get back with pictures in time for the afternoon edition.

Breathlessly, he raced to the airport and drove his car to the end of the runway. And sure enough, there was a plane waiting with all engines running and ready to go. He hopped aboard, and off they went. At about 5000 feet he got his camera out of the bag and told the fellow flying the plane to get him over the fire fast so he could take his pictures and get back in time.

From the other side of the cockpit there was a deafening silence. Then he heard these unsettling words, "Aren't you the instructor?"

A familiar feeling, isn't it? From the moment we were born, life has been confronting us with new questions we haven't answered before, new choices we haven't made before, new things to do that we haven't done before. What experience did any of us have at tying our shoes before we did it? What experience did we have at going to school before we went? What experience did I have at being a priest or you at being married before we got there? And what experience do we have of being middle aged, or old, or retired, or widowed, or dying till we get there? In a word, we've all had ample reason to say to ourselves many times, "there ought to be an instructor or at least an owner's manual here somewhere."

That's the very spot in which the apostles found themselves in today's gospel. Jesus had just told them to go out into the countryside on their own and preach the good news. "You just do what you've seen me doing," he tells them, "and don't take any money or supplies along with you. They'll just hold you down and get in your way."

Can you imagine how they felt, being told to act as stand-ins for Jesus? They were scared because they knew they weren't ready. They hadn't been with Jesus all that long; they hadn't yet taken his message all the way into their hearts; and they certainly hadn't done this before.

But, because Jesus asked them, they put on their sandals and tunics, took hold of their walking sticks and went. And, lo and behold, the Gospel tells us they were successful: they spoke the good news, they drove out demons and they cured the sick.

How did that happen? Not by accident. For, if in one way they were very unprepared, in another, they had all they needed – God had seen to that! Because they carried with them all the goodness and power that God had put in them when he made them human. And they carried with them the Lord himself – in their hearts.

And finally – since the Lord had sent them out two by two – each one had at his side a brother, a friend the Lord had given to walk with him and see him through his journey. So they completed their journey, not perfectly, not without mistakes, not even, I am sure, without their usual sins. But they did complete it and they did do much good. And God's kingdom drew a little closer to fulfillment.

Just as God did for them, we've been given everything we need to face whatever life brings. We're grasped us by the hand as ever so slowly, by trial and error, we find our way. And we're given us the unique gift of one another, to walk alongside and see us through our journey. None of us knows what life will ask of us before we sleep. All we can say for sure is that we will be asked, again and yet again, to travel along uncharted paths, that we've not seen before.

Can we be ready? Can we meet God's expectations of us as we wander those paths? Yes, we can! Because God doesn't expect that we be perfect or even sinless, but only that we open our hearts as wide as we can and draw upon the three great gifts already given to us: our selves, the divine self, and one another.

If we do that, we are ready for whatever life may bring. And God's kingdom will draw a little closer and we will know its joy. So set your foot on the path and don't look back. You will find your way.

Sheep without a Shepherd Need a Friend

Mark 6:30-34

Two pals are sitting in a bar watching the 11 o'clock news when a report comes on about a man threatening to jump from the 20th floor of a downtown building. One friend turns to the other and says, "I'll bet you ten bucks the guy doesn't jump."

"It's a bet," says the other. A few minutes later, the man jumps and the loser hands his pal a $10 bill.

"I can't take your money," says his friend. "To tell the truth, I saw him jump earlier on the six o'clock news."

"So did I," says the other. "But I just didn't think he'd do it again."

It's easy to get confused and tangled up and to say and do dumb things. At times it happens to us all. And sometimes our being tangled up and lost goes on so long that it gets to be a habit. It feels almost normal and we hardly even notice the mess in our head or our heart or our life.

If you doubt that, just think about some of the real-life crazy things you've seen or heard this week, especially the ones that are "Xerox copies" of last week or last year: the same folks making the same mistakes! And remember some of the confused, tangled parts of our own lives, which took us years to notice and years more to get straight. Remember?!

Jesus always knew what was in people's hearts; and now he sees clearly our inner tangles and confusions and self-deceptions, but none of that causes him to despise us or reject us. On the contrary, he says sadly, "What a shame to be wasting whole chunks of your life, wandering about in circles and going nowhere – like sheep without a shepherd. I know how bad that must feel," he says. "So let me show you the way out of your tangles; let me show you the way to a life that is a life. Let me help you see what really matters, and what doesn't matter at all."

What a true friend he is for us all!!! To love us when we're at our worst! But that's what he does, and it's what he's urging us to do. He's calling us to be the kind of friend that responds with an understanding heart to our neighbors' mistakes, tangles, and confusions – never jeering or sneering, never sniping from a safe distance, as we are wont to do, and never withholding love till our neighbor becomes perfect.

In being our friend, Jesus is calling us to become the kind of friend who responds with an understanding that flows deep and has its source in our recognizing our own foolishness and blindness and our own daily need for forgiveness. Jesus is calling us to be friends whose deepest instinct and habit is to reach out to help our brothers and sisters get better and grow whole in the sight of God.

That is our Lord's call, so let us answer it now! As he is a true friend to us, let us become true friends for one another.

Let God Be God for You

John 6:1-15

A woman arrived at the airport two hours before her flight. So to help pass the time she purchased a paperback and a bag of cookies at one of the newsstands. Then she settled into a seat in the terminal and quickly became engrossed in her book. After a while she noticed that the man sitting one seat over was trying to open the package of cookies on the seat between them. She was so stunned that a stranger would help himself to her cookies that she didn't know what to do, so she reached over and pointedly took one of the cookies and ate it.

The man didn't say anything. He just reached over and helped himself to another cookie. This really dumbfounded her, so, narrowing her eyes and wrinkling her brow, she took another cookie too. And so it went. When there was only one cookie left, the man reached over, broke it in half, ate the half, and left. The woman was thunderstruck at his nerve, but just then her flight was called and she marched on board. Still simmering, she settled into the seat and reached into her big purse for her book. And nestled there, right under the book, she found her unopened bag of cookies.

Now there's a real cookie monster!

Isn't it amazing how a simple incident like that can give us such a clear view into a person's heart – how it can reveal what a person really is. Well that's exactly what the event in today's gospel does for us in regard to Jesus. It lets us look straight into his heart and see what he really is. Look at him. Look at what he is letting us see. He isn't the least bit interested in being a king – that means nothing to him.

So what does matter to him? We do. Our needs do. He sees that huge crowd, so hungry that they're near fainting. And what is his reaction?

- "Gosh, that's a real shame – all those hungry people"? No.
- Or, "Sure glad I've got something to eat"? No.
- Or, "If those people had any sense, they wouldn't have come out here without any food"? No, not that either.

His reaction is simple and gracious: "These people are hungry. We've got to feed them. We've got to prevent their fainting on the way home." And that's exactly what he does. In fact, he provides for them so abundantly that there are twelve baskets of leftovers.

This single event tells us all we really need to know about Jesus and about the Father who sent him. It tells us how big the inside of God really is and how huge is God's affection for us. God truly delights in our being happy and in giving us whatever we need – food, friendship, comfort, reassurance and challenge, forgiveness and strength – all that and more, in abundance. There aren't narrow limits on what God's willing to give us, anymore than Jesus counted out how many loaves and fishes he was willing to give that crowd.

Now, if all that is true, and it is, then the fears and anxieties we sometimes have about God and about life are really crazy. Can you see how foolish it is to worry that God may not forgive us, or may abandon us, or may expect the impossible of us, or may not give us what we need? To give credence and power to those kinds of fears is to ignore a world full of evidence to the contrary.

It's time to stop shrinking our great God down to our own size. It's time to let God be God for us. We have seen God's grandness and graciousness to each of us a million times over. It's time to trust that graciousness, to trust that God's big enough on the inside to handle anything, even our smallness of heart.

So why not let God be all he wants to be and can be for you? It will change your life.

Don't Fall for the Lie: It'll Kill You

John 6:24-35

Two big cowboys were talking about a third cowboy. "He's a real tough character," says the one, "and quick on the trigger. He can shoot before his pistol clears his holster."

His friend was impressed. "That is fast," he says, "if he can shoot before his pistol clears his holster. By the way, what's his name?"

"Well," says the other fellow, "they call him Footless Frankie!"

What could be more stupid than to shoot oneself in the foot? And yet we see it happen every day, especially as we watch people interact with one another: people who should be natural allies, and neighbors who together could build wonderful lives, fall for the illusion that they don't need one another, the illusion that they can go it alone, and that neighbors are disposable. It's the ultimate shot in the foot! The ultimate in self-destruction.

Just think of Bosnia, Rwanda, Northern Ireland with generation after generation of people saying to their own neighbors and fellow citizens, "We don't need you. We can dispose of you and make a good life for ourselves." That is a world-class illusion, but people fall for it and act on it. And in doing so, they destroy all possibility of a good life, not only for their neighbors but for themselves, generation after generation.

But the madness doesn't end out there far away across the sea. All the statistics on violent crime in this country confirm that the great majority of victims are not strangers but friends and family members. And, still closer to home, as any priest or counselor or psychiatrist will confirm, most of the real damage to hearts and spirits happens, not at the hands of strangers, but in the family. In every case, whether far away or near, the illusion is the same. It says, "I don't need you or your help and you

have no claim on me. You are usable and disposable." What a perfect recipe for self-destruction!

Most of us would never speak that lie out loud, but all of us have spoken it wordlessly inside at times. And some of us may be speaking it there now, though probably without even noticing it. But no matter how often we've fallen for it, our hearts continue to tell us quite insistently, "That is a lie!" Our hearts hunger and thirst for something very different: for friendship, for real family that heals and doesn't harm, for communion, for a place of peace where no one need be afraid.

That hunger in our hearts is a gift from God, drawing us forward, drawing us away from the lies and illusions that can kill us, drawing us into true friendship with God and one another. That hunger in our hearts helps us see and feel the hunger in our neighbor's heart, and it tells us how to get a life that is a life. It tells us to lend a hand, to walk together, to share the gifts we bear, and to become coaches, not critics.

So let us listen to our hearts. God is speaking to us there. Let us build the family for which we hunger. Let us build the holy communion for which God made us.

Business as Usual Isn't Enough

Mark 9:2-10

There was a spoiled child who absolutely refused to eat, so his frantic mother took him to a psychiatrist. The doctor, who was one of the world's leading experts in such matters, coaxed the boy with every conceivable goody, but to no avail. In desperation, he finally asked, "Well, what would you like to eat?"

"Worms," came the reply. The doctor had no intention of being out-bluffed by a little kid, so he dispatched his nurse to the worm farm. Almost before you could blink, she was back with a huge plateful of the biggest, freshest, wriggliest worms you ever saw.

"Now eat the worms, sonny," smiled the shrink.

"But they aren't cooked," whined the boy. So the nurse took the worms around the corner to a French restaurant and very soon brought back a gourmet treat, "Worms Provencal." But the boy only snivelled, "I don't want a whole plateful, just one."

The doctor seized the plate, scraped off all but one worm, and hissed: "Eat the worm!"

"You eat half," said the kid.

And that's what the doctor did. Then he skewered the other half with a fork, and held it right under the boy's nose: "Eat!" But all the boy did was burst into tears. "Now what's the matter?" asked the psychiatrist.

"You ate my half," whimpered the tyke.

How easy it is to let our world shrink to worm size. How easy to let our hearts shrink so small that they can be filled all the way full with mini-thoughts and tiny grievances no bigger than, "You ate my half of the worm."

In Sunday's Gospel, Jesus challenges the apostles and us to break out of the tiny worlds and the tiny visions we make for ourselves. On the top of that mountain, Jesus lets his apostles see what he is on the inside. The vision is dazzling and larger than life. And Peter is so happy, so beside himself with joy at what he sees, that he wants that moment to last forever. He doesn't want to let it go. In fact, he wants to build a shrine on the spot for Jesus to stay in so the vision will never end; they'll all just stay there on the mountain top forever.

That's not at all what Jesus has in mind. For what he's just shown them is not only what he is inside. It's also what they and we are called to become: People who really look like God's own offspring—on the inside. That's a big vision. In fact, it is our life's work: Growing into the likeness of Jesus, taking on his inner shape, being transformed. That great life's work can't be accomplished by sitting around indefinitely on a mountain top, no matter how nice the view or how special the company. The apostles had to go back down the mountain, back to their lives, back to business, though not to business as usual.

Why did they have to go back down? Why couldn't they just stay forever in that happy, safe place? Because it's only in the give-and-take, the falling-down and getting-up, the forgiving and being-forgiven of daily life that our best selves grow into being. The fabric of greatness is woven out of ordinary thread. It is woven very slowly and always by hand, never by machine. And why couldn't they just go back to "business as usual"? Because once they'd gone to the mountain, "business as usual" would never be enough for them again. They knew now what they were about: They were about becoming heroes by doing the ordinary extraordinarily well.

That is the exact definition of our life task: Becoming heroes by doing the ordinary extraordinarily well, growing into full-fledged brothers and sisters of Jesus, filling in the sketched outline that is already drawn on our hearts. That is an awesome task, and not a little frightening. Lest we give up before we fairly get started and retreat to our little worm-worlds, remember what St Paul said so long ago, "If God is for us, who can be against us?" The fact is, God is for us. So the sky's the limit! No more little worm-worlds for us!

For for Pilgrims and Medicine for Sick People

John 6:41-51

There was a salty old-timer with a peg leg, a hook, and an eye patch, who was looking for a job as a sea captain. "You surely look the part," said the interviewer. "How did you lose your leg?"

"A shark took me leg," he grunted, "and now I wears a wooden peg."

"What about your hand?"

"Aye, laddy! I was in a sword fight and now I have a hook."

"How did you lose your eye?"

"T'was a terrible storm off Tortuga. The riggin' was all foul, and I looked up just when a sea gull was passin' over."

"And that put your eye out?"

"NO! – T'was the first day I had me hook!"

Most of us are in a lot better shape than that sea captain, and none of us are missing so many parts. But all of us – even the youngest – bear the wounds of body and spirit that come from just being alive and trying to make a life. Sometimes life deals us cruel blows that come out of nowhere like an assasin's dagger and cut deep into our hearts. Friends betray us, loved ones die, circumstances change and we are left out or forgotten or have no say and no sway. And sometimes we're just like that sea captain with his hook: doing ourselves grave harm without even noticing till the damage is done. Sometimes we wound others, but always we wound ourselves. And worse yet, we repeat the same wounding patterns over and over again. We are very slow learners.

Long before any of us were born, the God who created us to be like himself and to grow into his own image, knew we'd be like this, knew that our growing up would take a long time and would involve endless trial and error – endless mis-steps and stumbles and blunders, endless wounds to the spirit before, little by little, we'd find our way and build lives that make sense.

God knew all that before we were born, but let us be born anyway, and then didn't walk away, didn't leave us orphans. Instead, God gave us his son Jesus as our brother. And Jesus in turn gave us himself in the eucharist – his own body, his own spirit – to be received, taken inside us, and made a part of us as often as we need.

The apostles had two wonderful names for the eucharist. The first is "food for pilgrims," food for wanderers who are trying to find their way, and grow tired and hungry on the road. We know what that feels like, don't we. Sometimes we get so tired and weak it seems we can't walk one more step. The body and blood of Jesus is the food that keeps us going.

The second name the apostles gave the eucharist is "medicine for sick people," not "reward for the perfect" but medicine for people whose spirits have been wounded by life and by their own mistakes. We know what that feels like too, don't we. At those times, we don't need any more troubles or any more stuff. We need medicine that can bring us back to health. And that's what the eucharist is.

As Jesus restores our strength and cures our sicknesses with his holy food, there's something else very wonderful that happens. He helps us look at one another's wounds and weaknesses with kinder hearts. He helps us to be touched by others' pains and sadnesses, hungers and mistakes as if they were our own. And he helps us to do for one another what he has done for us: Heal and comfort, strengthen, encourage, and give new hope.

Not one of us deserves this holy gift – the Lord's own body becoming one with ours, and the Lord's own spirit drawing so very close to ours – but all of us surely need it. So let us receive the Lord this day with grateful and open hearts, and let him do his work within us so that we may do his work this day for one another.

The Ultimate Heart Medicine

John 6:51-58

In New Orleans in the French Quarter there was a wonderful little jazz club where the most talented musicians regularly performed. From the day the place opened, everyone complained about the terrible old piano with its missing keys and sour notes. The piano players hated playing it. The vocalists hated singing with it. And all the combos that played the club wished they could bring their own instrument. But nothing ever changed. Finally, after years of hearing everyone complain, the owner of the club decided to act and settle the matter once and for all. And so, at great expense, he had the piano painted!

Real change is always hard. And facing up to what we really need to change is even harder. That's why the eucharist is so important to us. The eucharist is our power source: food for our spirit. It gives us energy for the tough journey we're on and it keeps us going. But, even more important, it's medicine for our spirit, the ultimate heart medicine.

When taken as directed, it has the power to cure what's sick in us, and to heal what's wounded. But it isn't magic. We have to take it as directed. That means we have to receive the Lord, not just into our hands or on our lips, but all the way into our inmost being. And doing that takes close attention, inner quiet, and a great deal of trust.

But when we do welcome the Lord in that way, there, deep inside, with all the doors unlocked and all the nooks and crannies open, the Lord lights up our darkness. Deep inside us, heavenly warmth and light help us see and know God as absolutely devoted to us, utterly delighted at our successes, and anxious to see us get better, and happier, and more whole.

What powerful heart medicine God is for us. He doesn't just make us feel better. By his kind presence he gives us the courage and the confidence to look at what needs to be done and to see where we need to change, and not just close our eyes or look away from our unfinished work.

Change is always hard but it becomes possible for us when we trust the Lord enough to come into our hearts, shine a warm and kindly light on what we need to see, and take us by the hand and lead us where we need to go. And that happens when we receive the body and blood of the Lord without distraction or barrier.

So let us pray for one another:
May God help us to receive Jesus' holy body and blood, not just in our hands and on our lips but in the depths of our heart. And as we share God's company, heart to heart, may we be transformed into his likeness. Amen.

Reconnecting Is a Lifelong Task

John 6:60-69

One chilly, gray day a traveler saw a little sparrow lying on its back in the middle of the road. The man got down from his horse, bent over for a closer look and asked the little creature, "Why are you lying down there with your feet in the air like that?" "I heard the sky's going to fall today," the bird replied.

The man could hardly control his laughter, "So you think your spindly little legs can hold up that big sky?"

The determined little sparrow said simply, "One does what one can."

All of us are extraordinarily lucky—among the luckiest people ever to walk this earth. Yet we all have our troubles, sometimes just little ones: a summer cold, a leaky faucet, a sprained thumb. But sometimes: times of betrayal or financial ruin, of mortal illness or even death, or when a 1000 little things just add up, we get the feeling the sky has fallen or is just about to and there's nothing we can do.

No one is exempt. We all get our turn. So how do we survive, much less build a happy life? There is only one way: by connecting with trusting hearts to the only one who can give us life. We survive by rooting our hearts deeply in the Lord. This special connection to the Lord is like no other friendship we have. On the one hand, it will not make us immune to pain or trouble. But it will guarantee that no trouble will ever overwhelm us, and no difficulty, however grave, will ever have the power to take away our joy or our peace.

If that is true, and it is, why is there so much fretting and anxious worrying in our lives? Why so much despair and world-weariness and sadness of soul? Why do our troubles so often take control of us and define our lives? All that happens because we let our "rootedness" in the Lord erode and wash away. We let our connection with God grow weak, hanging sometimes only by a thread.

No wonder life can oppress us. No wonder Jesus says to us as he said to Peter, "Are you going to leave me too? You are barely with me even now."

Peter gave the perfect response for us all. "Lord," he said, "to whom shall we go? You have the words of eternal life."

What more is there to say? Our Lord has not only the words, but the essence of life itself to give to us, but God can't do it if we're not firmly connected to the Lord on the inside.

So there we have our task, a task that is never finished: the daily task of reconnecting with God and rebonding, rerooting our hearts in the one who has our names written in the palm of his hand.

That is our happy task each day, reconnecting with him. So let us begin it again.

It's Time to Get Our Insides in Order

Mark 7:1-23

There was a young woman who was recently separated and whose day was going badly. She was hot and tired, stressed and lonely and she barely had the strength to lift her little boy into his high chair for dinner. She put his food on the tray and began to read the mail – another bill she couldn't pay – it was the last straw. So she leaned her head against the tray and began to cry.

The little boy looked at his sobbing mother with a sad heart, then took the pacifier out of his mouth and pressed it gently to her lips. He gave what he had! And his gift came from the inside.

Today's gospel wrestles with a huge question: how do we build a good and happy life? Jesus gives us the answer: "Get your insides in order," he says. "Get your head and heart true and then follow where they lead."

But how do we "true" our head and heart? We start by looking very hard at what we've got and remembering where we got it. We name our gifts out loud and let our hearts be astonished at seeing close up what remarkable gifts we bear. And then we give thanks for being given so much we didn't earn.

Now thankfulness is an energy that needs an outlet. It says, "I've been blessed with so much, I need to carry my gifts to whoever needs them." Like the little boy with the pacifier, it says, "I need to give what I have."

So thankfulness gives us energy and the desire to give. But that leaves us with the question: who needs us? The answer is: lots of folks need us in lots of ways and not just the widows and orphans.

Some of us are creative. People need us. Some of us are wise and clear thinkers. People need us. Some of us are strong and calm under fire. People need us. Some of us are great mediators and reconcilers. People need us. Some of us are visionaries who think great thoughts. People need us. Some of us are practical folks who know how to make things happen. People need us. And some of us are good comforters. People need us.

Whatever our gifts, lots of people right here and now need us very much.

So it's time to look within and get our insides in order. It's time to see and name our special gifts with glad and thankful hearts. It's time to carry our gifts to whoever needs them.

It's time to build a happy life from the inside out. So let us begin!

God's Hospitality: A Comfort and a Command

Mark 7:31-37

A young student went to his rabbi with a question. "Rabbi," he asked, "how can we tell exactly the moment when night has ended and day has begun? Is it when it's so light that we can no longer see the stars in the sky?"

"No, my son," said the rabbi. "That is not how we tell that night is ended and the day has begun."

"Then how can we tell?" asked the boy.

The rabbi spoke softly. "We know that night has ended and day has begun when we look into the face of the stranger next to us and recognize he is our brother."

With God there is no night but only day. God looks at you and me seeing a much cherished child and never a stranger. There is nothing in us – nothing about us – that God does not see, and yet even on our worst days, God's attitude towards us never changes: "You are my dear boy, my dear girl; I love you, and I'll never give up on you, never call you stranger."

For those of us who have come face to face with our frailties and have seen and named our sinfulness, those words of the Lord are both comfort and healing, "you are my dear boy, my dear girl, and I'll never give up on you."

But those words are more than comfort and healing for us. They are also God's mandate to us. God, with gracious hospitality, has welcomed every single one of us inside a circle of love and left no one outside. God is asking us to do the same, to make the habit of hospitality the foundation of our lives: "As I have welcomed you into my life, so must you welcome one another and call no one stranger."

How different every part of our lives could be if we refused to label anyone "stranger." How different the way we'd drive and do business and even celebrate this liturgy. How different life could be if we said inside our heads, "I don't know her name, I don't know who he is – and I probably never will – but I do know she's my sister, and he's my brother. And I cannot call them strangers. I cannot fail to value them." How different life would be!

So let us pray for one another:
God grant that the night will end for us all. In his light may we look upon one another's faces and see there brothers and sisters to be welcomed and cherished always! Amen.

Give It Away If You Want It to Be Yours

Mark 8:27-35

A very nervous young couple were standing at the altar of their parish church, waiting to pronounce their marriage vows. The bride was pale, the groom was shaking, and both had forgotten everything they'd practiced at the rehearsal. Finally the moment arrived, and the priest asked the big question: "Do you, James, take Heather here present to be your lawful wife?"

With a shaky voice the groom responded, "I do???"

"Nice try, young man," said the priest. "Now, could you try it without the question mark?"

In Sunday's Gospel Jesus is urging us to try life without the question mark. He's pleading with us not to settle for half a life, but to be fully invested and hold nothing back. Listen to what he says: "Whoever would save his life will lose it. But whoever loses his life for my sake will save it." He's warning us about our ingrained habit of hedging our bets and holding back, keeping our eye on the nearest exit, and always making sure we've got a way out.

Now that's a great survival strategy for investors, poker players, and the Mafia, but it's a recipe for failure at the core of life. For if our real life work is to help one another grow into masterpieces, then nothing less than our best efforts will do. Nothing less than investing everything we've got in building up God's kingdom within us and around us. To let our fears cause us to withhold any part of ourselves from our life's work is a recipe for lifetime failure, sadness, and isolation. Holding tight to what we've already got is a sure formula for dying from the inside out.

Jesus is telling us we have an alternative – losing our lives in order to save them. It seems a strange paradox, but if we've been paying attention, we've probably already discovered a bit of how it works.

Just one example: At times we've all had the experience of connecting intensely with someone we trust. As we talked to that person and listened, it was as if the whole rest of the world fell away and ceased to exist. We forgot about ourselves, our image, how we looked, and whether we were hungry. For a few moments we gave our whole attention, we gave away our whole self to the other. And, in return for our gift, we found that we had become more on the inside.

The pattern repeats itself in every part of our life: When we give our best self into any moment, into any interaction, and hold nothing back and let all that is secondary fall away, we find to our surprise that we become more, much more. It is that "something more" that Jesus wants for us.

So let us pray for one another that we learn to give away our lives from the inside – give it all away – that we may have real life in abundance now and into eternity! Amen.

His Mission Is Not to Condemn

John 3:13-17

An elderly couple were celebrating their sixtieth wedding anniversary, and all through the day crowds of friends and relatives dropped in to congratulate them. So they were grateful when evening came, the last guest departed, and they were able to sit alone on the porch and watch the sunset. After a while the old man looked over fondly at his wife and said, "Agatha, I'm proud of you."

"What was that you said?" the old lady asked in return. "You know I'm hard of hearing. Speak up."

"I said I'm proud of you." But still she couldn't hear.

"Will you please speak up," she said.

This time he shouted, "I said I'm proud of you."

"Oh, that's all right, George," the old lady responded. "I'm tired of you too."

Most of us are lifelong Christians. That means we've heard the teachings of Jesus read to us every Sunday since we were toddlers. That's a lot of times. Yet I wonder how many of us have actually heard – inside – what Jesus has been saying. It may be that some of us are as hard of hearing as that old lady. I've been wondering about this a lot lately, because I've just read the results of a national poll of American Catholics. One question caught my eye: Why do you go to mass on Sunday? The answers were scattered all over the place: I go

- to hear the word of God
- to hear the sermon
- to hear the music
- to see my friends.

But the one answer given by nearly half of the Catholics polled said, "We go to mass on Sundays because it's our obligation. We have to go – there's a rule, the third commandment. And if we don't obey the rule God will punish us – perhaps eternally." In other words, those people are telling us, God is best understood as a rule giver and law enforcer, basically ill-tempered, always on the lookout for mistakes, and always poised and ready to punish. So the best advice is to keep a low profile and stay out of the way. Or try to get what you want by offering bribes in the form of prayers, novenas, scapulars and painful penances. In sum: Their God is an irascible policeman who takes bribes!

We've all seen some pretty unhappy faces – old and young – coming in the church door, Now we know what those faces are saying: I don't want to be here; but I'm afraid to stay away. I feel trapped in a relationship with a mean God.

Fortunately, that means God doesn't exist anywhere except in our imaginations. The real God is vastly greater – and nicer too. Listen to what Jesus has been trying to tell us about Him all along:

First, the real God's fondest desire is that we be happy. Therefore, his commandments are not arbitrary rules cooked up as a kind of obstacle course, a minefield to be tiptoed through to win heaven. His commands, especially the Golden Rule, are simply descriptions of the only way of living that works – if we want to be happy. They're a help, not a burden.

Second, nothing we can ever do can make the real God love us less. He's always reaching out to embrace us – even when we are at our worst. He will never reject us, never turn his back, never refuse to embrace. He will never punish us, because he doesn't have to. Our unloving choices always carry their own destructive consequences damage inside – to our hearts, and damage outside too. When we sin it is we who turn away, not God. It is we who damage and punish, not God.

Third, the real God doesn't need to be bribed. So we are wasting out time if we are trying to use our prayers and penances to turn aside his anger, improve his mood, or change his mind: he already wants the very best for us.

Our prayers – and our presence here at mass – are for out benefit, getting us in touch and keeping us in tune with the best friend we ever had. And we are the big losers, if we don't seize the opportunity. Jesus has told us all of this in a thousand different ways. But he said it best when he gave God a special name of affection that nobody had ever used for God before. He called him "Abba," which translates "my very dear Father."

That is who God is and that is who he wants to be for you and me. So, why waste our lives fearing a nasty tyrant who exists only in our imaginations? Instead, why not let God be for us what he has always wanted to be: A very dear father, a father who repeats over and over the invitation: "Come to me, all you who are weary and find life burdensome, and I will refresh you. . . . Your souls will find rest, for my yoke is easy and my burden light."

Jewel Makers

Mark 9:30-37

When I was beginning high school and was still on the first pages of my brand new Latin book, we read a simple story – our first in Latin. It was a tale about a poor but noble widow named Cornelia who was visited by two of her friends. Now the friends were described in Latin as *femina superba,* which sounds like "superb women," but in fact is best translated as "haughty witches."

From the moment of their arrival, these arrogant ladies flaunted their fine gowns and all their costly jewelry – rings, necklaces, and brooches. Finally they looked down their very long Roman noses and sneered at their hostess. "Now tell us, dear, where are your jewels?"

Cornelia nodded serenely and looked to the other side of the room. "There are my jewels," she said, smiling at her two young children.

Right on the mark! It is hard to get our values straight and even harder to keep them straight. The apostles make that all too clear in Sunday's gospel as they walk along with Jesus and argue about which of them is the most important! Is it the fisherman? The tax collector? Or perhaps the future betrayer? They're all small fries but still they argue about who's the most important!

We all want to feel like winners and look like winners. We all want to be somebody. And so, very early on, we try to figure out what it takes. In the beginning we're pretty sure a shiny, red tricycle or a Barbie with all the outfits would do the trick and make us feel important and whole on the inside. Of course, it doesn't. And before long our world gets bigger and bigger and we need sports cars and designer clothes, power boats and electric gates, board memberships and pictures in the paper to persuade ourselves we're important. Or maybe we go for prizes: a little gold star on my paper now, and a little Oscar for the mantlepiece later.

But whatever our gimmick, it never quite works, never quite satisfies. As nice as all life's goodies can be – and they can be pretty terrific – they never leave us feeling quite whole and full on the inside. Instead, after awhile we find ourselves feeling a little sad and maybe even a little betrayed by life.

God loves us very much but knows we're slow learners. So God helps us get our values straight by letting us feel the sadness that comes when we've invested our hearts in things that cannot fill us full; the sadness that comes when we've planted our gifts in fields that can yield no fruit.

Through that sadness and restlessness God is calling us, urging us to plant our hearts and invest our gifts in the only place where they will grow and bear fruit and make us real winners from the inside out. God urges us to invest our gifts in one another, and to become, like Cornelia in the story, real jewel makers.

It's our opportunity for happiness, our chance to become real winners: by becoming jewel makers. Let's not let this chance pass us by even one more day!

"Stranger" Is a Dangerous Word

Mark 9:38-48

About a dozen years ago, *Time* magazine reported on an experiment conducted by the sociology department at Stanford. Sociologists took a late model automobile into a nearby residential neighborhood and "abandoned" it for a week. In truth, because they were watching from a hidden vantage point to see what might happen. Nothing happened. Adults and kids walked or drove by, looked at the car, and obviously wondered whose it was and why it was there. But nobody laid a finger on it.

After a week, the observers ended their vigil and drove the car away. But not very far, just a few blocks, to a spot on the side of a well-traveled road that wasn't part of any particular neighborhood. Once again the car was "abandoned" and the observers took up their binoculars to watch from a distance. They hadn't long to wait. Well-dressed adults and teenagers in decent cars – the same kind of folks who lived in the first neighborhood – descended like locusts on that car and took what they wanted, tires, stereo, seats, doors, engine, the works! Within five hours only the frame remained.

The same car, the same community, two locations just blocks apart. What made the difference? The scholars thought about that and concluded the difference lay in a simple distinction: ours versus theirs. Even if we don't know the details, a car parked in our neighborhood is presumed to be one of ours. Whereas a car parked out in no-man's land is labeled "theirs," the property of one of the faceless "them," who have no connection with us, who are outside our circle, and thus merit no consideration from us.

That ugly little distinction, we versus they, ours versus theirs, is constantly in play, always trying to take over. It labels a person as a "stranger" - not one of us.

How could a person kill someone in a drive-by shooting? Easy. The victim generally a "stranger," not of the group, so that life just didn't count. How can airmen drop bombs on innocents below? Because they are strangers and not ours. How can we be so callous about the sufferings of the homeless and destitute? Easy! Because they are strangers, people without faces, not one of us. How can some of us be so rude and aggressive to other decent drivers on the freeway? Because those

drivers are strangers. Can you imagine acting that way if you knew the other driver was a friend or a client or your mother?!

The pattern shows up in even the tiniest of things. I've learned that even cigarette butts can tell us the same tale. Sunday mornings, when more than a thousand of our own parishioners have passed through church doors, hardly a cigarette butt is to be found anywhere on the grounds. But have a handful of visitors here for a thirty-minute wedding, and you'll find butts everywhere, even ground into the floor inside the church. To some of those visitors, we are strangers, not one of theirs, so anything goes.

In this gospel, Jesus had the disappointment of hearing his best friend John make this same ugly distinction, we versus they, ours versus theirs. "Jesus," he said, "we saw a man using your name to expel demons and we stopped him, because he was not one of ours!" What a disappointment for Jesus! John had already heard the Good Samaritan story at least as many times as we have. For nearly three years he'd seen Jesus befriending everyone he met, showing no preferences, making no distinctions, welcoming everyone into his life, and leaving no one outside the circle of his love.

John had seen and heard all that, but he hadn't taken it to heart. But Jesus didn't give up on him. He just told him again: for us there can be no such thing as a stranger, only brothers and sisters. For us there can be no "them," only an all-inclusive "us." The circle of our love has to grow so wide that no one is left outside. This is our life's task and we'll achieve it with God's help.

So let us turn to God in prayer.
Lord, we have set limits on our love and have been willing to call many of your people "strangers." Help our hearts to grow ever larger. Teach us to recognize all people as brothers and sisters, and show us the way to bring all people into the circle of our love. Amen.

They Know They're Little

Genesis 2:18-24

A newly-ordained priest was about to perform his first wedding, and he was very nervous. So he asked his pastor for help. The old monsignor told him everything he needed to know and then ended with some advice. "Father," he said, "if you get lost and can't think of what to say, quote scripture. It's always safe, and you'll never go wrong."

With that the young priest went off to church and did a fine job of conducting the wedding . . . until the very end, that is, when he was to pray the solemn blessing over the bride and groom. At that crucial moment, with hand outstretched and every eye upon him, he froze. He couldn't find his place in the prayer book. His mind was a blank. He had no idea of what to say. Then he remembered the monsignor's advice: if you get lost, quote scripture. So he ended the wedding by quoting most solemnly the only verse he could remember, "Father, forgive them, for they know not what they do."

Standing just inches away from a bride and groom as they exchange their vows, I find it difficult not to be awed and astonished at the immensity of what two fragile human beings are committing themselves to do and be for one another. To be faithful friends, to be truly one for better or worse, for the rest of their lives. How can such a thing be possible for mere human beings?

The same question always stuns me when a young couple present their new baby for baptism, and solemnly commit themselves to the immense task of being faithful models and guides for that child for decades to come. How can this be possible for ordinary humans? And the question rises yet again when I see a young man commit himself to serve faithfully as a priest for the rest of his life. How can this be possible for a mere human being?

Sometimes all of this surely does seem impossible. Sometimes all these solemnly-spoken commitments to be a faithful spouse, or parent, or priest seem just wishful thinking. And for all too many of us that's how things actually turn out. But in today's gospel, Jesus tells us that's not the way things have to turn out, even with all our flaws and limitations. In this gospel, Jesus says the impossible is possible: we can be part of his kingdom, we can become the wonderful spouses, parents, and friends

that we long to be, but so often have not been.

And how is this to happen? Jesus says quite simply, we must become like little children! But what are little children really like? And what makes them different from most of us? First of all they know they're little, and they know that in order to live they need the help of people who love them. It doesn't even occur to them to pose as invincible or to seriously pretend to be what they are not. Little children trust the people they meet, and they presume the best about them. (That's why they get all those lectures about taking no rides from strangers.) They don't label others as enemies before there's reason to do so.

Little children think of everything as possible and worth trying. You don't hear a little child saying "you can't do that" or "it'll never work." What you do hear is "when can we start"? Little children are compassionate to those who are even smaller and more helpless than themselves. Legions of stray cats, scrawny dogs, and birds with broken wings could testify to that.

Little children lack the attention span of adults. They have little physical strength, few skills, and only the sparsest of knowledge about the world. Yet they have what matters: they are transparently open and receptive to people, to God, to life. And that means that all that is good can get into their lives and help them.

Imagine what wonderful spouses, parents, and friends we could be – even with all our faults – if only our hearts were that open and receptive. No love, no joy, no person would ever be locked out. God and the whole universe would be inside working for us and filling in those parts of us that are damaged or weak. That is Jesus' promise: we will get all that just by doing what little children know how to do, by opening the doors of our hearts.

So let us begin now by opening our hearts in prayer:

Lord, hold us in the palm of your hand and show us once more how to be like little children. Help us to lay aside our masks and our pretensions, and teach us to trust, to hope, and never to fear. Let our hearts become so open, so transparent, and so wide that every person and every love may find there a home. Amen.

What Do We Know Now?

Mark 10:17-30

Not so long ago, I saw a little Peanuts cartoon that offered a chilling bit of insight into the human condition. Linus is philosophizing with Lucy. "Life is peculiar," he says. "Wouldn't you like to have your life to live over, if you knew what you know now?"

Lucy stares out blankly and then asks, "What do I know now?"

Good question! After all this living what do we know now? What have we learned about life? I suspect that most of us are like the rich young man in the Gospel: bit by bit we've learned that living by the rules, and following the commandments, makes sense – don't lie, cheat, or steal; don't murder; don't commit adultery, and so on. We've learned that the alternative to living by those rules is chaos or as the British philosopher put it, "the war of all against all," perpetual fear, daring to trust no one, being always on guard, never relaxing.

That's a nightmare and no way to live. So most of the time we work fairly hard at living by the rules. And when we succeed, everybody wins. So living by the rules is a giant step in the right direction, but as Jesus explained to the young man, it's not enough. Staying out of trouble and causing no one any harm are very good things, but it doesn't take us to the core of life. It brings us to the doorstep but it doesn't take us inside.

As Jesus keeps telling us, if we want our lives to be happy and fulfilling right now, we have to think big. We have to think like God, and that starts with knowing ourselves and our gifts very well, and then asking, "Who needs the gifts I have to give, and what's the best way to bring my gifts to them?"

Now we know from experience that when we let go and think big and start seeing ourselves as God's gift bearers, real joy comes: we know we're needed, we know we've got a purpose, we know inside what it means to be made in the image and likeness of God. So why do we pull back so often?

The reason, and the barrier to all the joy we ought to have is fear: fear that I may have no gift to share, fear that my gift is not needed, fear that in sharing my gift I will lose it and have nothing left for myself. Those fears are very real and often very powerful inside us, but they are lies that needlessly stifle and shrink our spirits and cut us off from the best parts of our lives.

Jesus is calling us to turn our backs on those lies once and for all. He's inviting us to redefine ourselves from the inside out and to remember that, like Jesus himself, we are God's gift bearers.

May we never forget that! May we never settle for anything less!

To Ransom Captives and Rescue Prisoners

Mark 10:35-45

Deep in the Middle Ages wave after wave of Christians went on crusades to the Holy Land to liberate the holy places from the Moslems. These crusades went on for several centuries and failed in the end. But in the meantime there were vast numbers of casualties: many thousands killed or injured in battle, tens of thousands – including a king of France – cut down by disease on the way, and thousands more – including a king of England – held captive for ransom. Whole religious orders of priests were founded with the sole purpose of ransoming captives and liberating prisoners from the clutches of the heathens. And sometimes those priests would even offer themselves in exchange for the prisoners!

Just an isolated moment in history long ago and far away? We might think so, but Sunday's Gospel disagrees. For, as we heard so clearly, Jesus defines his whole mission as ransoming captives. "I have come to give my life in ransom for the many." In defining himself in that way, Jesus also defines our vocation as his followers. So we'd better figure out what this business of ransoming captives and rescuing prisoners is all about.

First of all, what it's not about for us is dashing off to Lebanon or Iran or Iraq to negotiate with terrorists. Our task is more subtle than that, and our opportunities are much closer at hand. Jesus is asking us to do for one another what he tries to do for us. He's asking us to invest our very best energies in the task of setting one another free from whatever holds us captive.

To understand that vocation we have to look closely at the kinds of things that enslave people. Just think of the fears, and angers, and grudges that hold people captive. Think of the bad habits of a lifetime that are trapping so many. Think of the bad ideas that imprison so many. And think of the compulsive need for things, the need for stuff, which holds so many of us hostage and forecloses the possibility of a happy life. Just call up in your mind's eye the face of anyone you know, friend or foe, and you'll see there, even in the very best of people, the hints of prison walls, the need to be set free.

So how do we go about helping one another escape our prison walls? Tons of free advice will rarely do it – we've already learned that! The most powerful, liberating gift we have to give is our steadfast, compassionate presence. Our strength, our goodness, and our willingness to continue walking at the side of our friend can, in time, become strength and goodness and freedom for our friend.

That is a wonderful gift we have to give: strength, goodness, and freedom. What a sadness it would be if we failed to give it!

Lord, I Want to Sea!

Mark 10:46-52

For about 1500 years, from the time of Moses down to the destruction of Jerusalem by the Romans in 70 AD, Jewish worship centered on ritual sacrifices. There was a special sacrifice for every circumstance and each one was grounded in a key insight into human nature.

For example, every morning began with the holocaust sacrifice. An unblemished lamb and a loaf of the finest bread were burned on the altar, and a cup of choice wine was poured into the ground. Symbolically, the people were giving back to God the essentials they needed to live. In effect they were saying, "We know it all comes from you, Lord, and we're very grateful." How wise they were!

They had other sacrifices as well. Sacrifices of praise and of thanksgiving. Sacrifices for sins and for peace. Each one had its own prescribed ritual and special meaning, but probably the most interesting of all was the sacrifice for unknown sins.

This was more than just a bit of insurance in case a person had skipped the fine print and ended up breaking some obscure rule he knew nothing about. The sacrifice for unknown sins came from something the wise old rabbis had learned about human nature, and that is, sometimes we're all spiritually blind.

Sometimes we just don't see ourselves clearly or accurately. Sometimes we don't see what we're doing to others, what effect we're having on them. Sometimes we don't see the big patterns in our lives, though everyone else sees them. And sometimes we don't see the not-so-lovely ideas that are shaping our lives at the core. Sometimes our blindness lasts just a little while, and sometimes a whole lifetime. But always inner blindness is a hazard for every one of us. It can strike any one of us at a moment's notice! Now why is that so? Why do good people like us fail to see so much?

I think there are probably two reasons: First of all, very few of us were ever taught to ask carefully at every turn of the road, "What am I really doing, and why am I doing it?" We just weren't taught to look methodically for the truth about ourselves. And so, unseeing, we live on the outside of things.

Secondly, even those who were taught discover that quite often, as we begin to see, fear intervenes, and turns out the lights. Fear of the ugliness we may see. Fear of what we may have to change if we let ourselves see. Fear that whatever is wrong will be too much for us. Fear there's nothing of value within us. And, so out of fear, often we live unseeing on the outside of things.

Our fears would be entirely justifiable if we were walking this road alone. But we are not alone. The Lord himself is at our side with his hand outstretched to steady and encourage and strengthen us. We have no cause to fear now, and no reason to close our eyes any more, for there is nothing that we and the Lord cannot face together.

And so it is time for us to cry out with that blind man in the Gospel, "Lord, I want to see. Lord, I am ready to see whatever there is to see, because now I know for sure that I'm not alone!"

A Real Possibility

Mark 12:28-34

There was a congregation that was struggling to build a new church. Almost all the members had stepped forward generously with their pledges. But there was one major holdout, the town banker, and he hadn't given a penny. So, very reluctantly, the minister decided to make a personal call on the banker to plead his case.

The banker responded candidly. "I know you must think I'm a cheapskate, Reverend, but I'm really under terrible financial pressures at the moment. My son's at an Ivy League school at a cost of $25,000 a year. My mother's bedridden in a rest home at $60,000 a year. My daughter's husband abandoned her and the nine kids and she needs $40,000 a year. Now you've gotta understand, Reverend. If I've said 'no' to them, how can I say 'yes' to you?"

So much for the Golden Rule! In giving us his great commandment, "Love God with all your heart, soul, and strength, and your neighbor as yourself," Jesus is challenging us to think big, to give our all to life and to one another, and hold nothing back. It's an energizing challenge, full of hope and possibility. But it's daunting as well, almost too big to manage for ordinary mortals. And yet, Jesus who is always fair and always realistic about our weaknesses and limitations, is addressing those words to us. He's convinced that living and loving wholeheartedly is a real possibility for every one of us.

Now what do you think Jesus sees in us that gives him such hopefulness about us? First of all, he sees our longing for the very kind of wholehearted loving that he's prescribing. Now it's true that our longing to live and love with all our might may be buried under self doubt or fear, but it's there; and he sees it, and he speaks to our hearts, "Come out and live the only kind of life that's worth living. Stop settling for half a life that's locked up inside itself."

There's something else Jesus knows about us that makes him optimistic about our prospects, and that is we only have to handle one moment of life at a time – just one. Now, every one of us can do that. Even in the face of the multi-layered demands of everyday life, every one of us can take our moments one at a time, and give to each person there and to each task our whole attention and our best self – just for a moment . . . and then for just one more. When we do that, the outcome is always astonishing, because the moments we fill with life and love – one at a time – slowly come together into hours and days, weeks and years that literally glow. And slowly it dawns on us, we've made a life!

The full and happy life we long for is within our grasp. Jesus has given us the formula: wholehearted living and loving just a moment at a time. What a tragedy it would be to settle for less!

May that tragedy never be ours!

He Will Finish the Work If We Let Him

Matthew 11:25

A shy young man fell in love, but he was utterly tongue-tied whenever he was with the girl. A friend offered some advice: "Just memorize some great lines, expressing your total admiration, something like 'When I see your face, time stands still.' "

It made sense, so for weeks the young man practiced: "When I see your face, time stands still." Finally came the big date. They went to a romantic restaurant. The lights were low. His eyes met hers and he said, when I see your face, I, time, uh . . ." He forgot the words!

Again he tried, "Mary, when I gee your face, I, er, I mean . . .' Now he was totally flustered. Finally, in desperation he blurted out, "Mary, your face could stop a clock."

We laugh, but there's another part of us that's a little sad when we hear a story like that, because it reminds us of how much we're still struggling to get right. After all this time, we say to ourselves, "I'm still stumbling at the same old places in the road. Same old places. Same old cuts and bruises!"

It can be mighty discouraging and can even make us want to give up once and for all. But before we do that, it might be a good idea to see what God has to say to us on the matter. He's trying to catch our attention. He's calling us by name. Listen to him.

"I've been walking at your side from the very beginning," God says, "and following your progress with real hope. I know that you say yes to me sometimes and then get distracted or tired and your yes turns into a no. And, on the other hand, I know that sometimes you start with a resounding no to me and then your better self takes charge and you turn it into the beginning of a yes – maybe a little soft at first, but a beginning."

"I know" says the Lords "that sometimes you don't see the progress you're making; you feel disappointed that you haven't done better, faster. Dear child, I'm not surprised at all. These things take time. I knew that when I made you."

Look at how long it takes me to make a tree or even a flower! And that's simple when compared to all that I've dreamed for you. That will take a lifetime – a lifetime of you and me working together. And even when you reach the end of your road, I know in advance that I'll have to help you finish your work. And I will do just that, I promise.

None of us, no matter how perfect, will be entirely finished and complete when we reach the end of our pilgrimage on this earth. There will still be wounds in us to be healed and holes in us to be filled in. What we celebrate this day is God's loving desire to help all who have passed into his presence to complete their life's work, to let fall away anything left in them that may stand in the way of love, and to have all that is wounded be healed.

What we pray this day is not that God will help them – for God already intends that – but that they will open to God's help and will enter quickly into the joy that God so longs to share with them.

And so in the quiet of our hearts, let us speak the names of those who have gone before us and whisper to each of them: Hear our Father's invitation, come to him with open hearts, and enter forever into the fullness of God's joy.

What Kind of Heart Are You Making?

Mark 12:38-44

For those of us who read the newspapers and watch the nightly news, bad news is no novelty. We get it all the time. But once in a while something happens that is so monstrously evil that it almost stops our hearts. One of those dreaded moments came recently as we listened with horror to the confession of a young mother who strapped her two little boys in the back seat of the family car and drowned them – so she could be free! To us her actions seem incomprehensible, beyond belief. "She must be crazy," we say. But, in fact, there's a good chance she's not. There's a very good chance, indeed a likelihood, that her monstrous deed is quite comprehensible, almost predictable!

Big choices rarely come from outer space. They come from within. They come from the inner person that we have created – a tiny piece at a time – through thousands of choices across many years. Just as we are what we eat, we become what we choose. It happens so slowly that we rarely notice, but through our daily choices we shape our heart as surely as a sculptor shapes his clay. And our heart, in turn, impresses its shape on our deeds.

So, if a heart has slowly taken a shape that habitually says to itself, "I want what I want when I want it," can there be any surprise that when a big moment of decision comes, the choice is to seize what you want with no thought of what you may be doing to others? How could that be a surprise? The ugly deed is always "bought and paid for" well in advance.

But there's another side to this tale, and it's a happier one. Because gracious and true hearts are made in exactly the same way as vicious and selfish ones – through thousands of daily choices across many years. Not one of our thousands of tiny decisions to be compassionate, gracious and true ever gets lost. Every one of them is incorporated into the fabric of our heart, and piece by piece they help to shape the deeds that come after them.

The two widows in Sunday's readings had built gracious and true hearts in just that way over the years, and so when each was asked to give away all she had, the decision almost made itself. It didn't come from outer space. It came from the gracious inner person each widow had created one piece at a time.

We have, with God's help, the power to create for ourselves hearts and lives that are compassionate, noble, and true. We have the power to shape our future by shaping our present.

God has given us incredible power for good. Let us not waste it! Let us use it well this day and always!

Let Me Come to Your House Today

Luke 19:1-10

Here's a good question for you: How many bureaucrats does it take to change a light bulb? The answer is two, one to assure us that everything possible is being done, while the other screws the light bulb into the water faucet.

If you think about it, that's not a bad summary of many people's lives – perhaps our own lives: Assuring ourselves that everything possible is being done, and then screwing the light bulb into the water faucet. Certainly that is an apt description of Zacchaeus, the central player in Sunday's Gospel. Zacchaeus was one of the richest men in Israel. He held the position of chief tax collector, he moved in the highest circles, he was powerful, and he was also a crook.

Zacchaeus had always thought of himself as a model of success, but suddenly, at the height of his career, it dawned on him that his life wasn't working, that there was something missing at the core: There was no joy, just emptiness. And intuitively he understood that there would be no joy as long as he continued on the same course. He knew he had to change. So when he heard that Jesus was passing through town, he acted decisively. He abandoned all caution and all the considerable dignity of his position, and shinnied up that sycamore tree. He had to be sure to see and hear this holy man who just might be able to tell him how to find the joy he was missing.

The rest is history: Jesus looked into his eyes and said, "Let me come to your house today." He did, and Zacchaeus' life was forever changed. The story has a happy ending, but the seeds of that happy ending were sown much earlier when Zacchaeus recognized his emptiness, named it to himself, and decided to do something about it.

For every one of us there are parts of life that don't work, that are lifeless and yield no joy. For many of us that hasn't changed for many years, perhaps decades. The reason is that we're still hoping to get light out of a bulb screwed into a faucet, still looking for joy where it is not to be found.

If, in these failed parts of our lives, we can speak the hard truth as Zacchaeus showed us how to speak it, we will at that very moment hear the words that Jesus has been speaking to us all along, the words we've been drowning out with our self-deceptive assurances that everything's just fine. We'll hear him say, "I want to come to your house this day. I want live with you and not ever leave you."

We'll hear those words of Jesus at last, and at last the healing and transformation and joy will begin.

Will You Be Ready When the Future Comes?

Mark 12:38-44

There was a mother mouse who was scurrying across the kitchen floor with her brood of six little mice in tow. All of a sudden she came eyeball-to-eyeball with a very large and very mean looking cat. The mother mouse was terrified! But she pulled herself up to full height, squared her shoulders, and roared at the top of her lungs, "Bow wow!"

The cat nearly jumped out of his skin, and in the blink of an eye was scrambling up a tree two blocks away. Meanwhile, the mother mouse gathered her little ones around her and explained, "Now, my dears, you see what I've always told you about the importance of learning a second language!"

Sooner or later we all come face to face with our own version of that monster cat – face to face with an event or circumstance that tells us that our world and life as we have known it has come to an end. The ugly possibilities are endless: an irreversible illness, death of a spouse or child, rejection by our loved ones, abandonment by our friends, total loss of our fortune, utter failure in our life's work, the final triumph of all our enemies.

That's just the short list but the possibilities are endless and we've all had a taste of them. We all know what the Gospel means when it talks about the sun being darkened and the stars falling out of the sky. We know!

So it's of more than passing interest to discover how we are to survive when, inevitably, those moments do come. The Gospel gives us the key: "When all these things happen," it says, "you will see the Son of Man coming with great power and glory." That means that when our personal world falls apart and the bottom drops out of our lives, we'll be able to see past the ugliness and see through

the pain to the ultimate reality of things – which is: despite all appearances, God is still in charge, still cares, still has the power to make all things right, and still intends to do just that – in good time!

Now what is it that enables us to see all that so clearly when disaster has struck so hard? Faith! Only faith! Not some eleventh-hour grasping at straws, but a deeply ingrained habit of the heart that we've built a piece at a time over many years.

So what have our hearts been saying all these years? I hope something like this, "Lord, I know from living that you love me even more than I love myself. So, Lord, I entrust myself to you, and no matter what comes, I won't be afraid." If that is what our hearts have been saying – if that is the habit of our hearts – we have nothing to fear from the future because we're ready for it on the inside.

God never promised to insulate us from pain or sadness. But he does guarantee that, whatever comes, we will not be destroyed so long as we stay connected to him. Whatever comes, he will see us through and we will, in the end, prevail, so long as we stay connected to him.

So now is the time to speak our word of faith deeply from the heart. Now is the time to entrust our whole selves to him and never, ever look back.

And when at last the lights grow dim and our world fades away, we shall see him coming in power and glory! We shall see him face to face!

He Has Given His Word and He Won't Take It Back

John 18:33-37

I suspect that none of us has ever actually been invited to a coronation in Westminster Abbey. But we've all seen the film of Elizabeth's coronation there and we've marvelled at the majestic pageant: the monarch, vested in cloth of gold, wearing a sword encrusted with diamonds; receiving gold rings and bracelets dripping with rubies and sapphires; then the golden orb and the scepter – one for each hand. And finally, the crown, studded with price-less gems, placed on her head to the sound of trumpet and organ as she is seated on her royal throne.

We've all seen the pictures and been dazzled by the trappings of wealth and power. But very likely we've missed the core of the ceremony, a simple, symbolic act, which has its roots in the old testament, in King David's time. The king is anointed with holy oil – head, heart and hands – and by that symbolic act, he is bonded and wedded to his people – head, heart and hands – for the rest of his life, bonded to them as protector, defender and guide.

For Israel, and later for England, things never worked out quite that nicely in actual practice – the kings always got caught up in their wealth and power. But it was that idea of a king's absolute bondedness to his people that led Jesus to call himself a king – but a king like no other, for his commitment to us is total, irrevocable, and com-plete. It has no limits and no escape clause. It doesn't depend on our good behavior.

Jesus says very simply, "You are my people. And I'll stand by you and be for you always, even on your very worst days."

He holds nothing back from us – ever!

In giving us this undying pledge, Jesus, our Lord and our King, is also giving us a model. He is showing us how to live with one another, how to stick with and be for one another even when the journey gets very hard. He knows from his own experience how tired and discouraged we can get. He knows how strong the temptation can be to give up and walk away from one another and from our own special mission. He knows!

But he also knows where our final joy is to be found, and that is not in turning away from one another, not in turning away from challenge or even pain. He knows that our final joy will be found in standing firm with one another and continuing to carry our gifts to those who need them.

By his whole life Jesus has shown us the way, the only way. So let us walk with him and bring to bear upon every moment our very best – head, heart and hands – and never, ever turn back!

Cycle C

The Present

Luke 21:25-36

I have a little verse for you, just four lines. So listen closely.

> Yesterday is history.
> Tomorrow is a mystery.
> Today is a gift.
> That's why we call it the present!

So what are we going to do with this marvelous present that God keeps giving us? Will we fritter it away? Will we let it slip through our hands? Will we have nothing left when our present is all used up?

Just four weeks from now, on the day after Christmas, as we take down the tree, pack up the ornaments, clean up the mess, and look with incredulous eyes at the mountain of bills, will our hearts feel empty? Will we feel disappointed and somehow betrayed? Will we be wondering what all that shopping and cooking, decorating and dressing up was for?

The answer to all that is not for fate to decide. It's for us. Because what happens to us on December 26 – and how we feel then – hinges on our remembering now what all the shopping, cooking, and decorating are about. And what they're about is building communion!

All the work of Christmas is about renewing the bonds that bind us to one another and to the Lord, reweaving the ties that have been strained or broken, and reaching out with open hearts to build new bonds, new ties.

If we remember that we'll know inside how to handle "The Present" these next four weeks. The gifts we buy will make sense in the larger scheme of things. How we decide to spend these days and how we decide not to spend them will make sense. And so will the way we are hosts, and the way we are guests – reaching out and pulling everyone inside the circle of our care and concern. It will all make sense – if only we remember.

The calm we keep at our center during these busy days will tell all who see us that we know what "Our Present" is about, that we know what matters and what does not. And because of that, we ourselves will be a special gift to those who know us

Today is a gift, and that is why we call it "The Present." May none of us forget that as this wonderful season begins to unfold!

Time to Come in from the Cold and the Dark

Luke 3:1-6

Two little Martians landed on a country road on earth in the middle of a cold, dark night. "Where are we?" asked the one.

"I think we're in a cemetery," said the other. "There's a marker over here. It says . . . this person lived to be 108!"

"Wow! Does it give the person's name?"

The other Martian leaned closer and squinted, "Miles from Omaha."

At times we all feel like those Martians, far away from home, in a cold, dark place, with no familiar landmarks.

Sometimes the dark, unfamiliar place is the inside of our head. And we have the terrible experience of feeling cut off from our own self, a stranger to our self. It's a very lonely feeling.

Sometimes the cold, dark place is all around us as we find ourselves on the outside of love and friendship, wanting to get in but not knowing how. It's a sad and lonely place to be.

Our hearts know how life is supposed to be. There is something inside us, something God put there, that tells us that cold and darkness and being an outsider are not what we were made for.

There is something powerful inside us that tells us we are made to be family, the whole lot of us. Family, where everybody knows our name, where there are no strangers, where every face brightens when they hear the familiar sound of our step, and where we can feel the presence of our Father.

Family. It's what we long for and what we're made for. So why do we get so little of it? Why do we spend so much of our life as outsiders, cut off, in exile in the cold and the dark?

The answer is in Sunday's scripture: within us and between us there are places that are wounded and broken. There are gaping holes and lofty barriers in us and between us, and they keep us in exile, keep us from finding our way home.

So what are we to do? Sunday's scripture, which was written while the Jews were in exile in a distant land, gives the answer: name those sorry, wounded places within us and between us, and don't hold onto them. Name them and give them to the Lord who commanded "that every lofty mountain be made low, that the age-old depths and gorges be filled in, that the crooked places in us be made straight and the rough places in us be made smooth," that we may see the salvation of God, that we may, at last, find our way home.

That is God's promise and fondest desire for us all. So we simply must give all those sorry, wounded places to God, all the dark and empty places. Give them all to God and he will bring us home. God will bring us home!

Don't Forget

Luke 3:10-18

A few weeks before Christmas, a woman who lived in a New York apartment building found a greeting card taped to her door. "Merry Christmas from the custodial staff," it said.

"How nice," she said to herself and promptly forgot about it.

A week later she came home to find another card taped to her door. It was the same message, "Merry Christmas from the custodial staff." But this time, stamped right in the middle in big red letters, were the words, "Second Notice!"

We are all terribly forgetful. None of us is immune. As we immerse ourselves in our daily tasks – as surely we must – we can forget almost anything: birthdays, anniversaries, appointments, our bank balance, our glasses. You name it, we forget it. We make lists so we won't forget and then we forget the list.

But our forgetfulness isn't limited just to the little things. We forget the big things as well: who our real friends are, what really matters in life, who loves us, who needs us, what we were made for. We just forget and forget and forget.

That is why we need to gather here – week after week: to help each other remember who we are, remember what really matters, and remember that we aren't walking this long road alone. We're walking it with the Lord who is right at our side.

And what is this Lord like who walks at our side? Does God walk with us as a critic? a police officer? a judge? or maybe just an impartial observer? In fact the Lord is none of the above.

The Lord walks with us as a partner and mentor who wants to see us succeed and who understands that it's going to take us awhile. Now what more could we ask? How can we not celebrate and rejoice as today's liturgy urges us so insistently? How can we not be confident and hopeful and put all fears behind us. After all, God is with us and for us!

And there's still more. Having God walking with us as partner and mentor gives us the opportunity to be in close conversation hourly. With simple words like, "Well, Lord, what do you think about this?" Or, "Lord, can you help me see this more clearly?" Or simply, "Help, Lord, I can't do this one alone." Those are the kinds of words that partners and friends speak very often.

All of that is what we have come together here to remember. First, remember to rejoice and forget all your fears because God is with us. And second, remember to listen to and talk to God about the real stuff of our lives because God cares more than anyone else . . . and God knows the way home.

Trust the Lord, talk to the Lord, listen to the Lord. God knows the way home, and wants to see us safely all the way there. Thank God for sending us second notices! Thank God, indeed!

The Emptiness Will Be Filled

Luke 1:39-45

There was a terrible shipwreck and only one man survived, cast ashore on a tiny island with nothing but the clothes on his back. For a while he hoped for rescue. But in time he knew he had to make a life there on the island. And that is what he did. He taught himself to fish and hunt, to garden and cook, and he built himself a charming little cottage overlooking the bay. He even carved a tiny flute which he played every night after supper.

One day he hiked to the top of the mountain at the center of the island to see what he could see. As he reached the top, what he saw was a tower of smoke and his little cottage going up in flames.

He ran down the mountain as fast as he could. But it was too late. The cottage was in ashes – and his flute, his garden, his tools, his bow and arrows – everything he'd made with his own hands was gone, all gone!

He wept. He raged. He cursed God. He despaired. And finally, as night came, he collapsed on the sand and fell into a deep sleep.

The next morning he was awakened by sailors who had rowed ashore from a great ship to rescue him. "But," he exclaimed, "how after all this time did you know I was here?"

"Ah," said the captain, "we saw the smoke from your signal fire."

When all seems lost and we can feel our emptiness and feel our aloneness, God has a way of surprising us. If our hearts are open, God has a way of filling us in a way we'd least expect. That's the story of Sunday's gospel. Elizabeth, a childless old woman, and Mary, a peasant girl with no prospects, come together in a tiny country village to share a secret that no one else yet knows: God has not left them empty.

As they meet, God is filling the two of them with new life that will be a joy for all their people and that remains a joy for us today. And so they hug and kiss and cry for joy because they know that God has not forgotten his people or left them empty. And never will.

Jesus is God's living promise never to abandon or forget us, but always to be a lifegiver for us. God can give us life even in the worst and emptiest of times, even when all seems lost if we let go of the inner barriers of despair, anger, and distrust. God can open the doors of a new world for us and fill our emptiness full – just as he did for Mary and Elizabeth. God can do all that if we let him.

So let us pray with confident hearts:

Come, Lord Jesus, come now. Take away our emptiness. Fill us with your presence and make us your own! Amen.

He "Done It" for Love

Luke 2:1-14

It was Christmas Eve and a young mother was busy wrapping the very last packages. She asked her little boy to polish her shoes for next morning's Christmas Mass. And so off he went.

The little fellow was gone quite a while. But when he returned he was beaming as he presented the shiny shoes to his mother.

"What a perfect shoe shine!" she said. And with that she gave him a shiny new quarter for working so hard and doing so well.

The next morning, when she was dressing for church, she found something lodged in the toe of her shoe – something tiny, wrapped in a crumpled piece of paper.

Carefully she opened the tiny package, and inside she found the quarter she'd given her little boy for shining her shoes.

Written on the crumpled paper in his childish scrawl were these words: "Dear Mommy, I done it for love!"

That's why we're here to celebrate on Christmas: because he did it for love! All for love! So what more can we say but "thanks?"

Thank you, Lord Jesus, for becoming our brother! Thank you for taking on all our troubles! Thank you for keeping your promise to be with us and for us all the days of our life! In the quiet of our hearts, we thank you, Lord Jesus, this day and always! Amen.

Bearers of God's Grace

Luke 2:41-52

The French impressionist painter, Claude Monet, is well-known for his delicate painting "Footbridge over Water Lilies." What is less known is that the artist painted over 250 versions of this scene in his idyllic garden at Giverney. He painted the patterns of the changing light on the water at every time of the day, from early dawn to noon to late evening. The effect of changing light dancing on the waters intrigued and challenged Monet.

Once a well-meaning but unknowing visitor said to Monet: "You really ought to change the scene you are painting. It seems you are making no progress." The visitor's untrained eye missed the beauty of the similar yet vastly different canvases. Monet took no offense at the comment, but kindly replied: "Ah, progress. You are right, my hours on end in the hot sun do not move me to progress. But what a progression, minute by minute, the dazzling light makes upon the waters, calling forth from them new beauties at every shimmer and sparkle."

So much for what a world-class painting should be like. Today we are celebrating the Feast of the Holy Family which inevitably brings to the surface all manner of strong feelings about what a family should and should not be like. How wholesome and how realistic our ideas are varies greatly and that alone should impel us to ask if the gospel gives us any clue about how God intended our families to work. In fact it does.

Today's gospel says that after Mary and Joseph found him in the temple, Jesus went home with them, and there he "progressed steadily in wisdom, age, and grace." The key word is "progressed." He got better which means that on any given day he wasn't as good - wasn't as put together - as he would be later. He was less than perfect. He made mistakes like wandering away from his parents and frightening them half to death. And he learned from his mistakes, though not always right away. Just how fast did he learn? The gospel says he progressed "steadily." That is, slowly, a tiny step at a time - no huge leaps. Not an exciting process to watch; and often a wearisome one for parents to wait out!

Furthermore, do you really think that Jesus was the only one in that family who was progressing a small step at a time, and learning from his mistakes? Of course not! Mary and Joseph both had their learner's permits too, and that's all they had, and all that any of us will ever have in this life. Permits to learn by doing, by trial and error, all our life long.

And who grants those learner's permits? For the most part, the family; but not just any family. It has to be one whose love is big enough to look squarely at real faults and sins - and not deny their existence - and at the same time to see under all those faults the heart of a brother or sister, a parent or child or spouse who just isn't done yet, who we know couldn't possibly be done yet.

That's what a real family looks like: all its members unfinished and filled with imperfections, but not denying or covering up; making progress at a snail's pace, but bound together by a willingness to filter everything through understanding hearts. We have a wonderful gift to give to one another, if only we choose to give it. We can be the bearers of God's grace, liberating, encouraging, strengthening, empowering: drawing the best from one another, slowly drawing one another toward God.

Our time together is so limited and it passes so quickly.

Let us live together with understanding hearts so that we may die without regrets.

Our Journey Is Not Yet Finished

Matthew 2:1-12

A man was complaining to a friend about his job. "The stress my boss puts me under is killing me. I have migraines, my blood pressure is through the roof, I can't sleep at night, and I just found out I have an ulcer. If I stay on this job, the only question is whether I'll have a heart attack or a stroke!"

"So why don't you quit?" asked his friend.

"Well, you see," said the man, "we have this terrific health plan."

Making sense out of life and putting its pieces together well is no simple matter. It's a task that is never finished, even for the best and the brightest. No matter how old or wise we become, there is always one more question to be wrestled with, one more door to walk through, one more strange new room to enter and put in order.

Sometimes for awhile we can get away with ignoring the questions and refusing to look inside the new rooms opening before us. But eventually, life catches up with us and reminds us pointedly we are not done yet, we have not seen all that God has to show us, we have not yet become all that God hopes for us.

That is why this Feast of the Epiphany is made especially for us – this feast of three wise men who knew they weren't done yet, wise men who wouldn't settle for only half a life, three very wise men who were willing to travel afar to find the one who could tell them life's ultimate secret, the one who could tell them how to find purpose and peace.

At the end of their journey, they found Jesus who spoke not a word to them, but showed them – there in the stable in his fragile infancy – life's ultimate secret, which is ever so simple: God loves us very much!

Astonished and humbled at what it meant to find God in a manger, those wise men were changed forever on the inside. As the Gospel notes, "They went home by a different route," never to walk the same paths again.

God is speaking to us on this feast of the three kings, reminding us our journey is not yet done, and urging us to listen more closely to the secret he spoke to us by sending Jesus: "I love you very much. If only you'll take inside the love with which I've wrapped you round, your inside will be changed, the eyes with which you see the world will be changed, the face and hands with which you meet the world will be changed. Take my love inside you," God is saying, "and day by day the peace you seek will more and more be yours."

There it is. That is God's silent word to us. What will be our response? A simple one, I hope: "Come in, Lord. Welcome, Lord. Come in!"

You Are My Special Loved One

Luke 3:15-22

A family was spending a happy summer day at the seashore. As the house passed they surfed, built sand castles, played volleyball, and threw the frisbee to the family dog. They hadn't a care in the world.

And then a woman appeared far down the beach, her tangle of gray hair fluttering in the wind, her clothes hanging on her like a bundle of rags, her strange singing just barely audible above the sound of the waves, as she bent down every now and then to pick up God-knows-what from the sand and stuff it into her shopping bag. She was a strange creature, that bag lady, and she was drawing nearer and nearer.

The parents called their little ones back from the water and told them to keep a safe distance – who knows what she might say or do? And then she was upon them. She smiled a wrinkled smile at the children but they only shivered in return. So the lady continued on her way, searching in the sand; and before long she had disappeared from sight.

As they left the beach at the end of the day, the father asked some of the local folk about the "spooky" lady who had intruded on their day.

"Oh, that's Maggie," came the response. "She's a kind old soul. Every morning and afternoon she walks up and down the beach picking up bits of glass and sharp stones and shells so that little children won't cut their feet."

That family had looked into old Maggie's eyes but they hadn't recognized Maggie. All they had seen was a spooky bag lady – a potential threat. And the loss was not only hers but theirs as well.

Like that story, today's gospel is about recognition, but it has a happier ending. Jesus has just come down to the river to be baptised by John. He is listening attentively, as always, to the Spirit of God deep inside his heart and he hears these silently spoken words: "You are my beloved son; on you my favor rests." And with that, Jesus knows at last who he is. And he knows his mission: to help every single human being hear God speaking those very same words in his or her own heart.

Why is there so little peace among us? Why so little joy? Why is so much of life a cold war and sometimes a hot war of us against against them, of all against all? Because we have not recognized one another for who we really are. And who are we? God's very own, special people, whose innards are filled to the brim with the seeds of wonderful gifts that are just waiting to be discovered, valued, nurtured, and brought to flower.

Every time we fail to recognize in ourselves or in our neighbor the face of someone who is very special to God, someone who has a special gift to share, we are planting the seeds of conflict in fertile soil, and we are denying the seeds of peace and joy any soil in which to grow. We are saying, "You are nothing to me; and I am nothing to you; what happens to either of us is of no concern to the other." And that, of course, is a lie, for the Father of us all has tied our futures tightly together and made us family, like it or not.

The making of peace begins not outside, with diplomats, but inside, in the individual human heart, yours and mine. It begins with that moment of self-recognition when we hear and trust the voice of God's Spirit saying softly, "You are my special loved one." For at that moment we begin to value ourselves as great treasures ought to be valued.

But peace only begins there. It won't really happen until we recognize that God has spoken those very same words to everybody else too; and that every person we meet is a hidden treasure waiting to be discovered, valued, nurtured, and brought to flower.

Peace won't really happen till our hearts have grown big enough both to receive the smile of Maggie the bag lady – in whatever disguise she shows up – and to give that smile back with interest.

Only a Full-Time Partnership Will Do

John 2:1-12

There's a Peanuts cartoon which shows Linus listening attentively to his sister Lucy. Now Lucy has a really tough reputation, but it seems that she may have changed.

"I've decided that I should be an evangelist," she says. "You know that kid that sits behind me at school? I convinced him that my religion is better than his religion."

"No kidding!" says Linus. "How'd you do that?"

"Easy," says Lucy. "I hit him with my lunchbox!"

Some things never change! We say that often and with good reason. But Sunday's gospel urges upon us a very different way of thinking. As Jesus takes those jars of ordinary water and transforms them into an extraordinary wine, he's doing more than just a simple kindness for an embarrassed host. He's assuring us that God has the power to transform us, to take the ordinary in us and make it extraordinary.

God has the power and the desire. All that is needed is that we accept God as our full-time partner. You've heard our Protestant friends ask, "Have you accepted Christ as your personal savior?" This is what they are talking about: a serious partnership, with no exclusionary clauses, a partnership that puts everything on the table and is ready to do real business.

There's a long distance between that kind of intense partnership and the cool, arms-length, episodic relationship with God that we settle for so often. And that's a real tragedy because an occasional, arms-length relationship with God yields no growth, no change, and therefore no real satisfaction.

Why? Because it withholds so much, hides so much, and puts so much of life off limits that God can't even get close to the parts of us that need him most. In a word, keeping God at arm's length is a sure recipe for slowly rusting in oblivion, a sure recipe for sadness.

Jesus' miracle at Cana says, "Don't settle for rusting away or for the sadness and despair that go with it. Don't settle for what you call survival but that is not survival at all!

We are called to be extraordinary, each in our own way. And with God as our full-time partner, extraordinary is what we will become, slowly, one step at a time, in a partnership that will last for all eternity!

Building Blocks for God's Kingdom

Luke 1:1-4,4:14-21

There's an old story that makes its way around ecclesiastical circles from time to time. It seems that someone in the Vatican got word that the Second Coming of Christ was about to happen. Within minutes, of course, everyone in the Vatican had heard the rumor and the corridors and offices were crackling with tension and panic. Finally, one of the most senior cardinals knocked veryw quietly and very respectfully on the door of the pope's private apartment.

"Your Holiness," he said breathlessly, "we have reason to believe that the Second Coming of Christ is about to happen. What shall we do?"

The Holy Father looked up from his papers and said, "Look busy!"

Busy is what we are from day to day with the ordinary business of life. We have our regular routines and established patterns for just about everything. We read the same sections of the newspaper in the same order day after day. We come to mass at the same time, park in the same place, and sit in the same pew week after week.

We buy the same toothpaste and toast the same kind of bread month after month. We play cards and walk the golf course with the same friends at the same time on the same day of the week year after year. We eat the same menu from the same dishes every Christmas decade after decade.

No doubt about it, almost the whole of life is a series of habitual routines large and small that are rarely interrupted by anything more drastic than the newspaper's coming late or some "stranger" sitting in "our place" at the five o'clock mass!

Our habits and routines are like old shoes, comfortable and comforting. They get our daily business done – if not the easy or the best way – at least without a lot of thought or stress. And they give us a sense of stability and at-homeness which is quite a comfort when the world feels too big and too much for us.

But there's another side to our habitual routines that's not so pretty, and that is their power to blind us, to hold us hostage, to make us very poor on the inside. Our routines have the power to trap us inside tiny ideas and even tinier hopes, the power to persuade us that this is all there is, and that life is very small and very narrow indeed.

Over time, our routines and the endless cycle of everyday tasks that have to be done can persuade us that the best we can hope for is a life of quiet desperation.

That is why we need to hear what Jesus is saying to us in Sunday's Gospel: "I have come to give sight to the blind," he says, "to set captives free, and to bring good news to all who are poor – whatever the shape of their poverty may be."

Jesus is reminding us that our lives are meant to be very large inside. He's telling us that if we are being true to the gifts God has entrusted to us, every one of our moments has purpose – large purpose. Every one of those ordinary tasks that have to be done again and again is a building block for God's kingdom, a building block for eternity – if our eyes are open, if our hearts are open, and if we're being true to the gifts God has entrusted us to carry.

So let that be our prayer: Open our eyes, Lord, that we may see the immense value of each day. Open our hearts that we may give our best to each person and each task. And, in your good time, Lord, let us rejoice in the completion of the kingdom that you and we have been building together, one moment at a time. Amen.

Break Out into the Bigness of Life

Luke 4:21-30

A county truck pulled to a stop on a quiet street. A workman armed with pick and shovel climbed out and set to work. Laboriously he dug a large hole between the curb and the sidewalk. Then a second man exited the truck, filled in the hole, and tamped down the earth. And that was their pattern all the way down the street, the one carefully digging holes to just the right depth, the other filling them in and tamping them down to just the right height.

"What in the world are you doing?" asked a woman who had been watching them.

"We're part of an urban beautification project," was their reply.

"Beautification!" sniffed the woman. "I fail to see what's so beautiful about a row of filled-in holes."

"Well, you see," said the worker, "the man who plants the trees is out sick today."

God is very big and wants our lives to be big and full too. That's why we are made "in God's own image and likeness." But breaking out into the bigness of life is no easy task. So many things stand in the way: so many dumb ideas that we cling to for dear life, so many fears that we cherish as if they were best friends, so many crazy patterns of acting that make no more sense than digging holes and filling them up again.

God knows all this about us, and becoming one of us not only tells us but shows us how to break free of whatever is trapping us into tiny, cramped little lives. We want that so much. We want to be free and to enjoy a big, full life. But so often, just when we seem at the very edge of that breakthrough, our fears intervene and we pull back.

That is what we see happening in Sunday's gospel. The villagers' first reaction to hearing Jesus is delight. But then fear takes over, shuts down their delight, and chokes their momentary hope for a better, bigger life. Their fear of change is so great, in fact, that it rouses up a mighty, self-defensive anger within them. And those villagers drive this good man Jesus – and all his hopes for them – out of town and to the very edge of a cliff. The price of a bigger life was just too much for them.

The price of a big, full, whole life in the pattern of Jesus is always high and always the same: laying aside old fears and old habits, knocking down old walls and unlocking old rooms, stretching, reaching out, and becoming new on the inside.

That's a lot for a mere human to do. But we won't be doing it alone. The Lord Jesus, who has invited us to a bigger life and has shown us the path to it, will walk with us all the way to the end of the road.

All God's Creatures Are Straining to Tell You

Luke 5:1-11

A secretary was sitting at her desk one morning, when a co-worker came running into the office, all out of breath. "You won't believe this," he says. "I was almost killed a minute ago. I had just walked out of the deli, where I buy my egg sandwich every morning. A police car with its siren and lights on was chasing a car down the street.

"The police rammed the other car, then everybody jumped out and started shooting. And I was right in the line of fire! I could hear the bullets whizzing overhead. Windows were shattering, cars were careening onto the sidewalk, and everybody was running for cover. Let me tell you, I'm lucky to be alive!"

The secretary was quiet for a moment and then she replied. "So," she said, "you eat an egg sandwich every morning?"

She missed the whole point, and that qualifies her very nicely as one of us. Because missing the point, not seeing and not getting at the core of life is a problem we have every day.

As life tugs and pulls us in a variety of directions hourly, we forget what really matters; we bring only a part of our best selves to most moments; we are blind to the loveliest things around us and tone-deaf to what could make our souls sing.

At the bottom of it all is our failure to see what the whole of creation – every single piece of it – is straining to show us, and that is the awesome presence of God, who is the ground of our being, the ground from which we spring anew at each moment.

That is what Sunday's gospel is about: Learning to see and to recognize what has been here all along. Peter and his partners had looked for fish all night and had found none. Their nets were empty. So Jesus shows them where to look and how to look, and within minutes their nets are full to bursting.

Awed by the sudden, massive catch of fish where before there seemed to be nothing, Peter gets the point: This isn't about fish at all. It's about how vast, how awesome, and how close God is.

Peter sees through the details of the event, through those masses of fish, and gets the point: He is in the presence of God, God who was always there, God whom he'd hardly noticed before, God whose presence, if seen, can give every moment light and make every day a blessing.

The whole of creation is straining to show us what Peter saw that day. Look at the sunrise, the cool rain, my hand, your heartbeat, that flower, this sleeping infant, the vastness of space. They are all whispering the same message, the message of their maker: "I am good and beautiful and powerful beyond all understanding," whispers the Lord through creation, "and yet I am here, beside you and within you, sustaining you, and offering you light and life, joy and peace now." So speaks the Lord through creation.

Listen closely to creation, and you will hear the Lord. Look closely at what he has made and you will see his reflection. Take him in and walk with him, and his light and life, joy and peace will be yours this day. That is his promise!

Is Your Head AWOL?

Luke 6:17-26

There's a legend about a wise old dog who saw a young puppy chasing its tail. "Why are you chasing your tail?" he asked. The puppy answered with great seriousness, "I have studied philosophy and I have solved the problems of the universe which no dog has ever solved before. I have learned that the best thing for a dog is happiness and that happiness is in my tail. Therefore, I am chasing it and when I catch it I shall have happiness."

"My son," said the old dog, "I too have judged that happiness is a fine thing for a dog and that happiness is in my tail. But I have noticed that when I chase it, it keeps running away from me. But when I go about my business it follows me everywhere."

A wise old dog; a good bit wiser than most of us!

There is a restlessness in us that keeps us perpetually distracted, searching, and groping for something more. There's an empty place within us that cries out to be filled full, and in the course of time we try filling it with all manner of things. How often we are only half present to people or events, how often only our bodies are there because our heads have already moved on in the endless search for something more. How ironic that as we dash on in search of an undefined "something" that we fear we are missing, we end up missing the heart of life.

Sometimes with an old strategy or a new one we succeed in taking the edge off our hunger for awhile, but always the emptiness returns and with it disappointment, and our weary search resumes. Try as we may, nothing is ever big enough or good enough to fill us full.

All this might seem a curse, but in fact it is a blessing. For it is nothing less than God calling us from the inside, telling us over and over that the only thing that can ever fill us full is deep and abiding friendship with him and with his people. Nothing else will do.

Our vocation, our life's work, is to befriend one another into wholeness, to help build up good people and good bridges to connect them. It isn't easy or fast work but it's the work we were made for. And if we give it our full attention and our whole hearts, our bondedness with the Lord will grow, our hearts will fill up, and happiness will follow – as surely as a tail follows a dog!

The ancient Romans had a saying that was a kind of recipe for happy living. *Age quod agis,* they said. "Do what you are doing – with all your might." They were right!

So let us do the noble work that God has given us. Let us do it with all our heart, all our mind, and all our strength. And the immense happiness for which we were made will be ours.

Make Lemons into Lemonade

Luke 6:27-38

There was an old homesteader who had lived through the wildest days of the old West. He had seen herds of buffalo roaming the plains, and Indian warriors too, and he had panned for gold in California. And now he lay dying. His priest asked him, "Have you forgiven all your enemies?"

"Haven't got any enemies," he replied.

"Remarkable," said the priest. "But how did a red-blooded, two-fisted old fellow like you go through life without any enemies?"

"Easy," said the man. "I shot 'em!"

Sometimes we'd like to shoot 'em, and sometimes we have with our own special brands of ammunition: words, looks, checkbooks, and oh so much more. When we are hurt we know how to strike back, how to hit our target and make it hurt.

We are experts at getting even. There's just one problem: getting even won't get us where we want to go, where we want to live, and that is in family, in communion. The taste of revenge may be sweet but the aftertaste is bitter and it just won't stop. It can spoil an afternoon, kill a marriage, and ruin a continent.

So what's the alternative? What does Jesus suggest we do when someone has done us wrong? Roll over and play dead? No! Let the world trample on us? Definitely not!

"Use your imagination," he says, "and think big. If what you want out of life is peace and communion, then figure out what you can do to change your enemies into friends. Don't kill them, convert them."

Look at the examples he gives: turn the other cheek, give your shirt as well as your coat, walk the second mile. Those aren't rules. They're examples of strategies for shaming a person into taking a second look at his behavior, seeing its ugliness, and then changing.

Helping someone change isn't easy. It takes imagination and persistence. And in the end there are no guarantees. Some people have no reservoir of shame or good will for us to tap into; some aren't ready to even think about changing. But how can we be sure about that unless we try? How can we declare people our enemies for life or for the weekend, before we have given our best effort to bringing them around and making them friends?

There's another aspect to all this that we mustn't forget: we owe our forgiveness and our help to those who have wronged us because, even at this moment, that is what God is giving us: forgiveness and help.

God doesn't stop walking with us when we make a mistake, or erase our names from the palm of his hand when we sin. God sticks with us and gives us the support we need to get back on track, and in return asks only this: that we do the same for one another as generously as it is done for us.

And the payoff? The payoff comes a little piece at a time, but it is what we want most: family, communion, and peace. That is God's promise!

The Patterns Don't Lie

Luke 6:39-45

There was a conscientious young priest who wanted to be a really good preacher. So he asked a parishioner to listen to his homily each week and give him feedback. After mass the first Sunday the parishioner came to the sacristy and offered his judgment. "Warm," he said. "Warm!"

Now the priest was a people person so he liked this evaluation of his sermon very much.

The next week, the evaluation was exactly the same: "Warm," said the parishioner. "Warm!" Once again the priest was delighted. And so the pattern continued across many months.

Eventually the young priest began to get a little nervous. "Am I missing something here?" he asked himself. So he went to the dictionary and looked up the definition of "warm," which is, "Not too hot"!

Poor fellow! He heard what he wanted to hear all those months, which is easy enough to do – as we all know. And that is why Sunday's gospel is made for us. Jesus is asking us, "Do you know who you are on the inside?"

Our first impulse is to say, "Of course I know. How could I not know after all this time." But if we've learned anything from life, our answer will be more careful: "I know something of myself, but there's much of myself that I haven't seen yet, much I need to see."

"Ah," the Lord will say then, "that means we can do business. I can help you see if you are ready to look." And then he tells us how to look. "Look past your words, your wishes and your good intentions, and check out your deeds," he says.

There are always clear, identifiable patterns in our choices and in our deeds. And those patterns paint a very clear picture of what we're really like on the inside. Only very rarely does one of our deeds fall outside our established patterns. So, as

Jesus says, the fruit we bear does tell very reliably who we are.

And why is it so important to know who we are on the inside? Because we can't get better till we see where our trouble is. We can't get well till we see where our sickness is. We can't make our deeds match our words till we see where they don't match. Fine words and good intentions can set up quite a smoke screen and can fool the best of us. How often have we said, "I'm just fine," and meant it, and been dead wrong?

The Lord is asking us to take the time now to look closely at the real patterns in our life and not be distracted or beguiled by the surface noise of our talk, our wishes, and our busyness. He wants us to have lives that are big and satisfying. Coming to terms with our real selves – and leaving our imaginary selves behind – is the first step toward that big life.

Thank God, we don't have to do this work alone. Thank God, never alone!

Don't Betray Your Gifts

Luke 24:1-13

I have a riddle for you. What did Catherine the Great, Attila the Hun, and Pope Pius the Twelfth have in common? Answer: They all had the same middle name: "the"!

They had something else in common, something more important, which we all have too: They had what they needed.

To each of us is entrusted at birth a special and unique array of gifts. And with those gifts comes the power to construct a good and happy life. However, because our gifts – no matter how great – are limited, we are always ready victims for that lying inner voice that says, "What you have is not enough, not nearly enough to make a happy life."

That was the voice that Jesus heard during those long days alone in the desert. The lying voice that told him it wasn't enough for him to heal people's hearts, wasn't enough just to feed and forgive them, wasn't enough just to change people by loving them. That was the voice that whispered to Jesus from the inside, "If you really want to be happy, Jesus, If you really want to be big, you've got to be a showman and change rocks into bread; you've got to have "sizzle"; you've got to grab for the power."

It was an illusion and a lie, but that little voice had power because it tapped into the very core of what made Jesus special, and it proposed nothing less than to steal away the very heart of him. Imagine the tragedy for us all if Jesus had listened to that voice and betrayed the gifts that God was sending us through him! Imagine!

We are no strangers to that lying inner voice. To each of us it speaks quite often, "What you have is not enough for a happy life." It speaks in words subtly crafted to tap into the very gifts that make each of us special, the very gifts that make each of us powerful in our own way – just as with Jesus.

How ironic that we so often betray what is best in us and misdirect what is most powerful in us, thinking all the while that we are building something that is better and happier and more alive. How ironic that our greatest flaws are always distortions of our greatest gifts.

God has surely blessed us all with many gifts and for each of us those gifts truly are enough. If we are faithful to our gifts and let God's hand guide us, that inner liar who will always be with us will have no power to steal the heart of us, no power to trick us into betraying or wasting our gifts, no power to make us small where we are called by our gifts to be very, very large.

So let us give thanks for our gifts, and with God's good guidance, let us together build lives that are very large indeed!

He Is Bigger Than Any Sadness!

Luke 9:28-36

A man was crawling through the desert on his hands and knees, desperate for a drink of water. He came upon a person selling neckties. "Would you like to buy a nice necktie?" asked the salesman.

"All I want is a drink of water," croaked the man. The salesman had no water, so the poor fellow crawled on across the sand.

Eventually he came upon a beautiful restaurant. "It must be a mirage," he thought, but as he drew nearer he saw it was real.

With his last ounce of energy, he struggled up to the entrance and asked the doorman. "Please, sir, may I have a drink of water!"

The doorman replied, "Sorry. Gentlemen are not admitted without neckties."

Life is a marvelous gift, but at times it can seem awfully unfair and very hard. At those times – which can stretch on and on – we can all too easily lose heart and lose our way.

Sunday's gospel is about one of those times. Jesus and the apostles are on the road to Jerusalem and he has just told them that he is going to die there. They are crushed and confused and feeling mightily betrayed. Suddenly their life and the last three years with him seem like a huge waste. They make no sense.

Jesus understands this, so he takes them up to the top of the mountain and renews their hearts and their hopes by showing them where he is really headed, and that is to the resurrection. He helps them look through the pain that lies immediately ahead and see his destiny as God's son – resurrection. And it begins to dawn on them, "This is our destiny too."

Of course they want to stay right there on the mountaintop and set up shop with their own little shrines. But the work that will bring Jesus – and them – to the resurrection is not up there. It's down below, on the flat land, down below in Jerusalem. So together they walk down the mountain, pick up the fabric of their lives, and make their way to Jerusalem where they know what awaits them.

To each of us has been assigned the building of one piece of God's kingdom. The work is never fast and rarely easy. Too often it seems impossible and sometimes even pointless. We can lose heart and lose our way, and sometimes we do. But always in even the darkest times, our Lord is there, calling us for just a moment to the mountaintop, showing us yet again where we're headed, to the resurrection, and reassuring us once more we do not walk this rock road alone, we are not building these lives of ours alone.

The Lord is calling out to you this very moment from the top of the mountain. So, as the Gospel says, listen! Trust! And never give up!

The Lord is bigger than any pain! Bigger than any sadness!

The Two Saddest Words Ever Spoken

Luke 13:1-9

There were two friends who were ardent golfers. For years they wondered whether there would be golf in heaven. And they made an agreement that whoever died first would come back with the news.

Eventually one of them did pass on, and lo and behold, not more than a week later she appeared to her friend. "I have good news and bad news," she said. "The good news is there are superb courses heaven. The bad news is you're next on the tee!"

Sunday's gospel story about the fig tree has good news and bad news for us. The good news: God is merciful and forgiving. The bad news: the clock is ticking and our time is limited.

We have a limited amount of time to develop our gifts and carry them to those who need them:

- limited time to become the good husbands and wives our spouses need us to be for them;
- limited time to become the good parents our children need us to be for them;
- limited time to become the good friends so many people need us to be for them;
- limited time to grow into the people God always hoped we would be.

Even lots of time is limited time; and eventually it is no time at all!

Take another look at that shrivelled, fruitless old fig tree. Did that fig become a flop overnight? Not on your life! There were years of day to day neglect, years of no pruning, no watering, and no fertilizing before that final, sad spring when it failed to bear even a single piece of fruit. There was a lot of time, but time ultimately ran out!

Should that frighten us? Indeed it should because it shows exactly how we may be destroying our marriages, our children, our friendships, our very lives – without even noticing it. Not by being monsters, but by simple, day to day neglect, by just not getting around to seeing our gifts, seeing where they are needed, and then carrying them there; wanting to do so and intending to do so but just not getting around to it; and then . . . time's up.

That is frightening but it should also give us hope because it underscores what power we have in the form of the present. For if we can destroy the future by neglecting today, conversely we can save and transform our future by taking hold of this day.

"Too late" is a bitter phrase we have all had to speak; and we cannot change the past. But we need speak those words again, for we have the power with God's help to build a future that is worthy of us.

Our merciful God is giving us the second chance that farmer gave his fig tree, the chance to get our lives right, the chance to bear good fruit and lots of it, and the chance to be done with regret.

Let us not waste this second chance. Let us put our hands to the good work God has given us and never turn back!

What Is God Like?

Luke 15:1-3,11-32

Deep in the feuding backwaters of Appalachia, a feller was walkin' along when a bullet whizzed by. "Is that you, Lester?" he yelled.

"Yes it is," came the reply.

"Well, what in thunder are you shootin' at me for? We ain't got no quarrel."

"That's right," said Lester, reloading his gun. "We ain't."

"So why're you shootin' at me?" he asked again.

"Remember old Zeke Grubble and the feud you had with him?"

"Yes, I do. But old Zeke's dead."

"I know," said Lester, takin' aim again. "I'm his executor."

That's the way with so much of life: the anger and sadness keep rolling on and we keep feeding it. It's all so deadly stupid! That's why we need to hear what Jesus is telling us in today's gospel.

We usually call it the "prodigal son" story but actually it's about a father with two not very likable sons. The younger one wants his father dead so he can inherit right away. But the old fellow is still doing push-ups, so the boy demands his inheritance on the spot, gets it, squanders it, and then comes straggling home, looking and smelling like a pig pen.

And what does father do? He sees the boy from afar because he's been watching and waiting for him all the while. He runs out, embraces him, buffs him up, and throws a party. Not a single wag of the finger, not a single "shame on you." He's just glad the boy is back, and glad there is still time to help him get his life together.

And the other son? You know the type: always plays by the rules, dots the "i's" and crosses the "t's", but no heart, no spirit. (At least his brother was good at a party.) This one's specialty is pouting and hating; and that is what he does with intensity when "Pig Pen" comes home.

And what does father do this time? Once again, no wagging finger, no "shame on you", just an understanding heart that says, "I know what you're feeling, son. You think that maybe I don't appreciate you. But I do, and I want you to be happy, much happier than you are.

"You spend too much time out in the cold and dark of life, too much time on the outside of love. It is time for you to come in. Here now, you take my hand, and we'll go in together."

That is what God is like: compassionate, patient, willing to wait for us, never looking back, always ready to embrace, always reaching out his hand and saying, "Come on in now and don't stay out there in the cold anymore."

That is who God is and that is who God asks us to be for one another: compassionate, patient, willing to wait, never looking back, always ready to embrace, always reaching out our hand and saying, "Come on in now and don't stay out there in the cold anymore."

May God help us to be that for one another always! Amen.

He Sees No Losers

John 8:1-11

A little girl visiting her grandparents was playing with a stack of coins they had given her to use for treats. Three neighborhood rowdies passed by and noticing the coins determined to steal them from the girl. They approached her and began their bullying tactics, demanding she give them the money. Frightened but not out of her wits the girl hit on an idea. "I'll give you the money," she said, "but I have some larger coins in the house. I'll trade you those for the nickels." The boys though the little girl was dumb enough to trade her nickels for what they believed must be quarters, so they agreed. "Hurry up," they said. With that, she picked up the money, calmly climbed the stairs, and went into the house. She ran to her grandfather, crying, and told him the bullies were trying to rob her. Her grandfather wiped her tears and rising to his full stature, went outside. The boys were gone, their plot dissembled.

As they stood out there in the great temple courtyard, what were all those people thinking? What was going on inside their heads as they stood there in the early morning sun?

That mob of angry men. We can almost hear their thoughts: "She's trash! She deserves to die! If we could catch all the ones like her and stone the lot of them, our town could be a better place. Trash she is! Why can't she be like us?"

And the girl herself? She's no more than fourteen and already having an affair with a married man. Now, caught in the act and shaking, her sad, bruised, tear-stained face speaks her despair: "They're right," she says to herself, "I am trash and that's all I'll ever be. Maybe it's just as well they caught me, and this ugly life of mine will soon be over . . . over forever."

So there seems to be a consensus out there in the early morning sun: "She's a loser and her life is a dead end." But not quite a consensus, because there is a dissenter. His name is Jesus. And as he looks from face to face, he sees no losers, just ordinary confused people, the accused and the accusers, all blind, all mired in sad and hurtful lives.

He sees no losers and no dead ends! Instead, he sees an opportunity and he seizes it. "This can be a turning point," he says to himself, "a fresh start for every one of them, adulteress and mob alike."

And that is what he helps to happen. Ever so quietly and with condemnations for no one, he helps them to look within and see the truth about themselves and yet not despair. He helps them hope, as he hopes for them, and see the possibility of change, the possibility of a new life.

In holding out his hand to all of them so very long ago, Jesus is reaching out to us as well, inviting us to look within and see the truth about ourselves and yet not despair, but hope and change and live.

He is inviting us to let go of fear, let go of whatever is choking or shrinking the life that is trying to grow within us. He is inviting us to step out of the darkness and into the light, and he is making that possible by walking with us every step of the way. He never asks us to do the hard things alone.

His voice is clear. His invitation is from God. So let us take heart, put the dead ends behind us, and speak our "yes" to him! Let us accept the hand he holds out to us and walk with him into a new life!

All Will Be Well

We have just heard the story of the last hours of Jesus Christ, the best friend we ever had. As we listened to the reading of the Passion, we followed him, step by step, in our hearts through his last hours. And now, having heard Jesus speak those last, dreadful words, "It is finished," and watching his head drop upon his breast for the last time, we have to make sense of it all.

What does it mean, this good, kind, loving young man, the kindest man we ever met – barely in his thirties – dying in so ghastly a way, for no crime at all. What does it mean and what is it for?

What it means is that God loves us so much that he will withhold from us absolutely nothing – not even his own dear son. What it means is that no matter what, God will always be there for us, with ALL his love and power, comfort and grace.

There ARE no limits to his commitment to us, none at all. That's what God our very dear Father is saying to us through this terrible moment in Jesus' life. He's saying, "You can count on me. I'll never desert you, and there's nothing I won't give you, not even my son."

This Passion Sunday is, in one way, a very sad day: Walking with Jesus on this day can break your heart. But it's also the brightest of days, because it tells how very much we are loved, and because it reminds us who view it from the vantage point of the resurrection that, despite all appearances, ALL WILL BE WELL!

So let us rejoice, because, thanks be to our good God, ALL WILL BE WELL!

You Can Trust That Quiet Whisper

John 20:1-9

Two caterpillars were clinging to a leaf on a tall maple tree when a beautiful butterfly floated by. It was the first time either of them had ever seen a butterfly. The one caterpillar was awestruck by its beauty and grace. "How exciting it must be to have wings and to be able to soar like that!"

But the other did not share this enthusiasm. "Listen," the cautious one said, "there's no way in creation you're ever going to get me up in one of those things!"

There's a dark little voice deep inside us all that speaks words very much like that, "I'm a caterpillar and that's all there is for me – none of this soaring in the heavens. I'll inch along my assigned leaf for awhile and then one day some bird will get me, or I'll just fall dead onto the ground."

There is much in life that confirms that dark little voice: our fondest hopes get dashed, our best ideas come to nothing, our best things wear out and fall apart. We get sick and grow old, and fall apart and die. It seems that dark voice must just be right. But there's another voice within us that says, "Not so. There's more."

All our lives, at least when we've been paying attention, every one of us has heard a quiet whisper inside saying, "You are special! And you are destined for something more than dying." That inner whisper is always so quiet, so hard to put a finger on, that very often we hardly notice it or don't dare trust it.

But Jesus, when he came among us, talked to us about that inner whisper and told us we can trust it because it is God who is whispering to us and telling us that we are very dear children. Those are awfully comforting words! But can we trust them? Talk is so cheap.

The reason we really have something to celebrate this Easter morning is that Jesus did more than just talk. He acted and gave us a sign we can count on: his own dying and being buried, and rising from the dead as guarantee that his words to us and those quiet whispers in our heart can be trusted.

That is the message of Easter and of Jesus' resurrection: God didn't make us for pain and suffering, for sadness and dying, but for life, for exciting, eternal life in the divine embrace.

On this Easter morning, let us trust at last in this Good News that has always been there in our hearts. Let us trust in it, and rejoice in it, and be very, very glad!

Do I Add or Subtract?

John 20:19-31

As Jesus walked through that locked door and stood in the center of the upper room, can you imagine the thoughts that were churning around in the apostles' heads: Is this really Jesus? Maybe it's just a ghost? How did he get in here? Dear God, it really is Jesus! I'm so glad he's back.

Those are the first thoughts and feelings. Then some second thoughts take hold. The apostles start remembering, one by one, the last time they saw Jesus, or more correctly, the last time he saw them. Because they were looking the other way, running like crazy out of the Garden of Olives. The last thing Jesus saw of them was their backs. For Peter the memories are even worse, memories of a rooster crowing, and of seeing Jesus turn and just look at him in sad silence.

So now Jesus is back in the same room just inches away. And the apostles' heads are bursting with anxiety: What's he thinking? What's he going to say to me? He must hate me! What's he going to do? I wish I were back in Galilee! Get me out of here!

Jesus interrupts all those terrified and guilty thoughts with a single word that resolves everything. "Peace," he says. One at a time, he looks into the eyes of each of them and says, "Peace be with you." No scolding, no lectures, no finger-wagging, no judgments, nothing. He just wipes it all away. He forgives and he forgets. What a relief! It was the last thing they expected.

Before they can even catch their breath, Jesus spells out their life work: "I am sending you to do for others what I have done for you. I am sending you to become forgivers and healers of hearts." And he warns them, "If you fail to forgive, fail to offer healing, many will remain wounded, with hearts unhealed and imprisoned in their sinfulness."

With those few words Jesus defined for all time what it means to be a Christian in the real world, where the "rubber meets the road." If at any moment we wonder where we stand as followers of Jesus, he has given us the only measure we need, a few simple questions:

- Do I bring healing to people's hearts? By loving and accepting them, do I help them to come to terms with themselves and one another?
- Am I reconciling people and helping them to value one another more deeply, and so forgive one another more generously?
- Are the texture and fabric of my family and my community richer and fuller because of the graciousness of my ways?
- Do I add or subtract? Multiply or divide?
- Am I a builder? Is this moment and this place more because I am here?

None of us can give an honest "yes" to all those questions all the time. All of us falter and stumble. All of us need the Lord's healing, and the forgiveness of our brothers and sisters over and over again. But there's a blessing in disguise even in that. For as life teaches us how constant is our own need for second chances, our spirit slowly softens, and we come to know inside that we cannot withhold from others that same help and that same healing that we need for survival.

God has put the kingdom in our hands and has given us the power of forgiving and healing – the only power that can bring the kingdom to completion.

May God grant that our every breath and our every action speak to all the healing word that Jesus spoke so many times to his apostles and speaks to us each day: "Peace. Peace be with you all."

Are You Fishing Where There Are No Fish?

John 21:1-14

Two cowpokes bought a couple of horses which they rode happily all summer. But when winter came they found it cost too much to board them. So they turned the horses out into the countryside where there was plenty to eat.

"How'll we tell yours from mine when we come to get them in spring?" asked the one.

"Easy," said the other. "We'll cut the mane off mine and the tail off yours." And so they did.

When spring came and they went out to find their horses, they were dismayed to discover the mane and the tail had grown back. "Now what are we going to do?" asked the one, much perplexed.

Slowly and quite hesitantly the other proposed a solution, "Why don't you just take the black one and I'll take the white one."

It's easy to miss what is right under our noses. And when we do, there is always a price to pay whether it be frustration or disappointment, weariness or just plain sadness.

We get a good picture of that in Sunday's gospel. The apostles have labored all night and have caught nothing. They have worked hard and done their best but their nets are empty and so are they. Tired, hungry, and cranky, they are ready to give up.

The problem is they have been fishing where there aren't any fish, which is a sure guarantee of failure. So Jesus calls out to them and tells them where the fish are, over there on the other side. They shift their gaze and lower their nets. And you know the rest: instant and amazing success.

Like the apostles, we are no strangers to disappointment and sadness because all too often we try to "fish where there are no fish." We try to find contentment and peace where they are not to be found. Sadness and unease inevitably follow. But that is not a punishment from God. No, our weary disappointment is a gift from God. It is the Lord, calling us from the shore and telling us where the "fish" are, telling us where our hearts' desire is to be found.

So pay attention and listen carefully when that special kind of sadness strikes. Hear the quiet voice of our Lord whispering through your heaviness of heart. "I want you to be happy always," God says, "even when you face the hard things of life. And happy is what you'll be if you give your heart to what really matters. If you give your heart to me and to the brothers and sisters I've given you, I'll fill your heart full and you will know my joy now and always."

That is God's promise! And he always keeps his word!

That Bond That Makes All the Difference

John 10:27-30

A new supersonic jet was on its first flight and shortly after takeoff the captain came on the loudspeaker. "Those of you on the right side may notice that one of the engines is shaking rather badly, but not to worry, we have three more fine engines and we're cruising at 50,000 feet.

"You may also notice that the adjacent engine is glowing, or more precisely, one could say it's burning. But not to worry, we're at 40,000 feet.

"Now those of you on the left may have noticed that one of the engines fell off about ten minutes ago. But not to worry, we're cruising nicely at 30,000 feet.

"Some of you may also have noticed that a fairly large crack has opened up in the aisle and you can see the beautiful Pacific below. If you look very closely you'll see a small lifeboat that has been thrown from this plane. Once again let me urge you not to worry, because your captain will be on that boat monitoring this flight to the very end!"

So much for cheery words! The fact is that bad things do happen – to good people – all the time, sometimes very bad things: war, cancer, betrayal, car bombs. So what about this "Good Shepherd" talk we just heard in the gospel? Just wishful thinking? Not to worry???

Good question! Our answer is lurking in what was common knowledge in Jesus' time, namely, that shepherds and their sheep knew each other well and were bonded closely. And when the shepherd called, the sheep heard a familiar voice they knew they could trust, so they went with it and didn't hang back.

So that is what Jesus is telling us: the key to life is the bond of trust that helps us hear his voice from the inside, no matter what is going on outside; the bond of trust that helps us hear all he is saying to us – be it words of comfort, congratulations, or challenge.

The key to a happy life is the bond of trust that tells us it's safe to believe and to act on what he tells us because experience has taught us that he loves us even more than we love ourselves. That bond of trust gives us the confidence and the energy to overcome our natural and legitimate fears of all sorts, and gives us the hope and the energy to take the risks we have to take if we are to become our best selves and build God's kingdom.

Jesus, our Good Shepherd, does not promise to insulate us or immunize us from pain or disaster. Lightning does strike good people and the efforts of some of the nicest people on earth sometimes come to naught. Bad things do happen.

But for those who are truly connected to the Lord, who hear his voice deep on the inside, no trouble however great can bring them down; no sadness however great can destroy them or take away their deeply rooted joy.

"Stay connected to me," Jesus is saying, "and hear my voice inside you. And I will give you the power to build great things within you and around you.

"I will give you the power to laugh always, even in the face of death."

Too Late

John 13:31-35

I have a truly sad Mother's Day story for you today. Not so long ago I was called to the cemetery to officiate at the burial of a woman who had no parish and no priest. She was very old – 97 – and had been active to the end. But when the hour for the service came, there was only one mourner, her 75-year-old son.

"Tell me about your mother," I asked. "She must have been a positive, energetic woman to have lived so long entirely on her own."

"Not so," he said, shaking his head. "She was difficult. She had no idea how to love. She was never cruel to me; she was just nothing to me. And now she is gone."

And so he wept for what might have been, could have been, should have been. He wept and spoke softly to himself the saddest words in the language, "Too late."

Too late. May none of us ever have to speak those words. But how can we avoid it? There's only one sure path and Jesus laid it out for us in Sunday's gospel: "Love one another as I have loved you." A simple formula for a life without regret. And yet we misunderstand it all the time. We keep confusing the cheap imitations with the real thing. Infatuation, sentimental tears, the teenage crush, passion, that warm and cozy feeling – all very nice, but they're not love.

To love is to give a piece of one's heart and not take it back. Love sticks around on the good days and the bad ones. It does what needs to be done and never holds back. Love's work is done in tiny pieces and can be done even by the smallest of us.

Love has its bad days when its heart is cold and there are few cheery thoughts to warm it. But even then, love does not falter, and does not take back that piece of the heart that it gave away. Love's work is never done, but its yield is never ending.

True love will never have to speak the words, "Too late."

Long ago Jesus our brother gave his whole heart to us once and for all. May he help us to give our hearts to one another and never take them back. Amen.

Peace Is His Gift

John 14:23-29

I have a sad story for you, but deep down it isn't really sad at all. Recently one of our oldest and dearest parishioners passed away. She was spirited all her life and that hadn't changed at age 88. But she knew her day was drawing near. After mass just two Sundays ago she told me with great simplicity, "I'm failing, Father, and I don't think I can come out anymore."

She had been sick before, but somehow she knew that now it was time, so she relaxed, let go, and accepted it with peace. Wednesday mid-afternoon she received Holy Communion, whispered her prayers, and smiled her smile, and then precisely at 6 pm she breathed her last and went home.

Such peace! Such a wonderful ending. "I want to end like that," I said to myself. And then a voice inside me whispered back, "If you want to end in peace, you have to live in peace." That is something that no amount of securities or security gates, guards or alarms can give. Because they are all on the outside and what we long for is on the inside.

To live in peace is to be able at any moment to look in the mirror and not turn away. But what mere mortal can do that? "You can," Jesus says, because "peace is my gift to you, my free gift to you."

Jesus' gift is, in fact, his very own self and he won't take his gift back. No matter what we do he lives right here within us. And every day he gives us the chance to see the world and ourselves through his eyes – the chance to get things really straight in our head and heart – if we'll look through his eyes.

From inside, he helps us see what matters and what does not. From inside, he helps us let go of our fears and grievances, failures, and regrets.

From inside, he fills our hearts with thankfulness for all the good that is. He helps us see how and where our gifts are needed, and helps us say "yes".

From inside, he helps us look in the mirror and not turn away – not because we have become perfect, but because he has taught us that we are loved and forgiven, and that we have no need to run away or hide from anything anymore, not even from what we see in the mirror. With him dwelling within us we can do and be what is needed, and we know it.

That is the gift of peace that Jesus is offering us now, the gift of himself as mentor and friend, brother and guide.

May you receive his gift within you and life in his peace always. And when that day comes, may you give your spirit to him in the peace you have already known through many days. Amen.

Conscious Solidarity Is the Answer

John 17:20-26

There was a sea otter who sought an audience with the king. "My lord," he said, "you love justice and rule fairly. You have established peace among all the animals. But, sire, your peace has been broken!"

"Who has broken the peace!?" roared the king.

"The weasel," cried the otter. "I dove into the water to hunt for food for my children, leaving them in the care of the weasel. And while I was gone, my children were killed. I demand justice."

The king summoned the weasel. "Alas, my lord," wept the weasel, "I am responsible for the death of the otter's children, but it was an accident. I heard the woodpecker sound the danger alarm, and I rushed out to defend our homeland. In doing so I trampled the otter's children by accident."

The king summoned the woodpecker. "Is it true that you sounded the alarm with your mighty beak?"

"It is true, my lord. I sounded the alarm when I spied the scorpion sharpening his dagger."

The scorpion was next to be interrogated. "Do you realize that sharpening your dagger is an act of war?"

"Yes, I do, my lord," replied the scorpion, "but I didn't even think of preparing my weapon till I saw the lobster waving his sword."

At this the lobster interrupted, "Sire, I only began waving my sword when I saw the otter swimming toward my children, planning to snatch them for food as he does every year."

And so the questioning had come full circle, and the king turned back to the otter who was demanding justice. "It is you, not the weasel, who are to blame for the death of your children. Whoever sows death will surely reap it."

There are lots of things we want, so many things we'd love to have, but when we look into our heart of hearts, and tell ourselves the truth, there is really only one thing we long for, and that is communion – being deeply at peace and at one with everyone. That is what we're made for. It's the purpose of our life: deep, satisfying, bonded communion with one another and the Lord. Indeed, as Jesus gathered his apostles for their last meal with him, that was his final prayer for us – that we all would be one.

So why is there so little peace and harmony, so little true communion in our daily lives, and in our society? Why instead is there so much isolation, disharmony, and conflict, so much hurting and getting hurt, even within our own homes? I think today's story suggests the answer. Remember that indignant otter, who wanted someone punished for the killing of his children? He'd been killing the lobster's children for as long as he could remember. His daddy had taught him how, and he'd just never thought much about it. His thoughts had never gone beyond the otter family. In the end, of course, his thoughtless habit of violence caught up with him, and his own children were killed – caught in the crossfire. But even then he wanted to blame the tragedy on someone else, and was shocked when the king said he was the real killer of his own children.

So much of the time, we're like that otter, blandly content with ourselves, and indignant about the misconduct of others, but rarely conscious of how our own lifestyles and how the patterns of our own daily choices are killing our own chances and the chances of our society for communion, for peace, and for the at-oneness that is our destiny. We sow bad seed, we reap death, and then we are surprised and angry, again and again!

So are we doomed to an eternal cycle of this blind betrayal and disappointment? Not at all. The peace and communion we long for are within our grasp. The formula is simple. Indeed, there's only one ingredient, conscious solidarity: the habit of recognizing each human being as a brother or sister, and then making choices and setting a lifestyle that fit being a brother or sister.

Conscious solidarity. That's the magical insight that Jesus came to share with us, the insight that made him willing to endure the cross. That's the magical insight that will bring us communion and the only joy we really want or need. May God grant us the light to recognize we are brothers, and the wisdom to take our delight in building up one another.

Let Yourself Be Set on Fire!

John 20:19-23

Three men were walking along a beach when they came upon a lamp buried in the sand. They picked it up and rubbed it, and out popped a genie, straight from central casting. Now this genie had been around for a long time, so he had his lines down pat. "I'll grant each of you one wish," he said. The first man wrinkled his forehead in deep thought and then spoke his wish, "I wish I were ten times smarter."

The genie tapped him on the forehead and then announced, "You are now ten times smarter."

The second man thought even more deeply before naming his wish. "I wish I were a hundred times smarter."

The genie tapped him on the forehead and intoned, "You are now a hundred times smarter."

The third man, who really liked to think big, spoke his wish with gusto, "I wish I were a thousand times smarter!"

The genie tapped him on the forehead and announced in the most solemn tone, "You are now a woman!"

For a long time before Pentecost the apostles had been wishing that they were a lot smarter. Especially after the crucifixion, their own inadequacies were painfully clear to them. Even the miracle of the resurrection didn't change that. And Jesus' final disappearance when he ascended to heaven only made it worse. In those months if anyone wanted to find the apostles, they knew where to look – in the upper room, where the door was always locked and the windows shut, and the conversations were all variations on "if only . . . ," "I can't . . . ," and "He never taught us how to . . . ."

Then, suddenly on Pentecost, all that changed. That ragtag band of frightened little men became heroes and fearless liberators who would carry the Good News to the ends of the earth. What made the difference? The traditional answer is that the Holy Spirit descended upon them. But that is only half

right. It was the Holy Spirit that made the difference, but the Spirit did not "descend" or "arrive" on Pentecost as if by some pre-arranged schedule. The Spirit of God had always been there inside each one of them, from the moment they drew their first breath.

So what did happen? Where was the change? The change was in them. At long last they stopped holding back, stopped measuring out their commitment to the Lord in small doses. They stopped counting and calculating and just gave the Lord their whole selves. They lowered their guard and let themselves be touched in the deepest, most secret spaces of their hearts. And finally the Spirit could fill them up and transform them. And the church was born!

To some degree, we are in the same spot as those apostles were before Pentecost. The Spirit of God is within us – and has been within us since we drew our first breath, but in many ways, we haven't let ourselves be touched by that Spirit. We have entrusted mere fragments of our hearts to the Spirit. And so, many of the great works and great loves God has in mind for us have not happened.

This Feast of Pentecost is an invitation to rouse ourselves, and catch fire, and choose something more than an anemic little life. It is an invitation to invest and entrust our whole selves into the hands of the Spirit. The payoff will be huge and surprising, but the payoff will come only to those who invest all without hesitation, once and for all. There's an old saying: you cannot cross over a great chasm in two steps! Only a single great leap will do.

So let us pray for one another:

May God grant us the heart to leap across the great chasm of our fears and to let ourselves be set on fire. May we entrust our all to the Holy Spirit who has dwelt within us since first we drew breath. Amen.

Relax in the Lord

John 16;12-15

A few years ago a pack of wild dogs broke into the Omaha Zoo in the middle of the night. The area they invaded was inhabited by wallabies. And the next morning, when the zoo keepers made their rounds, they found all 23 wallabies were dead.

Upon closer inspection the keepers learned that none of the dogs had actually gotten into the wallaby cages. Not one dog had laid a paw or a jaw on a single victim. The wallabies were all dead from internal injuries suffered when their panic at seeing the dogs sent them crashing about wildly, bashing into the fences and one another.

Literally scared to death, fifteen adults and eight baby wallabies, dead of fear.

Fear, anxiety, anger, and doubt play far too large a role in all our lives, and sometimes they kill us. That is why this Feast of the Trinity is made for us. It's an antidote to the poison of our unhealthy fears, angers, and doubts. It's an invitation to relax in the Lord who is infinitely bigger than any problem or need of ours can ever be.

Relax in the Lord.

Relax and look at the stars in the vast, night sky and see there a reflection of the mighty God who made them.

Relax and look at the tiny fingers of a newborn child and see there a reflection of the tender God who made every child ever born.

Relax and look at the goodness of so many people around you and see there a reflection of the good God who made them.

Relax and look at the loveliness of a single flower and see in it a reflection of the gracious God who made every flower that ever blossomed.

Relax and look at all the goodness within your own heart and see there a reflection of the wonderful God who made you.

Relax in the Lord and know on the inside how vast is his goodness and how unfailing is his kindness. That vast goodness and kindness of God is more than just a comfort for us. It's also an invitation for us to grow very large on the inside, an invitation to grow into the very image and likeness of God.

That is God's invitation to us all every day: to grow very large on the inside, to lay aside all pretension, all fear and worry, anger and doubt, and to grow into God's image.

It's a wonderful prospect: to be like God. How could we settle for anything less?

Life Is Messy

Luke 9:11-17

A young man was strolling along when he stumbled on a magic lamp. In a flash a genie popped out and offered the usual three wishes. "Ah," said the young man, "first I wish for a Ferrari sports car. And second, I wish for $50 million."

Then, because he was a cautious fellow, he decided to think very carefully lest he waste his third and final wish. Driving along in his new sports car, he was pondering his options when, absentmindedly he began to sing along with a radio commercial, "Oh, I wish I were an Oscar Mayer wiener. . . ."

There's a fundamental messiness to life and it rarely moves forward in a straight line. Try as we may to "do our homework" and keep things tidy and in order, even the best of us do a fair amount of stumbling about. Even the best of us get caught off guard and laid low by our folly, our sinfulness, or simple bad luck:

- We study for hours – the wrong chapter.
- We drive carefully with seatbelts and someone drops a brick from the overpass.
- We arrive precisely on time – for last week's wedding.
- We expend a fortune on our kids' education. He becomes a surfer in Tahiti. She becomes Fidel Castro's live-in girlfriend.
- We build the house of our dreams and then wonder what we were thinking of.
- We succeed spectacularly in all our endeavors and then can't figure what all the striving was about.

Life is a wonderful gift. No doubt about it. But at times it can be very confusing and can leave us weary and exhausted beyond all telling. That's why this Feast of the Body and Blood of Christ is so good for us.

Our Lord knows how tired and confused we can get and how lonely and hungry our hearts can feel. He has always understood that about us. And so he gives us himself – all of himself – to be our food and to fill up our emptiness. He gave us his own body and blood to make us strong and healthy for this long journey that we're on.

The eucharist we share today is Jesus' silent promise for all our life long: "I'll always be there for you. No matter what happens, no matter what you think or do, I'll always be there, and I'll never leave you orphans."

That is God's promise: his own body and blood, food for us pilgrims, medicine for us sick people. He is enough for us now and always. Amen.

Don't Answer Too Fast

Luke 7:36-50

There's a fascinating tale written by H.G. Wells, about a bishop, a prosperous, elegant, white-maned old gentleman who could always be counted on for a pious platitude. The bishop had a favorite answer that always served him well when troubled or angry people came to his door. He'd assume his most pious pose, and speak in his best stained-glass voice, and ask, "Have you prayed about it, my child?" If spoken in just the right way, it silenced his questioner, and he was home free!

Now the bishop himself didn't pray much. After all, his life was quiet and uneventful, and he felt himself quite in charge of things. But one day the roof fell in, and he found himself, for the first time he could remember, quite overwhelmed. It occurred to the bishop that perhaps he ought to take his own advice and pray. So late on Saturday evening, he entered the cathedral, walked down the center aisle, genuflected and knelt in the first pew. He folded his hands, and couldn't help thinking to himself how wonderfully childlike and prayerful he must look. Then he began to pray, "O God, look down upon thy humble servant, bring me healing in this hour of my need. . . ."

Suddenly there was a voice, strong and firm, "Yes, my son, what do you wish?"

When the cathedral parishioners arrived for the early mass the next morning, they found their bishop still in that first pew, with an incredible look of surprise on his face, stone cold dead of shock! The bishop had said the words – prayed for healing – all his life, but he'd never really expected or even wanted an answer.

Sunday's Gospel is about healing: Our need for it, and Jesus' power to make it happen. The Gospel says that Jesus cured the sick and healed those who were possessed by demons. Now when the Jews used that term, "possessed by demons," they weren't talking about people being tormented by little red fellows with horns and pitchforks. They were talking about people whose spirits were troubled, people who were out of control on the inside. So Jesus was healing people whose bodies were sick and whose spirits were sick and wounded too.

There's a very practical question here: What do we have to do for *our* spirits to get healed? The answer is that we have to start by admitting our need for healing, admitting we're not whole, not finished, and that there are missing and broken parts in us. Well, that seems easy enough. Don't we admit that all the time? "I'm only human" we say. But that's a cheap admission, because it really has no content and thus no real value, except as an escape hatch. What we have to admit to are the ugly specifics of our woundedness: Our own special jealousy, or hatred, or cruelty, or treachery, or whatever. Our wounds are not pretty, but they must be named, by us, if they are to be healed.

But even that isn't enough, for there's yet another admission we have to make: Try as I may, I cannot heal myself. I cannot do it alone. If I doubt that, I need only take a look at my track record.

So is that it? Am I stuck where I am, wounded and unfinished? Our faith offers an answer, and it's a resounding "no". There is no wound too vast or too deep to be healed by our God, if we ask. And there's the rub, for as often as not our asking isn't asking at all.

Remember the prayer of St Augustine in his wild, wild youth: "Lord, make me chaste and pure, but not yet." Our asking has to be confident, but more than that, it has to be honest, single-minded, and without ambivalence. It has to be committed and determined to receive and take inside the healing grace the Lord will surely send. How often is our asking like that?

Every time we gather at mass, every time we say the Our Father, and lots of other times as well, we pray for God's healing of our inner wounds, and we do all this year after year. Do we in fact really want an answer to our prayer? Or are we like that pious old bishop who'd grown comfortable in his sinfulness?

If we do want an answer, if we do want healing, our course is clear. We need to:
- admit to our wound and name it,
- acknowledge that we are helpless on our own,
- ask for help with confidence, and
- show that our asking is true asking by preparing to receive the grasp that will heal us and raise us up.

We all need God's healing and God desires to give it. Only one question remains: Have we made ourselves ready to receive it?

Don't answer too fast!

Think Big, The Way He Does!

Luke 9:18-24

A traveler was stopped by an airport customs officer and was asked if he had anything to declare. "Not a thing," he answered.

"Are you sure?" asked the officer.

"Absolutely!"

"Well, what about that elephant standing behind you with a slice of bread in each ear?"

"Sir," said the traveler indignantly, "what I put in my sandwiches is my own business!"

That fellow knew how to think big! And that is what Jesus is urging us to do. But he says it in a way that requires some close listening. "Deny yourselves," he says. "Take up your cross each day and follow me."

Somehow that doesn't sound like a recipe for a big, happy life – unless you're really into suffering! But it's Jesus speaking, so let's see if we can make sense of it.

If you want to be happy, Jesus says, "Take up your cross." Now as everyone in Jesus' day understood, "cross" means simply "the true work of the day," which is the opposite of busy work or just hanging around.

And how do we know what the true work of the day is? Our gifts tell us, our circumstances tell us. And the Spirit speaks the word directly to our hearts. If we are listening, we will know each day what our true work is, and our joy will come from doing it.

If you want to be happy, Jesus says, "take up your cross." Don't run away from your life's work or from the true work of the day. Run toward it. Engage it. Give your whole self to it – as Jesus did.

Living that way has its price, of course, and sometimes, as with Jesus, the price is very high. But the spirit to whom we've given the direction of our life will give us what we need as we need it. The alternative, running away from our life's work and

betraying our gifts, will in the end bring only pain upon pain. That is no alternative at all!

If you want to be happy, Jesus says, "deny yourself," that is, forget yourself. Stop being the pawn of your own fragile ego.

Listen to the self-centered fears the ego uses to betray us: Do I look terrible? Am I too fat? Too old? Too dumb? Will they hate me? Will I fall on my face? Will someone else get all the credit? Will the cost be too great? Will it hurt too much? Will I win? Lose? How can I be sure?

Ego's self-absorbed fears lock us up inside ourselves and cut us off from the true work of our life, cut us off from happiness.

That is what Jesus is trying to help us see: "If you give in to fear and try to save your life by clinging to every piece of it tightly, you'll just lose it all."

Jesus' advice is, relax in the Lord. Forget yourself and your fears. Hand over your life to the Holy Spirit inside you. And then, with the freedom and energy that only the Spirit can give, spend your life – every last drop of it – spend your life on the good work our Father has given you. Happiness will follow as surely as day follows night.

Happiness will follow.

Put Your Hand to the Plow and Don't Look Back

John 9:51-62

A little rabbit was being chased around the neighborhood by a very big, very vicious dog. A crowd gathered to watch, and they cheered heartily as the rabbit dodged and weaved, cleverly evading the dog time and again.

As the minutes passed the rabbit held his lead, but he was tiring fast and he knew it. So he pulled up short in front of the cheering crowd and said with utmost courtesy, "I'm most grateful for your kind expressions of encouragement and support, but please, couldn't someone lasso that dog!"

Talk is cheap. It may be encouraging, as the rabbit noted, but it doesn't save lives and it doesn't make a life. Like the wind, talk passes by and then is gone without a trace.

The founders of our country knew that as they signed their names to the Declaration of Independence more than 200 years ago. Of itself their declaration was just talk. But behind the talk was commitment: their lives, their fortunes, and their sacred honor.

For seven long years they struggled, a third-world backwater against a superpower. Many of them lost all they had, many were wounded, many were killed. Till the very end they seemed destined to lose. And many were the days when even the great men like George Washington himself sank deep in depression. But they never took their hand from the plow, they never turned back. And in the end they prevailed.

Their model and ours is Jesus himself, who long ago showed us what faithful commitment looks like. It looks like that, the cross. And it says to us in deeds infinitely more powerful than words, "There's nothing I won't do for you. There's no limit to my commitment to you!"

What a comfort! But it's also a challenge to be more than mere spectators sitting on the sidelines of life. By his faithful commitment to us, Jesus is showing us the only way to live a real life, the only way to be happy: by committing ourselves totally, faithfully, and irrevocably to the noble work God has given us, and never turning back.

"Take those gifts our Father gave you," Jesus says, "and use them, all of them, generously. Commit your heart and your gifts to the noble work our Father has given specially to you. Put your hand to the plow and never turn back!

Be faithful and our Father who is faithful will give you life, life in abundance, now and evermore."

That is God's promise and God's challenge.

Make It Bloom!

Luke 10:1-9

Farmer Jones was working in his field of tall corn when his pastor came walking down the lane. "That's a mighty fine field of corn the Lord has given you," said the pastor piously.

"Well," said the farmer, "you should've seen it when the Lord was working it all by himself!"

To each of us is given – for a time – one small piece of this earth which we alone can make to bloom – we alone. Just as Jesus' disciples were assigned their specific towns and villages, we have our assignment in this time and place. And if we falter or run away, our part of God's kingdom will not come to be. God's help is essential, but we must do the deed.

It's no easy task the Lord has given us, and Jesus tells us just that straight out. "I am sending you as lambs in the midst of wolves," he says. Our life experience surely confirms that he knew what he was talking about. So his advice to his disciples as they set out on their journey merits our close attention.

"Travel light," he tells them. "You're going to be walking a long and hard road. So get rid of the excess baggage. Don't bring along anything that can slow you down or prevent you from reaching your destination and finishing the good work God gave you."

So what is this excess baggage that we think we need for our journey? What are we dragging along that is slowing us down or even bringing us to a full stop? Excess baggage comes in many shapes and sizes, and for each of us it's different.

For some it's fear or worry. For some it's ideas that have outlived their time. For some it's an attachment to persons or things that are no good for them. For some it's a heart of stone that weighs them down and stops them cold. The list goes on and on: old hates, old habits, old illusions, old blindness.

But whatever our excess baggage, we cling to it as if we could not make our journey and could not finish our life's work without it. What an irony that we cling to such trash so tightly that we cannot receive the treasures that would drop into our hands if only our hands and hearts were open and free! What an irony!

So there we have it, the Lord's challenge to us this very day. "Unpack your bags and see what you really need for this once-in-a-lifetime journey you're on. See what's slowing you down and wearing you out and keeping you from bringing to completion the good work the Lord has given you."

Get rid of that excess baggage and then get back on the road. The Lord will be with you and will be enough for you.

You *will* finish your journey well. And you *will* make your little piece of the earth bloom!

Is Everyone Inside Your Circle?

Luke 10:25-37

There were two friends who'd known each other since school days and had lived to a ripe old age. Finally they died and went to heaven, where they were astonished at what they saw. Each new street was more fabulous than the last; each mansion was bigger and more grand than the one before. "Isn't this wonderful!" said the one, totally overwhelmed.

"Yes," replied the other, "and to think we could've gotten here ten years sooner, if we hadn't eaten all that oat bran!"

Getting to heaven requires a little more than avoiding oat bran, but the formula is no mystery. As we heard Moses say in today's first reading from a distance of more than 3500 years, the key to heaven and to a happy life is not up in the sky or across the sea. We can find it right here, in communion, in loving God and loving our neighbor.

But how can we be sure whether we're really loving or not? Today's gospel, the Good Samaritan story, spells it out. If we really are loving:

- we'll include everyone inside our circle of concern and neighborliness, and leave no one outside;
- we'll be attuned to the needs of every person inside that circle;
- we'll do whatever is necessary.

Some of us may be shocked to find that there's nobody inside our circle of love, not even ourselves. For others, the truth is there's a fair-sized group inside the circle. But for all of us, the truth is that there are more outside our circle of concern than we'd care to count.

Who are these folks that we leave outside? In some cases whole segments of humanity that we've permanently banished to outer darkness, saying "You're not like us; and we have nothing to do with you." That's a terrible lie, but some of us live it.

Even closer to home are many others we may be locking out of our circle, many of whom are not strangers. The way we live and talk to one another within our own homes, the way we drive, the way we conduct ourselves in public places – restaurants, the golf course, and sometimes even in church – often shouts loud and clear, "I don't give a fig about the rest of you. I don't care whether this moment or the next hour of the rest of your life is happy or miserable. My circle of concern stops at the perimeters of my body, at the edges of my family, and at the boundaries of my property. So get lost!"

That sounds very harsh, and it is, but it's what many of our actions are saying every day, and no smoke screen of smiles or sentimental feelings will change that ugly fact.

This is not what we want our lives to say, which is why we gather here week after week. We come to remember that we are brothers and sisters, with no exceptions. We come to remember our own abiding need for the love, support, and help of others, our urgent need to be welcomed as a friend into the circle of our neighbors. With that truth in our hearts, we have a chance of remembering and recognizing how very much everyone else needs to be welcomed into our circle, and how great a blessing we can be to one another by welcoming always and never excluding.

May God bless our remembering and enlarge our hearts greatly to make room within us for all his people!

Are You Busy Elsewhere?

Luke 10:38-42

A husband and wife were sound asleep when they were awakened by strange noises downstairs. Because his wife insisted, the man went down to investigate. Armed with a putter and grumbling all the way, he found a burglar in the dining room emptying the silver chest.

"Stay right where you are," he said to the burglar. "I want to get my wife. She's been expecting you for the last thirty years!"

"Martha, Martha, you are anxious and troubled about many things!"

In Sunday's gospel Jesus is reaching out to the Martha in us. He knows that her complaint about getting no help in the kitchen is fair. But he also knows that is just a side issue. Martha's real problem is the way she's living her life. She seems to be doing all the right things – being responsible, honoring her commitments, doing her duty, striving very hard. Her work is getting done, but there's no joy in it.

Why? Because she has cut herself off from the present. Sometimes she looks backward at the "might've beens" and "should've beens." Sometimes she looks into the future at all the ugly and scary "what ifs." But the one thing she never does is focus peacefully on the present. Her anxieties about the future and her bitterness about "injustices" in the past detach her from the present.

Thus she never gives her whole self to anything because most of her is busy somewhere else, busy worrying, resenting, and mourning. And so she never receives from the person or the task or the moment at hand, the joy it has to give. What a waste!

What's the remedy for Martha and for the Martha part of us? How do we build a happier, calmer, more peaceful life and still get the bills paid, the meals cooked, the investments made, and the lawn mowed on time? We do it exactly the way Jesus did.

First, we decide what's worth doing. Next, we listen to the rhythms of life and get wise about timing. Remember what the Old Testament says? "For everything there is a season, and a time for every matter under heaven. . . . A time to be born, and a time to die. A time to plant and a time to uproot. A time to be silent and a time to speak." (Ecclesiastes 3)

There is a time for everything. So we have to listen to the rhythms of life and discover those right times.

Finally, knowing what matters, and knowing what this specific time is good for, we come to the "bottom line": we invest our whole attention, our whole selves peacefully, calmly, wholeheartedly in this moment as if it were our last – just as Jesus always did.

When Jesus was with someone, it was for him as if no one else in the world existed. No wonder those who accepted his friendship were so profoundly transformed by it. What a gift he gave and still gives! It's a gift we can give.

At the price of one moment at a time, well and peacefully lived, we can have – and we can give to one another – a taste of God's kingdom here and now. And, in God's good time, we can possess the whole of that kingdom together forever.

We can! Surely we will!

It's Time to Stop Working Alone

Luke 11:1-13

A little girl was telling her father how some "bad" boys in the neighborhood had set traps to catch birds.

"What did you do about it?" asked her father.

"I prayer that the traps wouldn't catch any birds," she replied.

"Anything else?" he asked.

"I prayed God would keep the birds out of the traps."

"Anything else?"

"Yes," said the little girl, grinning. "When the boys weren't looking, I went out and kicked those traps to pieces!

That's my kind of girl! Her instincts told her what real praying is about. It's not about talking. It's about changing and making things better. But who is prayer supposed to change? Well if you listen to a lot of our prayers, you might think it was God who was supposed to change and develop a more friendly attitude toward us. But that's just not true.

God already wants the best for us and doesn't need to be talked into anything. God knows what we need and he wants us to have it. God doesn't need to change, but we do – in all kinds of ways.

And that's what prayer is about: changing us, reshaping us, reconfiguring our insides to match God. It's about getting us in sync with God, getting us to stop rowing against the current. Prayer is about becoming like God on the inside, becoming whole and peaceful and happy on the inside.

All that can happen when we open our hearts to God, when we trust enough to be touched in our inner being and reshaped in God's own likeness.

Think of the crabby spouse who's driving you wild, or the whiny teenager, or the nagging parent. Think of your anemic investments or your sickly orange trees. Your prayer isn't going to change any of them – directly. But it can change you and the way you think about them and respond to them. And very often the new way you respond to them can change them too.

Our prayer, if it is true – if it really opens us to God, and realigns us with God, and puts us at God's disposal – our prayer can make things happen, powerfully good things. Because we are no longer living and acting alone. God is living and acting within us.

So isn't it time to stop living alone and working alone most of the time? Isn't it time to stop rowing against the current? Isn't it time to start experiencing life the way life was intended to be? Isn't it time to trust and let God all the way in?

It is time, definitely time! Right now!

Time to Weave a New Story

Luke 12:1-21

An airline pilot was flying high above the clouds with only three passengers aboard – a boy scout, a priest, and an atomic scientist. Somewhere in mid-flight, the plane developed engine trouble. So the pilot rushed back to the passenger compartment and announced, "We're going down! There are four of us, but only three parachutes. I have a wife and nine little children who need me!" And with that he grabbed one of the parachutes and bailed out of the plane.

Then the atomic scientist spoke up. "I'm the smartest man in the world. It would be a tragedy for all humankind if my life were snuffed out!" And with that he grabbed a parachute and bailed out.

With a sad but calm look on his face, the priest spoke to the boy scout. "My son, I have no family. I've had a long and happy life, and I'm ready to meet my Maker. You're still young with your whole life ahead of you. You take the last parachute."

The boy scout shook his head. "Thanks, Father, but that won't be necessary. We're both going to be all right. The smartest man in the world just jumped out of the plane wearing my knapsack!"

He wasn't as smart as he thought! And that's what today's readings are saying to us: we're not as smart as we'd like to think. A lot of what we do, a lot of our decisions and choices make no sense when examined up close. Indeed, a lot of what we do is a matter of simple inertia. And very often we don't even remember how or why we started going in this direction or that.

That poor fellow in the gospel story was very rich, very successful, but Jesus called him a fool because he had only one idea, he knew only one word, M O R E, and he never got beyond that. He was very good at what he did – maybe the best, and he was hard working too – so he got more and more and more. But in the end, more, even lots more, isn't enough.

When at last he came face to face with God, his hands were empty. All the stuff he'd invested his life in and hoarded so diligently, all the stuff that didn't really matter, had been left behind – as it always has to be. And he didn't have anything else! Empty-handed and naked he stood before God. And his emptiness was his own judge. God didn't have to speak a word. At that point, he never does.

Will you and I have to face God with empty hands? There's a quick way to find out. Our own inner moral compass will tell us the truth, if we ask it, and if we haven't already damaged it beyond repair. Here's how. Imagine for a moment that you discover today that you have just a few hours to live. It's too late to change anything, too late to do anything except say "goodbye." You needn't bother packing, because no baggage is allowed. All you'll be taking are your memories and your own heart – whatever you've become on the inside.

What would comfort you and give you peace at that moment? What memories would make you say, "I'm glad I lived; it wasn't a waste. I can't wait to see God and show what I've done with the life I was given"? What would allow you to say all that? It wouldn't be memories of a barn full of stuff, or memories of having built the biggest this, or bought the best that, or become the most powerful whatever. Only one kind of memory will warm and comfort you in the end: memories of having made life better and fuller and more fair and more beautiful for many people.

Are those the kinds of memories that fill your heart as you look within today? I hope so. But if the fabric of our memories seems thin and shabby, and if we find we've mistaken a stuffed knapsack for a parachute, maybe – just maybe – there's still time to build new memories, time to fashion a new heart. Perhaps there's time to weave a new story which one day we can tell with delight to our very dear Father.

God has been waiting to hear from our very own lips how we have spent this wonderful gift of life.

Trustees, Not Owners

Luke 12:32-48

A Texas oilman marched into the office of the local college president and announced, "I'd like to donate $10 million but there's a condition: I want an honorary doctorate for my horse."

"Your horse?" stammered the president.

"Yes, good ole Betsy has carried me faithfully for many years, and I think a doctorate is the least I can do for her."

"But we can't give a degree to a horse."

"Sorry," said the oilman. "No degree, no check!"

Within hours the board of trustees was locked in emergency session, and each member in turn roundly condemned the idea as an absolute disgrace. But finally, the oldest trustee spoke. "Take the money," she said. "It's about time we gave a doctorate to a whole horse."

That was a wise trustee! And that's what Sunday's gospel challenges us to be, wise trustees. Unfortunately, there are some obstacles to that. First of all, most of us think of ourselves as owners, not trustees. We talk about "my car, my house, my hair, my memory, my health," as if we owned all those things free and clear. But we don't own them, as life keeps reminding us.

Just take this homily time that we're sharing. This time surely seems like our own. We can look around as we please and listen or not listen as we please. But before you know it this homily time and this whole day will be gone forever. Entrusted to our care for a little while on a short-term loan, it will be gone almost before we notice. And all that remain will be our memories and a tiny difference in our heart: We'll be just a little more or just a little less.

The whole of life is like that. All we have, all that we are – even our bodies and our very breath – all are loans to us, gifts entrusted to our care for awhile simply because the Giver of All Good Gifts cannot even imagine not sharing with us.

And what does the Giver of All Good Gifts ask in return? Simply that we be good trustees . . . and not pretend to be owners. God asks that

- we see and name each one of our gifts with wonder and delight and thankfulness.
- we reverence all our gifts, and cherish them, and handle them with care.
- we share our gifts as generously and as freely as God shares them with us. "What you have received as a gift, give as a gift." (It's a matter of simple justice! But it's also the only way of living that fills the heart.)

Jesus speaks clearly about what it means to be good trustees: "When much has been given," he says, "much will be expected. More will be asked of those to whom more is entrusted."

Extraordinary gifts have been entrusted to our care, much more than most human beings ever dream of. The Giver of All Good Gifts has every reason to expect much from us, for we have been filled us with every good thing.

See God's gifts to you, and name them with thankfulness. Use God's gifts to you, and handle them with care. Share God's gifts to you, and they will be yours forever.

Don't Settle for a Cover-Up!

Luke 1:1-4,4:14-2112:49-53

A man came into a bar trying to sell his dog for $10.

"Get outta here," said the bartender.

But then the dog spoke up. "Please, sir, this man is mean to me; he never takes me for walks; he never feeds me, he coops me up for days . . ."

"Hey," said the bartender, "This dog can talk. Why're you selling him?"

The owner replied, "Because I'm sick and tired of all his lies."

Our lies are what today's shocking gospel is about. Our lies to ourselves. When Jesus says, "I have come for division, not peace," he's not giving up on love and forgiveness, and he's certainly not advocating holy wars or killing commies for Jesus! He's telling us that very often what we call peace is not that at all. Very often what we call peace is just a cover-up, a lie.

When Jesus speaks so graphically about five against two and two against three, he's not urging us to go out and stir up new troubles or start new battles. He's urging us to face up to the old ones, the old conflicts, the old sinfulness, and the old lack of at oneness that already exist inside us and in our relations with others. He's urging us to deal with those inner and outer conflicts, and not to hide from them or cover them up any more.

If our friendships and marriages, our families and communities are to live up to our high hopes, and if our life's work is to be worthy of us, then we have to let the Lord set us on fire with the energy we call "grace" – which is one part courage and one part love. With that holy fire warming and strengthening our hearts, there is no part of ourselves that we cannot confront; no sin in us that we cannot face; no failure in us that we cannot deal with.

With God's grace warming and strengthening us, there is no person to whom we cannot speak the whole truth because now we can speak it in love. With God's grace, now we can give the truth as a gift, and not use it as a weapon.

As we learn to speak the truth in love – first inside us, and then outside – and as we accept the challenge first of changing ourselves and then of helping others to change, the peace that God desires for us will slowly come to be.

By naming in love what divides us, we will have begun the building of bridges to join us together. We will have begun the building of the peace we long for.

This is not easy. And sometimes it very frighten ing. So let us pray for one another:

May God set us on fire and give us this day the strong, warm hearts of true peacemakers, who are ready to face the truth, and ready to work for change. With grace, may we build God's peace within us and among us! Amen.

He's Teaching. Are You Learning?

Hebrews 12:5-13

A little girl walked into a restauant and sat down at the counter. "What'll ya have?" said the cranky waiter.

"How much is a hot fudge sundae?" asked the girl timidly.

"Fifty cents," he growled.

The little girl pulled out her purse and studied her few coins. "How much is a plain dish of ice cream?" she asked in a tiny voice.

"Thirty-five cents," came the response. "So whatta ya want?"

Again she counted her coins. "I'll have the plain ice cream, please." The waiter took her money, brought the ice cream, and walked away. When he came back, the girl was gone. But there, placed neatly by the side the empty plate, were two nickels and five pennies – enough for a real sundae – his tip!

I wonder if he learned anything from that. . . . Today's epistle says, "Whomever the Lord loves, the Lord disciplines." Terrific! Now for a nice little homily on punishment? No! Discipline isn't about punishment. As its Latin root (*disco/discere*) tells us, it's about teaching. To DI-SCI-pline is to teach. And a DI-SCI-ple is someone who's trying to learn – trying to learn how to put a life together.

Now usually, when we think of putting a life together, we think of young people, who are asking questions like "what am I going to be when I grow up?" But, in fact, it's not just kids that have to work at putting their life together. All of us have to every day, because life is a constant process of inner building. When one phase is done, another has to begin.

So how does God teach and guide us as our inner building proceeds? Usually very quietly but always persistently because most of us are slow learners! God teaches us without using words.

Sometimes through our sadness the Lord may say, "You are squandering my gifts to you," or "You'll never be happy if you won't share the gifts I lent you."

Sometimes through our uneasiness, the Lords may say, "This isn't working, is it!"

And sometimes through our joy the Lord may say, "You got it right! Good for you!"

Always our Lord is there, quietly teaching, probing, showing the way. But are we learning? Sometimes not! Partly because we're not paying attention and partly because we often mistake our own voice for God's voice.

If we want the happy life that God wants for us, we have to learn to listen to what God is trying to teach us. That means being quiet on the inside, turning off the inner chatterbox.

It means putting aside our fears and all those "certitudes" that can distort what we hear from God, or even prevent us from hearing anything at all.

"Whomever the Lord loves, the Lord teaches." Always the Lord teaches, sometimes even through little girls with fifteen-cent tips.

Let us make sure we're listening! Let us make certain we're learning!

He's Given Us All the Tools We Need

Luke 14:7-14

A young college student had spent his entire semester at play, so as he faced the final exam in history, his mind was not cluttered with any facts. The exam was a single essay question: "Discuss in detail the Anglo-American conflict over Newfoundland fishing rights in the early 19th century."

The young man took pen in hand and responded bravely: "Too much has already been written about this conflict from the viewpoint of the English, and likewise too much has been written from the viewpoint of the Americans. Therefore, I shall discuss it from the viewpoint of the fish. . . ."

The ultimate escape – a familiar one to us all – flight from reality to a place where no one can "nail" us with the facts.

When a group of clergy get together, you can be sure they all know exactly what the pope should do about everything right now!

When lots of us get together, you can be sure we know exactly what the president should do about the economy, what the owners of the Padres should do about pitching, and what Mr. Boutros-Boutros Ghalli should do about Bosnia.

We're all "experts" on what's out there, only too glad to pontificate about what is safely beyond our reach because that requires no investment. And better yet, nobody can ever prove us wrong.

But that's not a life – just talking. Real life is right here, within our reach. And attending fully to what is here, investing our selves fully in this time and place is the only sure formula for a happy life.

No one ever did that better than Jesus. No one ever paid closer attention to the present; no one ever used his gifts more thoroughly. No one ever invested himself more fully in the people right in front of him than Jesus did.

As we bid farewell to summer and enter upon a new cycle of life, it is time to ask once again, how are we doing with the gifts that have been lent us? How are we doing in the here and now?

So let us look with open, honest, hopeful hearts. There's more giftedness within us, more opportunity right around us than most of us have ever guessed.

Let us try to see the work that God has assigned us by lending us these specific gifts and putting us in this specific place. And let us get on with building our share of the kingdom here and now. God's given us all the tools we need! You can count on it.

To the End of the Road, Together

Luke 14:25-33

Three young American priests were studying in Rome. And when Labor Day came along they were homesick. "Let's have a barbecue," said one, "just like we do at home."

"But where?" asked another.

"In the Vatican gardens," said the third. "The pope is still on vacation!"

So that's what they did. At the appointed hour, they sneaked their grill into the Vatican gardens, and before long the burgers were sizzling. But just at that moment, who should come along but the pope!

The two fast ones hid in the bushes, but the third had a little talk with the pope who appeared to be blessing the grill!

"Wow!" said the other two when the pope had gone, he blessed our grill!"

"That was no blessing!" said the third. "He was furious and as he was waving his hand he was saying, 'I want you and your grill and your two friends in the bushes out of here.'"

That's the opposite of what Jesus is telling us in today's gospel. He is saying, "Don't go. Stay with me but don't just hang around. Get with the program. And understand, it's going to cost you."

In effect he is saying, "You and I are going to build some great towers together, we're going to defeat some powerful enemies together, but it's going to cost a lot." That's what he's telling us, and life confirms that he's right. Nothing valuable is bought on the cheap.

It costs a lot to be a parent the way Jesus would be a parent. It costs a lot to be a husband or a wife, a banker or just a little kid the way that Jesus would. It costs a lot to be a friend the way Jesus would be a friend. Every great work costs a lot! And it means being like that little Energizer Bunny who just keeps going, and going, and going.

God gives to each of us a great work to do at each stage in our life. Some of us look at it, get frightened and run away. Some of us start with gusto and then fizzle out. Some of us just pretend to run the race, but never really start at all. And some of us grind slowly to a halt in sight of the finish line.

None of us is a stranger to faltering and to missing the most precious parts of life, and our brother Jesus knows that about us. So he's speaking to us all today, whether we're walking briskly, limping along, or just sitting down at the side of the road with our head in our hands.

"Come along, now," he says. "I know how tired and scared and frustrated you can get. Believe me, I know! The road is long, steep, and bumpy, and sometimes just plain boring. But you're not walking it alone. Here, take my hand. We'll walk all the way to the end of the road together."

It Takes Time and a Lot of Mistakes

Luke 15:1-32

A woman was critically ill and the doctor told her, "Only one thing can save you now, a brain transplant. But it's experimental and very costly."

"Money's no object," said the woman. "Can you get a brain?"

"Actually, three are available. The first was from a college professor and it'll cost you $10,000. The second was from a famous rocket scientist; it'll cost $100,000. The third was from a Washington bureaucrat and it goes for a half million dollars."

"Why so much for the bureaucrat's brain," asked the patient.

"Because," said the doctor, "it's never been used!"

A couple of brain transplants might be just the thing for those two sons in the gospel. A pair of hearts might help too. The younger son is an ugly blend of arrogance and stupidity. Imagine! Demanding a fortune he hadn't earned and the squandering it all in a matter of months.

And the older one is no better, a mean-spirited little accountant type who knows the rest of the fortune is his, but resents his brother getting even a party. Neither of them is very likable, yet their father loves them both – which is something of a mystery. What can he possibly see in them?

I suspect that what he sees deep down inside them is a bit of himself, a tiny seed of goodness that can be made to grow large if given enough care. So that father says to himself, "I know that good seed is there, because I put it there. I'm their father. So I'm going to help it grow. And I won't give up on

it if it doesn't grow right away."

That is what God is like. Looking down upon us, God sees tiny implants of goodness just waiting to grow. God sees all the possibilities and all the gifts we have. God knows we've got good "genes." There's no way God will give up on us just because we get in trouble or lose our way.

Knowing how we're made, God knows how long and hard we have to work to learn even the smallest of life's lessons. God knows that about us, just as we know it about our little children.

God looks into our hearts and says, "Don't give up. I've given you a wonderful destiny and all the tools you need to make it come true. But it takes time and a lot of mistakes to build a whole life and to grow into your full goodness.

"It always takes time. I know that, and I'll never give up on you. So now, don't you give up on yourselves. And don't give up on one another. I'll be with you on your way, and I'll see you all the way home."

Divided Hearts Are Sad Hearts

Luke 16:1-13

Imagine for a moment that for some mysterious reason a whole team of CIA people has been assigned to watch you night and day. Without your knowing it, they install secret cameras everywhere and hi-tech bugging devices too. They examine your garbage, track your accounts, and monitor your television. And before long, they know everything, right down to last night's heartburn and whether you put on clean socks this morning.

Finally, they're ready to make their report, ready to answer the CIA's big question: who are you? What are you about? The report starts like this: "Subject is attractive and friendly, appears normal in most regards. Financially secure, fair golfer, good bridge player, slightly overweight, allergic to broccoli.

"But after six weeks close surveillance," the report continues, "we can't figure him out, what makes him tick, what does he really care about. He says, 'Family, country, neighbors, and God.' That's what he says. But he spends most of his prime time on other things: Buying, getting, and having.

"Conclusion: Subject is restless and does not yet have a clear center. A likely candidate for trouble in the future. Should be watched closely."

To some degree or other, a report like that could be written about all of us, all of us good people. Because to some degree all of us have divided hearts, divided perhaps not very equally, between what really matters and what does not.

And because our hearts are divided, we rarely bring our whole self, our best self, to the parts of life that do matter.

This isn't a new problem, peculiar to an affluent society in an age of endless gadgets and unlimited shopping. It's a very old problem which Jesus saw lurking in the eyes of almost everyone he talked to. He saw it in their restlessness and in their under-the-surface sadness.

Listen to what he says to them, and to us: "No servant can serve two masters. He will either hate the one and love the other or be attentive to one and despise the other." The balancing act – living a divided life – can't go on forever because it just hurts too much.

So if we want to be happy, we have to choose the things that have the power to make us happy: loving, sharing, living with a thankful heart, naming our gifts with delight, and then taking delight in carrying them to the people for whom they're intended. If we want to be happy, we have to choose those things and then pursue them with all the vigor, intensity, ingenuity, and single-mindedness of that crooked manager in the gospel. That's what Jesus is saying.

"Choose!" says the Lord, "and then act with everything that's in you. Put your hand to the plow and don't turn back! Choose and don't ever turn back," says the Lord.

Not Intentionally Cruel, Just Asleep

Luke 16:19-31

A father went to tuck his little boy in bed. And the child said his prayers as he did every night: "Now I lay me down to sleep. I pray the Lord my soul to keep. And if I wake before I die . . . Ooops Daddy," said the little boy, "I got it backwards."

"No, son," said the wise father, "you said it just right. My deepest longing for you is that you do wake up before you die."

Some folks never wake up all their life long. They're not bad people, they're just asleep; and when they do finally wake up, they're shocked at what they see. "Where did all this come from?" they ask in dismay.

That's what the rich man asks in today's gospel. "Where did this huge chasm come from between Father Abraham and me?"

"You built it," comes the answer, "a piece at a time across many years."

"Well I certainly don't remember that, but can't you send someone over to help me?" he pleads.

"That is not possible because you built the chasm inside you. It is part of you now and no one can cross it."

We need not wait for eternity to see chasms like that or to watch master chasm builders at work. They are all around us, and some of them are us. Few weeks go by without our watching someone's marriage dying or sadly fading away. Few weeks go by without our watching somebody's kids "crash and burn."

The saddest part of these tragedies is that very few of them had to happen. Most of them were preventable if only someone had awakened and recognized in the mirror the face of a chasm builder – the face of someone who hadn't noticed that her spouse, his friend, or their kids were slowly starving to death on the inside.

Chasm builders are seldom intentionally cruel, nor are they more stupid than the rest of humanity. They just don't notice others' needs because they have eyes only for themselves, for their work, for their hungers, for their sadnesses, their grievances, and their needs.

They don't intend to hurt or kill, to starve or maim. They just do it in their sleep. And who are these sleepers? We are!

Jesus is calling out to us to wake up. Wake up and see one another's inner hungers, sadnesses and needs. Wake up and see the wonderful gifts you are carrying, gifts which just happen to match other people's hungers, sadnesses, and needs.

Wake up and know the joy of being, perhaps for the first time, a real brother, a real sister, a real friend – just like Jesus!

How to Survive the Rollercoaster

Luke 17:5-10

A little boy had been studying the Bible in religion class and he had some questions for his mother. "Is it true that we all come from dust?" he asked.

"Yes," said Mom, "we all come from dust."

"And is it true that when we die we all go back to dust?"

"Why, yes, dear, we all go back to dust."

"Well, Mom, in my bedroom under my bed, I think there's somebody who's either coming or going!"

There's a lot of comings and goings in all our lives, lots of little births and little deaths every day. Ask any first grader, any housewife, any businessperson. Ask your gardener, your doctor, your grandmother. They'll all tell you that life is a gift, but it's also a rollercoaster, an endless succession of highs and lows, laughing and crying, triumphs and tragedies. It's very confusing. And sometimes it can wear us down so far that it feels like we haven't got anything left inside.

So how do we keep going? How do we make something valuable out of the odd assortment of stuff that we find on our doorstep each morning? How do we survive success? And how do we live through the losses and pains that seem beyond endurance?

The answer is that we don't – not if we try to do it alone. What life asks us to do, to be, to give, and to endure is quite impossible – alone. But are we alone? Life at times tries to trick us into thinking so. But our larger experience of life tells us, "That's a lie!"

Listen for a moment to your own breathing . . . and feel your life's blood coursing through your veins. Look at what's right around you, marvelous things, great and small, intricate, complex, and beautiful. And through them all God is whispering, "You're not alone. I'm here and I love you. This life of yours, this place and all the places in your life, and these things that surround you are my gifts to you.

"So trust me – you've seen the evidence all round you – open your inner doors so that I can be your strength and your comfort. Let me have your heart, and I will make you whole. Slowly I will make you whole, and there will be nothing you cannot do, nothing you cannot survive."

That is what God is saying to us through the whole of creation and even through our very bodies. "I've given you good reason to trust me," God whispers. "So won't you trust me now?

And our response? "Yes! Yes, Lord. I do trust you. I entrust my life into your hands. And I know there's nothing we cannot do together, no ocean we cannot cross, no mountain we cannot move – together."

Sharing Gifts Reshapes Hearts

Luke 17:11-19

A famous gangster was on trial for murder. There were twenty eyewitnesses and tons of corroborating evidence. The case was airtight. So the judge almost keeled over when he heard the jury foreman pronounce the verdict, "Not Guilty."

"Not guilty?" croaked the judge. "But how? By what reason?"

"By reason of insanity, your honor."

"Insanity?" growled the judge. "All twelve of you?"

It's hard to keep a constant, firm grip on reality, and sometimes we all lose our grip. Subtle fears that we may not even acknowledge can make us flee to our own little world beyond the clouds where no one can bother us with the truth.

Nowhere is this more visible than in our use of the word "my." *My* house, *my* coin collection, *my* orange trees, *my* life. That's the way we talk. But that's talk from outer space! For the truth is that none of those things – including our life – are really ours.

They're all on loan, given to us a day at a time by a preposterously generous God. We haven't earned them. They're not owed to us. We have no title to them. They are simply gifts, given not because of our goodness but because God is a father who wants the best for his children.

So how can we not be grateful? How can we stop the gratitude from welling up inside us? The answer is we can't if we're letting the facts get through to our brain. We have to give thanks. Our heart insists on it.

But how do we give thanks to a father who already has everything? Pretty words won't do it, and we can't send flowers! All we have are his gifts, and that's our clue. The only thanks God really wants is that we use our gifts well, and share them with one another as generously as God shares them with us.

Thankfulness is ever so much more than just words. It's a whole way of living. It starts with our marveling at the vastness of God's kindness. And it slowly comes to completion with the gradual reshaping of our hearts into the image and likeness of our generous father. We become like God by doing what God does. Sharing gifts reshapes hearts. And hearts like that are ready for heaven.

May God give us thankful hearts, that see our gifts with joy, and share them with delight. And as each day draws to a close, may the Father see ever more clearly his own face reflected in our soul. Amen.

Afternoons of Life

Luke 18:1-8

Alan Bennett, the English playwright who wrote the "The Madness of King George," has a line in his autobiography that needs sharing. He says, "The majority of people perform well in a crisis and when the spotlight is on them; it's on the Sunday afternoons of life, when nobody is looking, that the spirit falters."

Isn't it so! The Sunday afternoons, the et cetera parts of life, those flat places where there's nothing of interest in sight and no visible curves in the road around which something wonderful might be about to appear. The spirit does falter, and whispers of "why bother" and "what's the use" echo in our ear.

Those are the times we have the least heart for praying, but they are the times we most need to pray. Why? Because those are the days we most need to see the world through God's eyes. That is where good prayer always starts, trusting God enough to let go and look through his eyes – the eyes of a wise Father. If we do that and if our hearts are open, we'll begin to see what God sees, and hope as God hopes. We'll begin to want what God wants, and do what God does.

That's what praying in faith does inside us. It slowly reshapes our ideas and our perspectives to match God's, slowly reshapes our values and our expectations of life to match God's.

Ever so slowly praying changes us, and in time it even changes the way we pray. And precisely because real change comes only very gradually, we have to stick with that inner conversation with our Lord, even and especially on the Sunday afternoons of life – which sometimes last all week long!

God has so much to show us and to teach us. We have so much to learn, so many new doors that need to be opened, and so many old ones that need to be closed permanently.

So where do we begin? By telling God our story once again, all the parts of it this time, both the grim and the bright. And then by speaking the words the prophet Samuel spoke in darkest night so long ago, "Speak, Lord. Your servant is listening."

If we are listening from the heart, we will change. Even the most gnarled parts of us will change!

"Speak, Lord. Your servant is listening!"

A Dangerous Mix of Fact and Fiction

Luke 18:9-14

A psychiatrist was telling a friend about his toughest case: "I had this patient who lived in a total fantasy world. He was absolutely convinced that somewhere in South America he had a fabulously rich uncle who would someday leave him a fortune. All day, every day, he just waited and waited for a letter telling him to come down and claim his fortune. He just sat around and waited!"

"Amazing!" said the other doctor, "were you able to help him?"

"It was an eight-year struggle, but with determination, skill, and insight, we made excellent progress – until. . . ."

"Until what?"

"Until the stupid letter arrived!"

Illusions! We all have them, but in most cases there's no letter.

The pharisee in today's gospel gives us a good look at how powerful and how dangerous an illusion can be.

There was a good bit of truth woven into his illusion. It was perfectly true that he was not greedy, crooked, or adulterous. It was also true that he fasted twice a week and gave ten percent of his income to charity. All good stuff! But mixed in with it was a piece of sheer fantasy: "I am not like the rest of men!"

That was sheer fantasy, but it seemed plausible to him because it was mixed in with a lot of truth. And that made it doubly dangerous: not only was the illusion harder to detect, it was thereby harder to escape.

The consequences for the pharisee's life were enormous:

- How could he ever grow and get better if he thought he was already a finished product? -
- How could he ever be forgiven if he was blind to his faults?
- How could he forgive others if he'd never experienced the pain of needing to be forgiven?
- How could he ever be a real friend if he lived on Mt. Olympus?
- And how could God himself ever reach him if he lived in a fantasy fortress where truth was never let in?

The answer to all those questions is he couldn't.

We all have our illusions, all different, but all dangerous mixtures of fact and fiction that lock us up inside our own head and cut us off from life and love, cut us off from growth and from healing.

Behind every illusion stands fear, fear that reality may be too big or too ugly to handle. And indeed it often could be if we were alone. But we're not alone. Our Lord is with us and there is nothing we can't look at, nothing that can't be forgiven, nothing we can't handle together.

So isn't it time to let go of the illusions we've been hiding in, whatever they are? Isn't it time to be free of the fears that hide us from ourselves and choke our life? Indeed it is time. Jesus is holding out his hand, and if you listen closely you can hear him speak your name and say, "Don't be afraid anymore. You don't need to hide anymore. Just step out into the light."

The Good Will Grow

Luke 1:1-4,4:14-21

A young boy was in a very serious accident and his survival was in doubt. After a few days his teacher went to visit him at the hospital and she was horrified at what she saw: his whole body was covered with terrible burns and he was in great pain. She wanted to run out the door, but instead she said, "Tommy, I've come here to teach you about nouns and verbs. That's what we're studying in class now and we don't want you to get behind."

The next afternoon when the teacher returned, the nurse pulled her aside. "What did you do to that boy yesterday?" she asked. The teacher was alarmed but before she could offer any excuses the nurse said, "We've been so worried about him but ever since you were here his whole attitude has changed. It's as if he's decided to live!"

A long time later the boy himself admitted that he had given up but that his teacher's visit had changed that. "After all," he said to himself, "they wouldn't send a teacher to work on nouns and verbs with a dying boy, would they!"

Someone hoped in him and then he began to hope in himself.

That is exactly what Jesus did for Zaccheus in Sunday's gospel. Zaccheus was a fabulously wealthy tax collector who had made his fortune mainly by pushing around poor people who were too powerless to fight back. In many ways he was not a nice man.

And yet when Jesus looked up in that tree, he saw through all the cheating and extortion. Lurking under it he saw a person with a great potential for good, a person who was ready to build a new life. Jesus hoped mightily in that goodness and extended his hand. And Zaccheus began to hope in himself again, and his old life began to fall away.

The power of Jesus' friendship and power of all the goodness hidden inside Zaccheus becomes clear when we see what he does next. He faces up to the consequences of all the evil he has done across so many years, and he decides on the spot to begin making it right: he gives half of his wealth to the poor, and 400% restitution to all the people he cheated! Zaccheus was serious about making a new life, and for the first time in years he was happy.

Life can wear us down, and never more thoroughly than when we look at our mistakes which so easily erase the memory of our goodness. Jesus knows our failings full well. But he also knows all the good that is lurking inside us.

With all the power and enthusiasm of the ultimate best friend, he calls out to us: "Believe in the good our Father implanted in you," he says. "Help it come forth. And just as I hope in you, you must hope in one another. Don't give up on each other. Don't turn away. The good will grow if you help it. The good will grow."

We Stand on Their Shoulders

The top executive of a major corporation was out for a drive with his wife when he pulled into a shabby little gas station with a single pump. The lone attendant filled the tank and checked the oil while the executive went inside to make a phone call. Upon his return he found his wife chatting amiably with the attendant. "Did you know that guy?" he asked his wife as they drove away.

"Oh, quite well," she said. "In fact, we dated seriously in our last year of high school."

"Boy, aren't you lucky I came along," bragged the husband. "If you'd married him, you'd be the wife of gas station attendant instead of the wife of a millionaire."

"No, dear," replied the wife. "If I'd married him, he'd be the millionaire and you'd be the gas station attendant."

As we stand here today, on this Feast of All Saints, we are all standing on the shoulders of generations of splendid, heroic, yet for the most part unnamed and unknown people, anonymous heroes who are the ones who really make the world go round. For each of us, there are specific individuals who have been foundation stones for our lives, rocks upon whose goodness, hopefulness, wisdom and moral strength our own life's work has been grounded.

Think of the heroes in your life, the ones that really made a difference:

- the granny who comforted you when all the world seemed hostile;
- the uncle who played baseball with you when nobody else liked you;
- the priest who said, "Of course God loves you," when all the world thought you were a jerk;

- the teacher who saw what was in you when nobody else saw anything;
- the neighbor who embraced you – when everybody else was keeping their distance – and said, "You're a fine person. You just keep going and don't worry."

Little heroes, all of them, but heroes who helped us survive. Heroes without whom we might not be here today. That's why we have this feast of All Saints! To remember and honor those almost-invisible heroes who gave us life.

So in the quiet of our hearts, let us look yet again upon those dear faces and remember what they were and what they did for us. Let us speak our thanks to them and to our Very Dear Father for giving us such friends. And let us pray to our Father that we may, in our turn, be for those who need as, true saints who give life, joy, and peace, saints who lend our shoulders to those who need to stand on them.

Look at Those Faces

Luke 20:27-38

In traditional Catholic teaching the age of seven has been regarded as the age of reason. So that's the age when children are allowed to receive their first communion. In times past it's also the age when they were deemed to have sufficient understanding to commit a mortal sin and thus lose their immortal soul.

There was a fine little boy named Johnny who had just reached the age of seven. His birthday party was in progress, "Happy Birthday" had just been sung, and he'd blown out all the candles in a single breath.

Up came his older brother with a smile and a pat on the back, "Congratulations on your seventh birthday, Johnny. Now you can go to hell!"

That wouldn't have bothered the Sadducees because they didn't believe in hell – or heaven. In fact, they didn't even believe in the Bible except for the first five books which imposed the temple tax that supported them!

So their question about which of the seven brothers got the wife in heaven wasn't just silly. It was cynical as well; and it also revealed how poor they were on the inside. Their image of God was very small – downright inconsequential. And matching it was a shrunken idea of their own destiny: utter nothingness.

How can smart people end up with such anemic, shrunken hopes of life? By shutting their eyes to what the whole world is showing them and by closing their ears to what their own hearts are telling them.

We come to know God by looking at creation. The scope of creation is vast and beautiful, but God's best works are people. So if you want some hint of what God is like, and if you want an answer to the question, "Is there life after death?" just call to mind the faces of all the good people you've known.

One by one remember how they have struggled to build good lives, to create good families, to be good friends. Remember their love and how hard they try to get life right, even when the best they can do is by trial and error. And remember, even in the midst of their fair share of errors, how much goodness there is in them.

If these are the creatures that have tumbled from God's hands, what must God be like? Immensely, astonishingly wonderful! No doubt. And if that is so, can there be any doubt about their destiny – and ours? Can our immensely good God allow what is good to die? Can God let it burn out like a dying candle?

Our heart tells us the answer: love survives and goodness lives on because God is good beyond belief: every creature tells us so.

Our hearts know that. So listen to your heart and life in hope. You can live in hope because it is the truth!

Dare to Dream Great Dreams

Luke 21:5-19

Some years ago when our liturgy was being changed from Latin to English, a pastor was rehearsing the changes with his people.

"Now," he said, "when I say, 'The Lord be with you,' you all reply, 'And also with you.' Okay, let's try it: The Lord be with you," he said.

"And also with you," they replied.

"Very good."

So Father went back to the sacristy to vest and then came out to begin mass: "In the name of the Father, and of the Son, and of the Holy Spirit. Amen." With that he frowned and tapped the new microphone: "There's something wrong with this microphone!"

To which the people responded on cue: "And also with you."

Eventually life "gets" us all, even the luckiest of us. Our bodies, with their traces of broken bones, missing teeth, and scars large and small, are living records of the direct hits we've taken.

And our wounded spirits have their own stories to tell – stories of failures, tragedies and betrayals, and sometimes just years of silent desperation. Sometimes we get hit so hard or for so long that it feels like "The end": we've got no more to give. We just want to say good-bye and disappear.

Jesus knew that feeling and knew that at times each of us would feel that way. So he speaks to us quite pointedly in today's gospel about the experiences that can feel like the end. He catalogs the terrible things that can happen – plagues, famines, earthquakes, wars, and even betrayal by our own parents and friends. And yet, he says, "Not a hair of your head will be harmed. You will save your lives by patient endurance."

What is he talking about – "not a hair on your head"? These battle scars of ours are real!

Yes, they *are* real. But Jesus is not promising to insulate us from life's troubles: Bad things do happen to good people. He is promising to give us what we need in order to face our trials and to prevail over our troubles, however terrible they may be.

"Don't quit," he's saying to us. "Don't run away, and don't just sit there – that is not patient endurance. Hold to the task and persist to the end. I will give you what you need as you need it and life will never be too much for you – even though you face death."

We live in a complicated, sinful, troubled world, and yet God is inviting us to dream great dreams. He's offering us the joy of seeing the best and truest of our dreams begin to come true here and now. And that is exactly what will happen if we trust him enough to keep going, keep walking with him till our journey is complete.

So let us pray for one another:

"May God support us all the day long
till the shadows lengthen and the evening
    comes,
and the busy work is hushed,
and the fever of life is over,
and our work is done.

Then in His mercy,
may He give us a safe lodging
and a holy rest
and peace at last. Amen."

(Cardinal Newman)

Don't Live with Your Eyes Closed

Luke 23:35-43

A group of American tourists were on safari in deepest Africa. In meeting some of the local tribesmen, the women on the tour were fascinated by the natives' jewelry, especially the unusual kind of necklace worn only by the chieftain. "What's that made of?" asked one of the women.

"Alligator teeth," replied the chieftain.

"Oh," said the woman breezily, "I suppose they have the same kind of value for you that pearls have for us."

"Not quite," scowled the chieftain. "Anyone can open an oyster!"

I suspect we wpould be quite content to settle for the oyster – and its nice little pearl. But unfortunately, life demands that we face the alligator, look him – or her! – square in the eye, without blinking, and pull teeth! And where is this alligator we have to confront? We see it in the mirror first thing every morning. The alligator we have to face is ourselves, our inner selves, not the skin we're wrapped in, but what's inside our skins.

God gave us the power to know, not only what is outside us, but what is inside us. We have the power to reflect upon ourselves, and to live consciously – to see accurately who we are and where our life path is leading, to recognize what we're doing and why we're doing it.

In giving us this power to know ourselves, God made us like himself! So why does using this power feel like facing down an alligator? Why does looking inward frighten us so? Because we know in advance that it will bring us face to face not just with our goodness but with our unfinishedness, our darkness, and our need for change, which at times may seem just too much for us.

Sometimes a tiny voice inside us will call out insistently, "Something's not right! Better take a look!" We get scared, so we whistle in the dark or turn on the television or pick up the phone or shop till we drop to drown out that little voice.

Sometimes we succeed for years or even for a lifetime in drowning out that little voice, keeping our eyes firmly shut, living in the dark, never knowing ourselves, and therefore never filling out the wonderful image that God dreamed for us on the day we were born. That is world-class tragedy, and it happens every day.

Today's Gospel gives us a look inside two men, two thieves who had lived their whole lives with their eyes closed, and had never known themselves. As they hang on their crosses at either side of Jesus, with the last minutes of their lives ticking away, the one clings to the habit of a lifetime, keeps his eyes closed, and angrily lashes out at Jesus, as if he were to blame: "It's your fault we're stuck here. Why don't you do something, Jesus?" And he dies in his angry blindness.

The other thief breaks the habit of a lifetime. He opens his eyes, sees the sad truth about himself and speaks it, first of all to himself. And the truth sets him free to ask Jesus for the help that God had been waiting for so long to give. So he hears the words, "This day you will be with me in paradise!"

There is much good in us to rejoice over and much unfinished in us to weep over. But there is nothing in us to fear – except the inner blindness which fear sometimes makes us choose. That blindness strangles life, stunts growth, and kills God's wonderful dreams for us. But we have no reason to choose blindness because we have no reason to be afraid of what we may see.

We can afford the luxury of looking within because we know the Lord is with us with his strength and compassion. And there is nothing the two of us cannot face together, nothing we cannot prevail over together – no alligator, no power in heaven or on earth.

May God grant us the grace to open our eyes and step out into the light, to see all that God sees and leave our fears behind that we may begin to grow into the beautiful image that God dreamed for us the day we were born. Amen.

You Always Find God in the Strangest Places

Luke 1:57-66

A long time ago, there was a beautiful old monastery that had fallen on hard times. Its buildings were still magnificent and in good repair. Its library was still filled with the finest of leather-bound books. Its tower stood tall and its bells could still be heard round the countryside. But despite all that, the monastery was dying, for no young monks had come to join its community for many years. All that remained were the abbot and four brothers – all over eighty. The end seemed close at hand.

One day, the abbot in desperation went into the nearby woods to ask the advice of a wise rabbi who lived in a tiny hut. The two of them prayed together, and then the rabbi spoke these strange words, "The only thing I can tell you is the Messiah is one of you."

When the abbot returned to the monastery, the monks were waiting breathlessly and asked in a chorus, "Well, what did he say."

"Not a thing," replied the abbot, "except that the Messiah is one of us. I don't know what he meant."

In the days and months that followed, the old monks pondered the rabbi's words. And the thoughts of each went something like this: "Did he really mean one of us monks here in this monastery? I wonder which one. Maybe the abbot? Yes, that's it. The abbot has been our leader for more than a generation." On the other hand, he might have meant Brother Thomas. Thomas is certainly a holy man. Everyone says he's a man of light. Maybe.

"Surely he couldn't have meant Brother Elred. Elred's always criticizing and disagreeing. But come to think of it, even though he's a pain sometimes, he's almost always right and he's prevented a lot of big mistakes. Maybe the rabbi did mean Brother Elred. Definitely not Brother Philip. Philip is so passive, a real nobody. But then, he has this gift for always being there when you need him. He just magically appears by your side and pitches in. Maybe Philip is the Messiah.

"Of course, the rabbi didn't mean me. He couldn't possibly have. I'm just an ordinary person. Yet, what if he did? Suppose I'm the Messiah. Dear Lord, not me. I couldn't do that much for you, could I?"

As they continued their thoughts along these lines, the old monks began to treat each other with extraordinary respect on the off chance that one of them might be the Messiah. And on the off-off chance that each monk himself might be the Messiah, they began to treat themselves with extraordinary respect. In the days of its decline, the monastery received few visitors, though once in a while, people still came to picnic on its lawns, to wander along its paths, and even to pray in its empty chapel. After the abbot's visit to the rabbi, the few who still came began to sense something new, a different atmosphere, of extraordinary respect, that radiated from the five old monks and filled the whole place. They found themselves drawn back to the monastery more and more frequently. They began to bring friends, and their friends brought friends. Then it happened that some of the younger men who visited the monastery started to talk about their lives, hopes, and dreams with the old monks. And after a while, one asked if he could join the monks. Then another, and another. So within a few years, the monastery had become once again a thriving place, a vibrant center of spiritual light and life for the whole kingdom – thanks to the wise rabbi's simple words.

Today we are celebrating the birthday of John the Baptist, who is worth remembering because he was the first one to recognize that God was present in a most unlikely place, in his cousin, the carpenter's son Jesus.

We celebrate John's birthday, because we need to learn how to do what he did, and that is to look for and to recognize what is Godlike in the most unlikely of places: At the core of every human heart. And then, having recognized the likeness of God in the heart of our neighbor (or in our own heart), we need to learn to affirm that holy presence, hope in it, and treat that person with such extraordinary respect, that the Godlikeness that lurks within will be drawn out, will surge forward, and come at last to full flower.

For those old monks in the story, recognizing and cherishing the Godlikeness in themselves and in one another meant transformation and a second chance for themselves and their dying monastery. It could mean the same for us all!